My Life as a Quant

Reflections on Physics and Finance

Emanuel Derman

WILEY

John Wiley & Sons, Inc.

Published by John Wiley & Sons, Inc., Hoboken, New Jersey

Published simultaneously in Canada

For general information on our other products and services, or technical support,
please contact our Customer Care Department within the United States at
800-762-2974, outside the United States at 317-572-3993 or fax 317-572-4002.

Wiley also publishes its books in a variety of electronic formats. Some content that
appears in print may not be available in electronic books.

For more information about Wiley products, visit our Web site at www.wiley.com.

Library of Congress Cataloging-in-Publication Data

Derman, Emanuel.
  My life as a quant : reflections on physics and finance / Emanuel Derman.
    p. cm.
  Includes biographical references and index.
  ISBN 978-0-471-39420-4 (cloth)
  ISBN 978-0-470-19273-3 (paper)
  1. Derman, Emanuel 2. Investment advisors—Biography. 3.
Physicists—Biography. 4. Options (Finance) 5. Quantum theory.
6. Mathematical physics. I. Title.
  HG4621.D47   2004
  332.6'092—dc22

                         2004007664

Printed in the United States of America

10 9 8

To the Memory of My Parents

Ambition is a state of permanent dissatisfaction with the present.

Contents

The Two Cultures

■ Physics and finance ■ What quants do ■ The Black-Scholes model ■ Quants and traders ■ Pure thought and beautiful mathematics can divine the laws of physics ■ Can they do the same for finance? ■

MODELING THE WORLD

If mathematics is the Queen of Sciences, as the great mathematician Karl Friedrich Gauss christened it in the nineteenth century, then physics is king. From the mid-seventeenth century to the end of the nineteenth, Newton's Law of Gravitation, his three Laws of Motion, and his differential calculus described with apparent perfection the mechanical motion of objects in our world and the solar system.

In 1864, two hundred years after Newton, the Scottish physicist James Clerk Maxwell formulated the compact and elegant differential equations that described with similarly astounding precision the propagation of light, X-rays, and radio waves. Maxwell's equations showed that electricity and magnetism, formerly separate phenomena, were part of the same unified electromagnetic field.

We cannot simply look at the world around us and deduce Newton's Laws or Maxwell's equations. Data on its own does not speak. These equations were triumphs of the mind, abstracted from the world in

1

some miraculous confluence of hard thinking and deep intuition. Their success confirmed that pure thought and beautiful mathematics have the power to discover the most profound laws of the universe.

At the start of the twentieth century, the pace accelerated. Einstein, pondering the conflicts between the Newtonian and Maxwellian views of the world, proposed his Theory of Special Relativity that amended Newton's mechanics and made them consistent with Maxwell's equations. Fifteen years later Einstein trumped Newton again with his proposal of the General Theory; it corrected the Law of Gravitation and described gravity as a large-scale wave in space and time. At almost the same time, Bohr, Schrödinger, and Heisenberg, with help from the ever-prodigious Einstein, developed the quantum mechanical theory of the small-scale behavior of molecules, atoms, and subatomic particles.

It was Einstein who perfected this mental approach to discovering the laws of the universe. His method wasn't based on observation or empiricism; he tried to perceive and then enunciate the very principles that constrained the way things should work. In a 1918 speech on the principles of research given in honor of Max Planck, the discoverer of the quantum, Einstein captured the magus-like appeal of trying to see through a glass, darkly, when he said: "There is no logical path to these laws; only intuition, resting on a sympathetic understanding of experience, can reach them."

What is the purpose behind the search for scientific laws, in any field? Clearly, it's divination—foretelling the future, and controlling it. Most of the modern technologies we enjoy, rely on, detest, or fear—cell phones, electric power grids, CAT scans, and nuclear weapons, for example—have been developed by using the basic principles of quantum mechanics, electromagnetic theory, and relativity, all of which were discovered by cerebration. The classic tools of twentieth-century divination have indeed been those of physics. More recently, physicists have begun to employ the same tools in finance.

For the past twenty years, throughout Wall Street and the City of London, in most major and many minor financial institutions, small groups of ex-physicists and applied mathematicians have tried to apply their skills to securities markets. Formerly called "rocket scientists" by those who mistakenly thought that rocketry was the most advanced branch of science, they are now commonly called "quants."

Quants and their cohorts practice "financial engineering"—an awkward neologism coined to describe the jumble of activities that would better be termed *quantitative finance*. The subject is an interdisciplinary mix of physics-inspired models, mathematical techniques, and computer science, all aimed at the valuation of financial securities. The best quantitative finance brings real insight into the relation between value and uncertainty, and it approaches the quality of real science; the worst is a pseudoscientific hodgepodge of complex mathematics used with obscure justification.

Until recently, financial engineering wasn't really a subject at all—when I entered the field in 1985, it didn't have a name and was something one learned on the job at an investment bank. Now you can get a master's degree in the subject at scores of institutions—the Courant Institute at New York University, the University of Michigan at Ann Arbor, and the University of Oregon in Eugene, to name a few. Since July 2003 I have been a professor of the subject at Columbia University. Engineering schools, statistics and mathematics departments, and business schools organize these one- to two-year programs; they promise to transform students, in exchange for about $30,000 per year, into employable financial engineers. So popular are these degrees that some universities run several similar programs in distinct departments.

Nowadays, managers on Wall Street receive daily calls and emailed résumés from PhDs seeking jobs in finance. Physics journals publish increasing numbers of papers on financial economics. And increasingly, physicists and mathematicians working on the quantitative side of banking have been joined by PhDs and faculty members from finance departments and business schools. Two of the best graduate finance departments in the country, the Sloan School at MIT and the Haas School of the University of California at Berkeley, have each lost several of their best young finance faculty to the banking and trading worlds.

Part of the reason for the influx of physicists to other fields was the 1970s collapse of their traditional job market: academia. Thirty years earlier during World War II, the invention of radar and the construction of the atomic bomb confirmed the usefulness of physics to postwar governments. Shocked by the successful voyage of Sputnik, the Depart-

ments of Defense and Energy began to fund pure research more copi-
ously, and physicists seeking grants to do such research weren't above
playing up the spin-off benefits of their work. Physics departments in
the 1960s grew and academic posts multiplied. Inspired by the subject
and supported by scholarships, a wave of ardent graduate students
entered the field.

The good times didn't last. By the end of the Vietnam War a deteri-
orating economy and a public revulsion with science in the service of
war put a large dent in research funds. During the 1970s and 1980s,
many theoretical physicists who had once hoped to devote their lives to
fundamental research were forced to become migratory laborers if they
wanted to remain in academia, taking temporary short-term positions
in universities and national laboratories wherever they became available.
Many of us eventually gave up the struggle to find even a low-paying
semipermanent academic job and turned to other areas. We sought
physics-related jobs in a variety of fields—in energy research or telecommunications, for example. Former colleagues of mine began to work
on alternate power sources at the Solar Energy Research Institute in
Golden, Colorado, or on the mathematics of oil retrieval at Schlumberger in Ridgefield, Connecticut. Others helped develop advanced
switching systems at AT&T's Bell Laboratories in New Jersey.

Coincidentally, some of the same forces that compelled physicists to
move out of academia made Wall Street begin to embrace them. The
Arab oil embargo of 1973 caused fuel prices to soar and interest rates to
climb; soon the fear of inflation propelled gold prices above $800 an
ounce. Suddenly, financial markets seemed to become more volatile.
Bonds, a traditionally conservative investment, were suddenly seen as
much riskier than anyone had imagined. The old rules of thumb no
longer applied. Understanding the motion of interest rates and stock
prices became more important than ever for financial institutions. Risk
management and hedging were the new imperative and, in the face of
so much freshly perceived risk, complex new financial products that
provided protection from change proliferated.

How could one describe and understand the movement of prices?
Physics has always been concerned with dynamics, the way things change
with time. It was the tried-and-true exemplar of successful theories and
models. And physicists and engineers were jacks-of-all-trades, simultane-

ously skilled mathematicians, modelers, and computer programmers who prided themselves on their ability to adapt to new fields and put their knowledge into practice. Wall Street began to beckon to them. In the 1980s, so many physicists flocked to investment banks that one head-hunter I know referred to them as "POWs"—physicists on Wall Street.

THE MOST SUCCESSFUL THEORY

What is it that physicists do on Wall Street? Mostly, they build models to determine the value of securities. Buried in investment banks, at hedge funds, or at financial software companies such as Bloomberg or SunGard, they tinker with old models and develop new ones. And by far the most famous and ubiquitous model in the entire financial world is the Black–Scholes options pricing model. Steve Ross, a famous financial economist, options theorist, and now a chaired professor at MIT, wrote in the *Palgrave Dictionary of Economics* that "... options pricing theory is the most successful theory not only in finance, but in all of economics."

The Black–Scholes model allows us to determine the fair value of a stock option. Stocks are commonplace securities, bought and sold daily, but a call option on a stock is much more arcane. If you own a one-year call option on IBM, for example, you have the right to buy one share of IBM one year from today at a predetermined price: say, $100. The value of the option on that future date when it expires will depend on the prevailing value of a share of IBM. If, for example, a share sells for $105 on that day, the option will be worth exactly $5; if a share sells for less than $100, the option will be worth nothing. In a sense, the option is a bet that the stock price will rise.

An option is a special case of a more general *derivative security*, a contract whose value is *derived from* the value of some other simpler *underlying* security on which it "rests." A derivative security's payoff at expiration is specified in a contract via a mathematical formula that relates the payoff to the future value of the underlying security. The formula can be simple, as is the case with the stock option just described, whose payoff is the amount by which the final stock price exceeds the value of $100, or it can be extremely complicated, with a payoff that depends on the prices of several underlying securities through detailed mathematical expressions. During the past twenty years derivative securities have become widely used in the trading of currencies, commodities, bonds, stocks, mortagages, credit, and power.

Derivatives are more intricate than unvarnished stocks or bonds. Then why do they exist? Because derivatives allow clients such as investment banks, money managers, corporations, investors, and speculators to tailor and fine-tune the risk they want to assume or avoid. An investor who simply buys a share of IBM takes on all the risk of owning it; its value waxes and wanes in direct proportion to IBM's share price. In contrast, an IBM call option provides potentially unlimited gain (as the share price rises above $100) but only limited loss (you lose nothing but the cost of the option as the stock price drops below $100). This asymmetry between upside gain and downside loss is the defining characteristic of derivatives.

You can buy or sell options retail on specialized options exchanges, or you can trade them with wholesalers, that is, the dealers. Options dealers "make markets" in options; they accomodate clients by buying options from those who want to sell them and selling options to those who want to acquire them. How, then, do dealers handle the risk they are forced to assume?

Dealers are analogous to insurance companies, who are also in the business of managing risk. Just as Allstate must allow for the possibility that your house will burn down after they sell you an insurance contract, so an options dealer must take a chance of a rise in IBM's stock price when he or she sells you a call option on IBM. Neither Allstate nor the options dealer wants to go broke if the insured-against scenario comes to pass. Because neither Allstate nor the dealer can foretell the future, they both charge a premium for taking on the risks that their clients want to avoid.

Allstate's risk strategy is to charge each client a premium such that the total sum they receive exceeds the estimated claims they will be obliged to pay for future conflagrations. An option dealer's risk strategy is different. In an ideal world, he or she would simply offset the risk that IBM's price will rise by buying an IBM option similar to the one he or she sold, from someone else and at a cheaper price, thereby making a profit. Unfortunately, this is rarely possible. So instead, the dealer *manufactures* a similar option. This is where the Black-Scholes model enters the picture.

The Black-Scholes model tells us, almost miraculously, how to manufacture an option out of the underlying stock and provides an estimate of how much it costs us to do so. According to Black and Scholes, making options is a lot like making fruit salad, and stock is a little like fruit.

Suppose you want to sell a simple fruit salad of apples and oranges. What should you charge for a one-pound can? Rationally, you should look at the market price of the raw fruit and the cost of canning and distribution, and then figure out the total cost of manufacturing the hybrid mixture from its simpler ingredients.

In 1973, Black and Scholes showed that you can manufacture an IBM option by mixing together some shares of IBM stock and cash, much as you can create the fruit salad by mixing together apples and oranges. Of course, options synthesis is somewhat more complex than making fruit salad, otherwise someone would have discovered it earlier. Whereas a fruit salad's proportions stay fixed over time (50 percent oranges and 50 percent apples, for example), an option's proportions must continually change. Options require constant adjustments to the amount of stock and cash in the mixture as the stock price changes. In fruit salad terms, you might start with 50 percent apples and 50 percent oranges, and then, as apples increase in price, move to 40 percent apples and 60 percent oranges; a similar decrease in the price of apples might dictate a move to 70 percent apples and 30 percent oranges. In a sense, you are always trying to keep the price of the mixture constant as the ingredients' prices change and time passes. The exact recipe you need to follow is generated by the Black-Scholes equation. Its solution, the Black-Scholes formula, tells you the cost of following the recipe. Before Black and Scholes, no one even guessed that you could manufacture an option out of simpler ingredients, and so there was no way to figure out its fair price.

This discovery revolutionized modern finance. With their insight, Black and Scholes made formerly gourmet options into standard fare. Dealers could now manufacture and sell options on all sorts of underlying securities, creating the precise riskiness clients wanted without taking on the risk themselves. It was as though, in a thirsty world filled with hydrogen and oxygen, someone had finally figured out how to synthesize H_2O.

Dealers use the Black-Scholes model to manufacture (or synthesize, or financially engineer) the options they sell to their clients. They construct the option from shares of raw stock they buy in the market.

Conversely, they can deconstruct an option someone sells to them by converting it back into shares of raw stock that they then sell to the market. In this way, dealers mitigate their risk. (Since the Black-Scholes model is only a model, and since no model in finance is 100 percent correct, it is impossible for them to entirely cancel their risk.) Dealers charge a fee (the option premium) for this construction and deconstruction, just as chefs at fancy restaurants charge you not only for the raw ingredients but also for the recipes and skills they use, or as couturiers bill you for the materials and talents they employ in creating *haute couture* dresses.

LIFE AS A QUANT

The history of quants on Wall Street is the history of the ways in which practitioners and academics have refined and extended the Black-Scholes model. The last thirty years have seen it applied not just to stock options but to options on just about anything you can think of, from Treasury bonds and foreign exchange to the weather. Behind all these extensions is the same original insight: It is possible to tailor securities with the precise risk desired out of a mix of simpler ingredients using a recipe that specifies how to continually readjust their proportions. The readjustment depends on the exact way in which the ingredients' prices move.

Because bond prices don't move exactly like stock prices, the recipe for a bond option must differ from that of the classic Black-Scholes model. But this is a subtlety—when a new product is first created, a crude Black-Scholes-like model often suffices. Then, an arms race begins. As competitive pressures increase and spreads tighten, quants at different firms refine and extend their first pass at the model, adding new and more accurate descriptions of the motion of the ingredients and obtaining better recipes for the salad. Extending the model demands a grasp of financial theory, mathematics, and computing, and quants work at the intersection of these three disciplines.

The life of a practitioner quant in a trading business is quite different from that of a physicist. When, after years of physics research, I first came to work on Wall Street at the end of 1985, my new boss asked me to take a second pass at a problematic Black-Scholes-like model for bond options that he had built a year earlier. I started out slowly and carefully, working like a physicist; I read the relevant papers, learned the theory, diagnosed the problem, and began to rewrite the computer program that made the model work. After several weeks he became impatient with my lack of progress. "You know," he said a little sharply as he took me aside, "in this job you really need to know only four things: addition, subtraction, multiplication, and division—and most of the time you can get by without division!"

I took his point. Of course, the model used more advanced mathematics than arithmetic. Yet his insight was correct. The majority of options dealers make their living by manufacturing the products their clients need as efficiently as they can—that is, by providing service for a fee. For them, a simple, easy-to-understand model is more useful than a better, complicated one. Too much preoccupation with details that you cannot get right can be a hindrance when you have a large profit margin and you want to complete as many deals as possible. And often, it's hard to define exactly what constitutes a "better" model—controlled experiments in markets are rare. Though I did ultimately improve the model, the traders benefited most from the friendly user interface I programmed into it. This simple ergonomic change had a far greater impact on their business than the removal of minor inconsistencies; now they could handle many more client requests for business.

Although options theory originated in the world of stocks, it is exploited more widely in the fixed-income universe. Stocks (at least at first glance) lack mathematical detail—if you own a share of stock you are guaranteed nothing; all you really know is that its price may go up or down. In contrast, fixed-income securities such as bonds are ornate mechanisms that promise to spin off future periodic payments of interest and a final return of principal. This specification of detail makes fixed income a much more numerate business than equities, and one much more amenable to mathematical analysis. Every fixed-income security—bonds, mortgages, convertible bonds, and swaps, to name only a few—has a value that it depends on, and is therefore conveniently viewed as a derivative of the market's underlying interest rates. Interest-rate derivatives are naturally attractive products for corporations who, as part of their normal business, must borrow money by issuing bonds whose value changes when interest or exchange rates fluctuate. It is much more challenging to create realistic models of the movement of interest rates, which change in more complex ways than stock prices; interest-rate modeling has thus been the mother of invention in the theory of derivatives for the past twenty years. It is an area in which quants are ubiquitous.

In contrast, quants have been a rarer presence in the equity world. There, most investors are concerned with which stock to buy, a problem on which the advanced mathematics of derivatives can shed little light. Fixed income and equities have fundamentally different foci. When you walk around a frenetic fixed-income trading floor, you hear people shouting out numbers—yields and spreads—over the hoot-and-holler; on a busy equities floor, you mostly hear people shouting company names. Fixed-income trading requires a better grasp of technology and quantitative methods than equities trading. A trader friend of mine summed it up succinctly when, after I commented to him that the fixed-income traders I knew seemed smarter than the equity traders, he replied that "that's because there's no competitive edge to being smart in the equities business."

I don't mean to suggest that all quants work on the Black-Scholes model. Increasingly, some of them work on statistical arbitrage, the attempt to seek order and predictability in the patterns of past stock price movements and then exploit them—that is, to divine the future from the past. Hedge funds, private pools of capital that seek out subtle price discrepancies in odd and unexplored corners of markets, have become major employers of quants during the past five years, and continue to hire them to do "stat-arb."

Risk management is also in mode, and for good reason. A decade ago, in 1994, a sudden unexpected rise in global interest rates caused severe losses on many proprietary bond trading desks whose bets turned sour. This led banks to enlarge their previously rudimentary risk management efforts, and caused regulators of the securities industry to focus on risk limitation. Many quants now work within each investment bank's centralized-risk group, whose job it is to aggregate all the firm's positions and so estimate quantitatively the current risk and probable future losses. But probabilities are necessarily extracted from past events; they provide notoriously poor estimates of the likelihood of future catastrophes. Market crashes are not randomly occurring lightning bolts; they are the consequence of the madness of crowds who are busy avoiding the last mania as they participate in what will turn out to be the current one. Despite the losses of 1994, many firms again lost vast sums on their speculations during the worldwide withdrawal of credit following Russia's 1998 bond default. More and more, therefore, the market for quants is in risk monitoring and management.

THINKERS VERSUS DOERS

I didn't fully realize that the word *quant* had negative overtones until I leafed through a dictionary of finance terms several years ago and saw the entry "quant—often pejorative." Often is right. When I first came to work at Goldman, Sachs and Co. in 1985, I instantly noticed the shame involved in being numerate. Sometimes, talking in a crowded elevator to another quant, you might start to say something about the "duration" or "convexity" of a bond. These are relatively low-tech bond-math terms that describe the sensitivity of a bond's price to changes in interest rates. If the colleague you were talking to had been at the firm a little longer than you, then he—most quants are male—would shift uncomfortably and try to change the subject. "Futures dropped more than a handle today!" he might say, imitating the confident vernacular of a genuine bond trader. Soon, you began to realize, it was bad taste for two consenting adults to talk math or UNIX or C in the company of traders, salespeople, and bankers. People around you averted their gaze. There was something terminally awful about being outed.

Even in the mid-1990s geeks were fair game. One afternoon a colleague and I were standing on either side of one of the narrow aisles between the banks of trading desks on the floor when one of the chief traders walked between us, his head momentarily between ours. At that instant he winced, clutched his head with both hands as though in excruciating pain, and exclaimed, "Aaarrggh-hhh! The force field! It's too intense! Let me out of the way!" In the same vein, I lost count of the number of times some junior traders heading for lunch entered the elevator to see a group of quants standing there and then reflexively uttered some variant of "Uh-oh! Isn't there some rule against all of you getting in the elevator at once?"

Traders and quants are genuinely different species. Traders pride themselves on being tough and forthright while quants are more circumspect and reticent. These differences in personality are reflections of deeper cultural preferences. Traders are paid to act. All day long they watch screens, assimilate economic information, page frantically through spreadsheets, run programs written by quants, enter trades, talk to salespeople and brokers, and punch keys. It's hard to have an extended conversation with a trader during the business day; it takes an hour of standing around to have five minutes of punctuated repartee. Part of what traders do has a video game quality. In consequence, they learn to be opinionated, visceral, fast-thinking, and decisive, though not always right. They thrive on interruption.

Quants do not. Like academics trained in research, they prefer to do one thing from beginning to end, deeply and well. This is a luxury that is difficult to enjoy in the multitasking world of business, where you have to do many things simultaneously. When I moved to Wall Street, the hardest attitude adjustment for me was to learn to carry out multiple assignments in parallel, to interrupt one urgent and still incomplete task with another more pressing one, to complete that, and then pop the stack.

Traders and quants think differently, too. Good traders must be perpetually aware of the threat of change and what it will do to the value of their positions. Stock options in particular, because of their intrinsic asymmetry, magnify stock price changes and therefore suffer or benefit dramatically from even small moves. Quants think less about future change and more about current value. According to financial theory, at any instant the so-called fair value of a security is an average over the range of all its possible future values. Fair value and change are therefore two sides of the same coin; the more ways in which a security can lose value from a future market move, the less it should rationally be worth today, and hence the mantra: more risk, more return. This difference between the quant's view of value as an average versus the trader's need to worry about any change makes this kind of professional cross-communication difficult.

Tour de France cyclists don't need to know how to solve Newton's Laws in order to bank around a curve. Indeed, thinking too much about physics while cycling may prove a hindrance. Similarly, options traders need not be expert quants; they can leave the details of the recipe for manufacturing options to others as long as they have the patience to thoroughly understand how to use it and when to trust it, for no model is perfect. One trader I know used to say, "You can't give a person a Black-Scholes calculator and turn him into a trader," and this is true; it takes study, understanding, intuition, and a grasp of the limits of the model in order to trade wisely. You cannot just follow formulas, no matter how precise they appear to be.

A good quant must be a mixture, too—part trader, part salesperson, part programmer, and part mathematician. Many quants would like to cross over to become traders, but they face the formidable obstacles of scholarly backgrounds, introspective personalities, and hybrid skills.

One of the theories about what makes an animal nonkosher is that it transcends categories. In the book of Genesis, the creation categorizes animals by both their species and location, referring to "birds of the sky" and "fish of the sea." Occupying both categories is what makes some animals nonkosher. Shrimp, for example, live in the sea but aren't fish and don't swim. Ostriches are birds, but do not fly in the sky. Both are nonkosher. Similarly, cloth made from a mixture of linen (a plant) and wool (an animal product) is also proscribed. Those who were brought up keeping kosher can feel nauseated at the thought of eating category-violating food.

Quants are the nonkosher category violators of Wall Street, half-breed players who make pure traders or undiluted information technology managers uncomfortable. Quants are amateurs with no clear professional role model. While traders and programmers in investment banks have distinct ladders to climb and clearly marked rungs to ascend, the quant professional ladder is short and often ends in midair.

Nevertheless, in the twenty-first century, as universities have initiated financial engineering programs and financial institutions have embraced risk management, being a quant has slowly become a more legitimate profession. The overheated tech-stock market of the late 1990s cast a warm, reflected glow on geeks of all types, as did the droves of hedge funds trying to use mathematical models to squeeze dollars out of subtleties. The guts to lose a lot of money carries its own aura. D.E. Shaw & Co., a New York trading house that was rumored to be making substantial profits doing "black box" computerized statistical arbitrage before their billion-dollar losses in 1998, and Long Term Capital Management, the quant-driven Connecticut hedge fund that ultimately needed a multibillion-dollar bailout, have both contributed to this more glamorous view of quantization. And indeed, many of the Long Term Capital protagonists are back in business again at new firms. The capacity to wreak destruction with your models provides the ultimate respectability.

THE SACRED AND PROFANE

There is an almost religious quality to the pursuit of physics that stems from its transcendent qualities. How *does* a planet know that it must obey Newton's Laws, or an electron perceive that it must move according to the principles of quantum electrodynamics? Do tiny internal homunculi program internal nanocomputers to spit out the electron's next position? It's hard not to have a sense of wonder when you see that principles, imagination, and a little mathematics—in a word, the mind— can divine the behavior of the universe. Short of genuine enlightenment, nothing but art comes closer to God.

When I was a graduate student at Columbia in the 1970s, physics was the great attractor for the aspiring scientists of the world. Bearing witness to this was the large box of documents kept near the entrance to the physics department library. We referred to it as the "crank file." The box contained the unsolicited typewritten letters, manuscripts, and appeals that poured steadily into the mailbox of the department's chairman. Eccentric though the documents were, they made fascinating reading. There were eager speculations on the nature of space and time, elaborately detailed papers refuting relativity and quantum mechanics, grandiose claims to have unified them, and farfetched meditations that combined physics with more metaphysical topics. I remember one note that tried to deduce the existence of God from the approximate equality of the solid angles subtended by the sun and the moon when observed from the earth, a remarkable circumstance without which there would be no solar eclipses.

None of these papers had much chance of getting past a journal referee. Few of the writers had much hope of even getting into graduate school. They may not have wanted to. The letters were mostly a *cri de cœur* from isolated and solitary physicist *manqués* all over the world.

Most of my classmates laughed at the naiveté of the letter writers, but as I skimmed through the crank file I found it hard to feel superior. Instead, peering into the box of manuscripts, I always saw my pale reflection. Out there, beyond academia and industry, were people like us, similarly in thrall to the same sense of mystery and power that lay behind the attempt to understand and master the universe with only imagination and symbols. They were cranks, those letter writers, but they were also genuine amateurs, lovers of the field interested in wisdom and magic rather than money.

There are amateurs in the financial modeling world, too, but they often come in more mercenary flavors, and why not? Because I used to run a group called Quantitative Strategies at Goldman Sachs for many years, after a while almost any letter from the outside world addressed to the "Quantitative Something-or-Other" at Goldman found its way

to me. Once every few months I received a note from someone isolated and far away who thought he or she had made some great breakthrough in financial theory. Often, they would explain, it was a
breakthrough whose exact details they were unwilling to divulge without being given a contract promising them a share of the future profits they were certain its use would guarantee. I sympathized with them.
They, too, believed in the power of imagination.

Theoretical physicists are accustomed to the success of mathematics
in formulating the laws of the universe and elaborating their consequences. The universe does indeed seem to run like some splendid Swiss
clockwork: We can predict the orbits of planets and the frequency of
light emitted by atoms to eight or ten decimal places. But when a physicist first pages through a graduate economics or finance textbook, he or
she begins to feel aghast. The mathematics of economics is so much
more formal than the mathematics of physics textbooks—much of it
reads like Euclid or set theory, replete with axioms, theorems, and lem-
mas. You would think that all this formality would produce precision.
And yet, compared with physics, economics has so little explanatory or
predictive power. Everything looks suspect; questions abound.

When physicists pursue the laws of the universe, it seems selfless. But
watching quants pursue sacred laws for the profane production of profit,
I sometimes find myself thinking disturbingly of worshippers at a black
mass. What does it signify to use the methods of physics and the language of mathematics to model the economic world? Is it justifiable to
treat the economy and its markets as a complex machine? How can
traders put their faith in this stuff? Isn't value determined by people?
And how can people be described by equations and predetermined
rules? Isn't this endeavor the misguided consequence of some sort of
physics envy, an inappropriate attempt to model messy human systems
with the wrong paradigm? Is social science, as the economic historian
Robert Skidelsky once observed, merely a compendium of flawed
thinking disguised as scientific understanding? If mathematics is the
Queen of Sciences, is quantitative finance a science at all? And finally,
are quants scientists or cranks?

This book is an account of my experiences as a scientist, quant, and,
on occasion, a fellow traveler of cranks.

Chapter 1

Elective Affinities

■ The attractions of science ■ The glory days of particle physics
■ Driven by ambitious dreams to Columbia ■ Legendary
physicists and budding wunderkinder *■ Talent*
versus character, plans versus luck ■

I expected New York to glitter. Instead, when I arrived on that hot
August afternoon in 1966, the city was grimy and littered, disap-
pointingly unmodern. I was jet-lagged and weary, and the sweaty cab
ride from Kennedy airport to upper Manhattan tilted me towards depression. The cramped Formica-filled rooms in International House,
a graduate student dormitory established by the Rockefeller Foundation
on the far reaches of New York's Upper West Side, bore little resemblance
to the spacious-looking illustrations in the brochure they had sent to me
in South Africa. The sickly green-and-white walls in the corridors and
the guards at the back entrance added to the prison sensibility. It took
several months before habit obscured all of this ugliness. "I. House," as we
all called it, was actually a very good place for foreigners.

A few hours after stepping off the airplane, I descended into a state
of acute loneliness. It must have had something to do with the sudden
perception of distance and time; I had been away from home many
times before, but never this far, and never for so undetermined a
period. For weeks, verging on months, I walked around with a lump
in my throat that threatened to overwhelm me. This welling-up sensation took a long time to pass, and when it finally did, I missed the

painful intensity that the sadness and longing had brought to my existence. A few years later I read *Young Törless* by Robert Musil, and
recognized the adolescent protagonist's piercing and yet delectable
unhappiness. The echoes of that first loneliness never totally faded away.
Ever since, whenever I've had to start out in a new city alone, I feel
again the resonances of those desolate days, at least for a short time.

I spoke to almost no one during those first few weeks in I. House,
which was virtually empty in the quiet lull before classes began. Ever
cautious, I had arrived three weeks early, compulsively planning to settle down and get acclimated before starting my PhD program in physics.
Instead, I felt isolated from everyone I had ever known. It is almost
impossible today to be as cut off from any place in the world as I was
from Cape Town during that first year in New York. There were almost
no telephones in I. House—one extension in a badly soundproofed
booth in the corridor served a floor of fifty people. Phone calls to South
Africa were expensive and had to be booked in advance through an
operator. I never called home; instead, I wrote letters to family and
friends several times a week. Finally, mercifully, my first semester at
graduate school started.

A blind but avid desire for success in physics spurred me to leave
Cape Town; simple chance brought me to Columbia. I had entered the
University of Cape Town four years earlier at the age of 16. We were
educated in the British style: You had to choose your major area—
science, arts, medicine, or commerce—before you began your studies.
I chose the natural sciences. In my freshman year I took four separate
year-long courses in Physics, Pure Maths, Applied Maths, and Chemistry. There was not much choice of subtopics; you studied everything
they chose to teach and then received a grade based on the grand final
exam at the end of each year. By my final year I had decided on a joint
major in Applied Maths and Theoretical Physics. Foolishly, the school
had permitted me to study only theoretical physics from my second
undergraduate year onwards, and so I emerged with no experimental
skills. It was a premature specialization that no good American university would have tolerated.

In late 1965 I suddenly noticed that the more ambitious students
in my class were planning to apply to graduate schools abroad. Serendip-

itously, I stumbled on a path to the United States through a bad case of acne. By coincidence, my sister, a clinical psychologist, had helped my dermatologist's young nephew successfully overcome "poor concentration" ten years earlier. The dermatologist took a benevolent interest in me, and encouraged me to apply to study physics abroad. I took his advice without really understanding what I was embarking on, and began to apply for scholarships to programs in the United Kingdom and the United States. The Cape Town physics department was insularly lukewarm about the benefits of study abroad, but I did not let them dissuade me.

If not for the acne, I might have remained in South Africa. Ever since, I've liked to believe that the course of my life, the old friends I parted from and the new friends I made, my marriage and my children, were the consequence of a random case of acne.[1]

Particle physics is the study of the smallest and most fundamental constituents of matter. Even in Cape Town, 5,000 miles from Europe and civilization, we knew that we were in the glory days of the field. As the 1960s passed, each year brought yet another triumph. At accelerators around the world, experimentalists clashed ultrahigh-speed protons against each other like cymbals and discovered a multiplicity of new particles emerging from the collision. Richard P. Feynman once said that doing elementary particle physics is a lot like banging two fine Swiss watches against each other and trying to figure out their workings by examining the debris. That was the challenge.

The proliferation of new particles made it difficult to know which were elementary and which were compound. The mystery was a recapitulation of the great puzzle of nineteenth-century chemistry, when the similar proliferation of new substances provoked the quest to understand chemical structure. That pursuit had culminated in Mendeleyev's construction of the periodic table, which arranged all the elements in an understandable order based on their chemical qualities. Empty spots in the table corresponded to as-yet-undiscovered elements whose qualities,

---

[1]The dermatologist's poorly concentrating nephew was Jonathan Dorfan. A few years later he, too, came to graduate school in the United States, where he is now head of the Stanford Linear Accelerator Center, one of the few great global laboratories for experimental particle physics.

associated with their place in the table, suggested how to find them. Now, in the twentieth century, the race was on to find an analogous table for the qualities of so-called elementary particles. So many new ones were being discovered in cosmic rays or man-made colliders that some serious physicists (from California, of course) began to propound holistic sorts of models in which no particle was more elementary than any other and any particle could be considered a composite of all the rest.

In Cape Town in the summer of 1964, we heard popular lectures about the work of physicists Murray Gell-Mann and Yuval Ne'eman, both modern-day Mendeleyevs, who each invented their own periodic table of particles. Some of the subtables in their system contained eight distinct particles. Gell-Mann dubbed his model the Eightfold Way, a sophisticated and hip allusion to the eight Buddhist principles of living. By looking at the properties of the unpopulated gaps in their table, Gell-Mann and Ne'eman had predicted the observable properties of a very strange new particle called the Omega Minus. Shortly thereafter, exactly as forecast, the particle was created in a collision in the particle accelerator at Brookhaven National Laboratories on Long Island. It was recognized by the characteristic trail it left in a giant bubble chamber, a signature whose properties matched the exact predictions of the Eightfold Way. It seemed you could apprehend the universe with thought.

I became deeply attracted to particle physics and general relativity, subjects that dealt with the ultimate nature of matter, space and time; a life spent studying these topics would be a life devoted to the transcendental. Like many of my physics friends, I began to develop an almost religious passion for fundamental physics. But beneath my passion was an even greater desire for fame and immortality. I dreamed of being another Einstein. I wanted to spend my life focusing on the discovery of truths that would live forever. Sometimes, I felt arrogantly superior to people who were headed for more mundane professions.

My mother encouraged me to devote myself to academic pursuits. My father, though he was more naturally scholarly than my mother, might nevertheless have been happier if I had gone into business with him. I myself would have laughed quite disbelievingly, at age 16, 21, or 34, if someone had told me that I would be working at an investment bank at age 40.

At registration on the first day of my first semester at Columbia, my assigned course advisor was Professor Henry Foley, himself a near-famous physicist who had been part of a classic 1940s experiment that verified Feynman's Nobel Prize-winning theory of electrons. Foley, a charmingly cynical man, quizzed me briefly about my knowledge of atomic physics and discovered how little I had learned in Cape Town about the details of the spin-orbit interactions of electrons. Then he commanded me to register for G4015, the introductory Columbia graduate course in atomic physics and quantum mechanics.[2] Most physics majors at American schools had taken the equivalent subject in their junior or senior year of college, so here I was starting off a year or more behind the rest of the pack. It was a disheartening setback, the beginning of three long, tedious, and unexpected years of coursework and examinations at a time when I had expected to soon embark on original research.

Foley was right, though—I didn't know enough. In Cape Town in the early 1960s we had learned a shallow rudimentary version of modern physics and quantum mechanics. The physics professors there, for the most part, seemed uncomfortable with everything that had developed after 1930. Their attitude—that you were lucky if you ever got to *really* understand quantum mechanics—stayed with me a long time. Physics in the United States was much more professional, hard-nosed, and businesslike, Columbia's physics department, I saw over and over again, didn't think of modern physics as something esoterically advanced and difficult, to be revealed to you only when you crossed some threshold and finally became an initiate. They expected you simply to plunge right in.

The one subject I had learned really well as an undergraduate was Applied Mathematics, a slower-moving subject easier to keep abreast of in distant, isolated South Africa. In Cape Town, the closed-book, year-end exams were fashioned after the famous Cambridge Tripos examination on which many of the British-educated faculty had been reared.

---

[2]You may think me pedantic to list the actual course number. But even now, more than thirty years later, each prosaic course number still conjures up a vivid subworld of a certain year, a particular classroom, a specific professor, a sliding chalkboard, and a noisily clanking steam radiator, together with the exciting sensation of being on the threshold of mastering some new and arcane alchemical subject.

Rapid, practical problem solving as well as memorization were heavily emphasized. Everything was done thoroughly. In each successive year we were taught progressively more advanced versions of classical mechanics and electromagnetic theory. I can still recite some of the indefinite integrals and Fourier transforms we had to learn by heart in order to take the final exams.[3]

The physics department I entered at Columbia in 1966 was legendary. The first thing that struck me was their direct connection to so many groundbreaking episodes of twentieth-century physics. The recipient of the first PhD degree ever awarded by the department, at the start of the century, had been R. A. Millikan. Later he received the Nobel Prize for his precise measurements of the invisible electron's charge by ingeniously measuring the deflection of tiny oil drops carrying an unseen electron or two's worth of static electricity.

When I arrived, I. I. Rabi, the grand old man of physics in the United States after Oppenheimer's death, was nearing the end of his reign over the Columbia department. He had received the Nobel Prize in 1944 for finding a method of measuring the magnetic properties of nuclei. Rabi was the intellectual father of a whole generation of American physicists, a respected government advisor, and one of the creators of the Brookhaven National Laboratory, where Gell-Mann and Ne'eman's Omega Minus particle was finally discovered. Now near retirement and seemingly garrulous, he struck me as more comic than genius. But I was young and a little arrogant then, and I had no conception of his wisdom and influence. Recently, I saw his old quote that "If you decide you don't have to get A's, you can learn an enormous amount in college."

The late Enrico Fermi, a 1938 Nobel Prize winner, was regarded as the spiritual father of the Columbia physics department. His black-and-

---

[3]During my last few years at Goldman, Sachs, I interviewed undergraduates applying for jobs in investment banking, and I was often surprised at how little of their coursework some of them recalled, how little a sense they had of the essence of their field. I met juniors majoring in statistics who couldn't define standard deviation and students who had taken several courses in electromagnetic theory but couldn't remember Maxwell's equations. What I had learned I had learned well. Theirs sometimes seemed a wasted education.

white three-quarter profile photograph graced the seminar room on the eighth floor of the Pupin Physics Building; he had been on the faculty there during World War II and the Manhattan Project. Fermi was the experimentalist who had created the first self-sustaining nuclear reaction at the University of Chicago, a step on the way to the bombs that leveled Hiroshima and Nagasaki. Amazingly, he was also the theorist who, in the 1930s, had predicted the existence of the neutrino, a massless and chargeless particle that interacted so weakly with ordinary matter that it wasn't detected until some twenty years later. He was one of the last physicists to make major contributions to both theory and experiment, an eclectic Goethe of the field.

Columbia had also been the wartime home of the beautiful Maria Goeppert-Mayer, who later received the 1963 Nobel Prize for her theoretical proposal that the nucleus of an atom, like the atom itself, consisted of shells of orbiting particles. Because of Columbia's antinepotism laws—her husband Joseph Mayer was a professor of chemistry—she had been only a member of the research staff of the university, and not a full faculty member.

Closer to the present, Columbia had been at the center of the postwar development of relativistic quantum electrodynamics (QED), the fabulously accurate theory of how electrons emit and absorb light that I would soon struggle to learn. Atoms and the electrons inside them are so small that physicists can only indirectly examine their structure. You cannot actually "see" the inside of an atom; instead, in much the same way that doctors used to tap a patient's chest and listen to the quality of the sound emitted in order to figure out the state of the patient's insides, so physicists must poke at an atom and then diagnose the character of its internal electrons from the light they emit. Until the late 1940s, QED was riven by such deep mathematical and conceptual inconsistencies that, in many cases, calculations of the frequencies of emitted light led to literally infinite results.

In the late 1940s, Feynman and Julian Schwinger in the United States (and, unknown to them, Shin-Ichiro Tomonaga in Japan), in a *tour de force* of insight and mathematical prowess, showed how to mend the theory of QED. They were then able to predict correctly minuscule and previously unsuspected corrections to the wavelengths of the light emitted by the internal electrons as they jumped from one orbit in the atom to another.

Willis Lamb and Polykarp Kusch, both at Columbia in the late 1940s, had carefully and accurately measured a variety of these almost infinitesimal corrections, and they found perfect agreement with Feynman and Schwinger. Lamb and Kusch each received a Nobel Prize, as did Feynman, Schwinger, and Tomonaga a while later.

It didn't take me long to learn that not all Nobel Prizes are equal. In 1968, when I was the teaching assistant for Kusch's junior-level course on electromagnetic theory, I met with him regularly. Soon I began to notice that people in Pupin treated him as though his Prize was somehow worthy of less respect than those of the other faculty members. A few years later he left for the University of Texas.

Also at Columbia, but not yet Nobelists at that time, were Leon Lederman, Jack Steinberger, and Mel Schwartz, all of them renowned even then for a host of elegant experiments and discoveries. In 1988 they received their Nobel Prize for having shown, almost thirty years earlier, that there were not one, but two different types of the neutrino that Fermi had proposed. (The discovery of a third type of neutrino in 2000 was less astonishing and definitely not Nobel-worthy.)

Finally, fiercely brightest among all the stars in the Columbia firmament was Tsung-Dao Lee, the embodiment and perhaps even the cause of all the good and bad qualities of the department. He had won his Nobel Prize in 1957, at the age of 31, for theoretical investigations that led to the startling discovery of the so-called nonconservation of parity. Lee and his fellow Prize-winner C. N. Yang had intrepidly suggested that nature's laws were not symmetric with respect to the seemingly arbitrary human definitions of "left" and "right." It was an almost unbelievable hypothesis, but they proposed experiments to test it. In less than a year they were proved correct. When I arrived at Columbia only eight years later, the consequences of this discovery were still working their way through the framework of physics.

"T. D.," as everyone called him, was Pupin's version of the Pope and the Last Emperor of China rolled into one. He was a holy terror, self-centered and intense. About ten years ago I saw a photograph of him in the literary magazine *Grand Street*, taken as part of a series of photographs of scientists writing on blackboards. One was of Feynman, lively and jovial, lecturing on QED. Another featured Mitchell Feigenbaum of the Rockefeller University, examining his doubling equations that revealed the hidden order behind apparently chaotic phenomena. Most of the physicists looked prosaic, even Gell-Mann himself. But T. D.'s photo was different. Taken in the 1950s, it showed his fervent young face glowing with light as he spoke, for all the world looking like Moses descending from Sinai. T. D. set the tone at Columbia. His presence could inspire, but it could consume, too.

The faculty were not the only extraordinary beings at Columbia. Many of the students seemed to be *wunderkinder*, too. My graduate classes, even the advanced ones, always contained a smattering of precocious smart-aleck American undergraduates. I was envious and wary of them. Some, sporting crewcuts and narrow-shouldered dark suits with ties, were relics of the Fifties; others had lank, long, hair and dressed in faded jeans and sweatshirts. But whatever they wore, they all raised their hands in class to ask questions whose answers they already knew.

I was awed by these people who knew more than they had been taught. In South Africa I had mastered only a limited number of skills really well, and that knowledge lasted a lifetime. There, I had waited obediently year after year to get to the level at which "they" would begin to teach "me" the things I was able to handle. It had never occurred to me that I could learn what I wanted when I chose. In America, I was alarmed to see students who set about learning things on their own. I'm still embarrassed to admit to myself that I almost never studied anything I wasn't officially taught. I recall one major exception. In my fourth year of college I spent many months studying unified field theories of gravitation and electromagnetism for my honors' thesis. My independent investigation of the extension of Einstein's theory of gravitation exhilarated me, but this autonomy was an exception.

In 1966 and during subsequent years, I dreamed ambitious dreams about success on the scale of T. D. Lee. By this unrealistic measure, few of the *wunderkinder* fulfilled the full magnitude of their intimidating promise. One became a think-tank military analyst whom I was pleased to recognize on television during the Gulf War following the Iraqi invasion of Kuwait. Another completed a PhD in physics, moved to medical school, began a residency in psychiatry, and finally became a well-known neural-net theorist. A third, after winning the prize for the best physics undergraduate at Columbia, struggled with manic depression. Determined to keep studying, he would keep a running daily log on his canary-yellow legal notepad of the exact number of minutes he had spent actually working at full concentration. Each time he paused or took a break, he stopped the clock and he wrote down the number of minutes he had worked since the last interruption. At the end of the day he computed the total. Compulsive myself, I was sympathetic to his counting; I knew how few were the hours in the day one actually works seriously and undistractedly, and was momentarily tempted to start my own time sheet.

I learned one lesson from the fates of both the professors and students I met at Columbia: In the end, character and chance counted at least as much as talent. Luck, combined with what my mother called *sitzfleisch*, the capacity to persevere, played an overwhelming role.

First in Cape Town and then in New York, I had been steadily learning what kind of physics suited me.

Like most physicists, I was a reductionist: I believed that you can explain complex things by reducing them to their constituents. Biology depends on chemistry; chemistry is merely the physics of molecules and atoms; atoms are made out of electrons and nuclei; nuclei contain protons and neutrons, and protons and neutrons seem to be made of quarks. What are the ultimate subnuclear particles at the putative root of this hierarchy, and what are the laws that determine their behavior? These questions are the domain of particle physics.

Particle physicists are snobs who think that their field is the source of the most fundamental knowledge, and take some mischievous pleasure in denigrating other messier or more complex areas of physics. Gell-Mann, the codiscoverer of the Eightfold Way and the discoverer of quarks, succinctly summarized the latent prejudice of most particle physicists about the superiority of their enterprise when he famously referred to solid state physics, the apparently more mundane study of bulk matter and its variety of forms, as "squalid state physics."

Nowadays, not everyone agrees with Gell-Mann's clever *bon mot*. Over the last twenty years physicists have discovered a deep commonality between large-scale bulk matter and small-scale particle physics.

Much of what is new and interesting in both fields seems to emerge from what is called their "many-body" nature: Both bulk matter and tiny particles can each be viewed as resembling a medium, each made out of a very large number of similar constituents. When many similar constituents are clumped together, their collective behavior can display completely new and unexpected characteristics. A drop of water can suddenly freeze and turn solid in a way that no single water molecule can. A ripple of excitement or a hush of expectation can sweep over a crowd but not over a single individual. In the words of another Nobel Prize-Winner, P. W. Anderson, "More is Different!" He, and many other "squalid-state" physicists believe that there is no single grand reductionist Theory of Everything.

It is unlikely one will ever know who is right, but, like most aspiring physicists of the postwar period, I was immensely attracted by the reductionist point of view. I wanted to be the ultimate reductionist, a particle physicist.

Technically, I still had to choose between being a theorist or an experimentalist, but for me, this wasn't much of a choice. The essence of theoretical physics is the attempt to look at the universe, and then mentally apprehend its structure. If you are right, you emulate Newton and Einstein: You find one of the Ten Commandments. You write down a simple set of laws that, plucked from nowhere, miraculously describes and predicts how God's world works. This was the struggle to which I aspired. Anything else would have been a compromise that I was not prepared to make.

Even within theoretical particle physics there are further refinements. Pure theory is the search for abstract laws, for a formulation of the divine commandments that rule the world. But, for every Moses descending from the mountain with a valid new law, there are countless well-intentioned prophets whose proposed laws turn out to be wrong. So how does one tell when a theory is right?

Beauty, even mathematical beauty, is not enough. Physicists must test a new theory by elaborating the ways in which it manifests itself in the world. Physicists who do so-called phenomenology work out the detailed and observable consequences of a theory, providing the practical link between principles and experiment, between mind and matter. Phenomenologists elaborate the theory; they create heuristic approximations to engineer the theory into a pragmatic tool; they propose experiments to validate or refute a theory, using the theory itself to compute the expected results. Phenomenologists deal a little more with the ripples on the surface and a little less with the laws beneath it.

Though I wanted to do pure theory, I ultimately ended up spending much of my life in physics as a phenomenologist. Over the long run, this stood me in very good stead. When I moved to Wall Street, I found quantitative finance to resemble phenomenology much more than it resembled pure theory. Quantitative finance is concerned with the techniques that people use to value financial contracts and, given the fluctuations of the human psyche, it is a pragmatic study of surfaces rather than a principled study of depths. Physics, in contrast, is concerned with God's canons, which seem to be more easily captured in the simple broad statements that characterize profound physical laws.

I had a passion for the content of physics, but I was also possessed by a hungry ambition for its earthly rewards. Both passion and hunger persisted over the years, despite the inevitable disappointments. Ten years later, as a postdoctoral researcher at Oxford in 1976, I experienced a minor epiphany about ambition's degradation. At age 16 or 17, I had wanted to be another Einstein; at 21, I would have been happy to be another Feynman; at 24, a future T. D. Lee would have sufficed. By 1976, sharing an office with other postdoctoral researchers at Oxford, I realized that I had reached the point where I merely envied the postdoc in the office next door because he had been invited to give a seminar in France. In much the same way, by a process options theorists call time decay, financial stock options lose their potential as they approach their own expiration.

Chapter 2

Dog Years

■ *Life as a graduate student* ■ *Wonderful lectures* ■ *T. D. Lee,*
the brightest star in the firmament ■ *Seven lean years*
■ *Getting out of graduate school only half-alive* ■

I f you didn't mind wasting the best years of your youth, graduate student life at Columbia was paradise. Once you got over the first two hurdles—passing the PhD qualifying exams and obtaining a research advisor—no one seemed to give a damn about what happened to you. Being a graduate student was not a bad sinecure. The university just kept funneling you a small but livable stipend and hoped you stayed out of their way. I spent seven biblically-lean years in the physics department. One friend spent ten. We both got out alive.

Some didn't. It wasn't long before we had all heard the legend about the graduate student who had shot his PhD advisor. Several years ago I read a *New York Times* article about two graduate students who committed suicide while studying in the Harvard laboratory of Nobel Prize-winner Professor E. J. Corey. In a subsequent letter to the Sunday *New York Times* magazine of December 20, 1998, Linda Logdberg of Upper Nyack, New York, wrote in to comment on life as graduate student:

> . . . Perhaps even more now than then, graduate education is an
> extended adolescence during which highly intelligent young
> people see their world shrink to fit the dimensions of their advi-

sor's laboratory. . . . With their identities bound to the outcome of the thesis project, graduate students are socialized to view other options (teaching, industry, even changing to another type of work altogether) with contempt. Wanting a decent wage and meaningful work that occupies, say, only 50 hours per week are considered signs of selling out.

It's an accurate description. We went into science for the love of it and thought nothing else was half as good. Some failed the PhD qualifying exam and left at the end of one year. Others passed the exam and then gave up before getting a thesis advisor. Many threw in the towel mid-thesis. The remainder struggled through and went on to a life of itinerant postdoctoral research. Few of us had an easy time. Ms. Logdberg is especially accurate in acknowledging the undeclared self-hatred we felt in looking down on those of our friends who, like failed novitiates in a nunnery, shamefacedly transferred their efforts to less ambitious endeavors. "Shame is Pride's cloke," I read in Blake's *Proverbs of Hell*; I understood exactly what he meant. But that was later.

The first year at Columbia consisted of four courses per semester followed by "the quals," the general PhD qualifying examination one had to pass in order to be allowed to continue with the doctoral program. To be a theorist, you also had to pass a special theory section on the quals. Without this formal admittance, no advisor would take you on.

I knew little modern physics so that, even if I were to pass the quals and be admitted to the rarified world of theory, I would have to spend another two years taking a host of preparatory courses. If I had gone to graduate school in Cambridge, England, where there was less required coursework, I might have finished my PhD in three or four years. Now I would have to wait that long before even beginning research! I had taken one step forward, but now faced two disappointing steps back.

Given that I wanted to be a theorist, there was little choice. Without the proper education, it is impossible to do theoretical research. I half-envied my budding experimentalist friends who were able to contribute something useful as soon as they started their apprenticeship—they could build particle detectors, write computer programs, and analyze data. Despite their worm's eye view, they had something constructively rewarding to tackle. We theorists seemed to be dishearteningly useless and alone.

Years later, when I moved to Wall Street, I especially liked the ways in which one could be usefully busy in quantitative finance. There was always a program to write, a trading interface to design, a calculation to do. It was nice to be able to contribute without having to be extraordinary.

Meanwhile, as I settled down into New York in 1966, life gradually improved. Every morning I rose to WNEW AM's Klavan and Finch, who pretended to be the men in the traffic helicopter that WNEW did not possess; one of them read printed traffic reports over the rotor noise simulated by the other. I still meet people who recall their endless pitches for "Dennison's, a men's clothier, Route 22, Union, New Jersey, open 10 A.M. to 5 the next morning. Money talks, nobody walks!" The Route 22 I imagined as I heard this was some exotic Kerouac cross-country highway, with a touch of the tawdry charm of Nabokov's *Lolita* motels. In 1980, when I finally decided to leave physics, I found myself driving down the same Route 22 en route to my interview at Bell Laboratories in Murray Hill, New Jersey. It didn't totally disappoint.

I liked New York's Upper West Side, its almost Caribbean atmosphere and vibrant street life. Manhattan was a marvelous place in which to be lonely. You could walk all the way down Broadway from Columbia to Times Square, watching people, stopping for a solitary coffee at soon-to-be-extinct Automats or Hopperesque Chock-Full-of-Nuts diners, and never feel isolated. Hope lurked on every block. The Puerto Ricans around I. House sat on the steps of their brownstones until late on hot summer nights. My friend and fellow student Eté Szüts, a 1956 refugee from Hungary, taught me the ropes. After an evening of doing homework problems, we would walk down to 123rd Street and Broadway for a midnight slice of pizza made by a small dapper Italian man in a white apron and T-shirt who combed his elegant grey hair while he looked at himself admiringly in the mirror as his enormously fat wife observed him resentfully from a thin metal folding chair that somehow supported her. The jukebox, I remember, played "There's a Kind of Hush (All Over The World)."

Some aspects of life in New York took getting used to. I was surprised by the easy and familiar kidding around between whites, blacks, and Asians in I. House. Twenty-one years of seeing blacks regarded as the invisible backdrop to white life in South Africa had left its mark on me, which only then began to fade.

I was also struck by the discrepancy in styles of cursing. I had never actually heard the word "motherfucker" uttered until a few weeks after I arrived in Manhattan, when two ten-year-old boys imperturbably called each other just that on the 104 bus that ran up and down Broadway. Heard for the first time, it sounded shockingly literal.

Finally, I was impressed by the exceptional independence of American graduate students. At the University of Cape Town, textbooks were regarded as auxiliary material. We took careful lecture notes and studied them thoroughly, and that was usually enough. In my second week at Columbia, I was shocked to discover that one assigned homework problem was totally unrelated to any material covered in class. Thinking that the professor had erred, I walked down the I. House corridor to query Eté, who told me that the relevant material could be found in the last section of the second chapter of our textbook. I was momentarily dismayed at the notion that someone might set problems on topics that were never discussed in class. From then on, I focused as much on textbook reading as I did on note-taking.

At Columbia, the classes I liked best were taught by people who gave you a feel for what it was like to discover something new, as well as a sense of how it had been done.

In my first year, I took a course in advanced electromagnetic theory from Richard Friedberg, a dishevelled-looking *wunderkind* who, as an undergraduate, we heard, had cracked a famous unsolved problem in logic and number theory. The method he used to solve it is still called Friedberg numbering. Now a young professor, he was one of a stable of young whizkids who had studied under T. D. Lee and then joined the department as faculty.

Friedberg was unkempt, distracted, and pale. He often closed his eyes for long periods in class as he tried to concentrate. Eté delighted in telling me that Friedberg was a true genius. In keeping with his persona, he quickly put his own stamp on the course he taught. Instead of taking the standard didactic approach to electricity and magnetism, Friedberg plunged us into thrilling intellectual history. We were each told to buy a Dover reprint of the Dutch physicist Lorentz's early-twentieth-century classic *The Theory of Electrons*. The book, based on Lorentz's lectures at Columbia in 1906, was an account of his heroic pre-Einsteinian intellectual struggles to resolve the contradictions between the laws of Newton and the laws of Maxwell on which all of physics was then based.

Maxwell's late-nineteenth-century theory of electromagnetism described the propagation of light waves through a stationary material fluid, the ether, that supposedly filled all of space. Newton's seventeenth-century laws of mechanics described the motion of all matter, and hence the motion of the ether itself. Step by painful step, Lorentz explained how to combine the two theories so as to predict how light would propagate in moving fluids or how it would change its appearance to moving observers. There were paradoxes in Lorentz's stitched-together theory that he could eliminate only by making modifications to the assumed structure of matter itself. He deduced that moving objects would have to contract in size as they moved through the ether. These painstaking conclusions brought him closer and closer to the formulas of Einstein's 1905 theory of special relativity, but without the insight about space and time to match it.

Lorentz's theories were relegated to the footnotes of history, and he never fully grasped Einstein's radical insights. Friedberg's lectures brought Lorentz's struggles to life; they gave me an immense appreciation for how Einstein's cerebral and yet intuitive analysis eliminated or sidestepped the confusion that came before. Ever since, I have been curious about *how* breakthroughs occur. No discovery, in physics or finance, is as obvious as it seems to the people who read the textbooks written even a few years later.

It amazed me that, using Einstein's formalism, I could so easily solve problems about the motion of light in moving fluids that had once been too complex for anyone to tackle. Somehow, Einstein had transformed almost inconceivable mysteries into mere formalism and rules. Now, after a little education, any first-year graduate student could, like an organ-grinder making music, calculate the correct answers to questions that couldn't have been posed a few decades earlier. I became ever more constantly aware of the gap between creator and disciple. Everything looks simple once you have been taught it. However, it is only when you have struggled amidst the chaos of the sensible world on your own that you can understand how difficult it is to impose or discern an order that eventually, in retrospect, looks deceptively obvious.

I still have a copy of my 1967 blue examination book for Friedberg's course, filled with my handwritten essay on Lorentz's attempts to explain the propagation of light through the ether. Once every few years I like to take a look at the complimentary comment Friedberg wrote in the margin, saying that my answer had gone beyond the question asked, but that it dealt "with the required points as well as the superfluous material in a completely clear and intelligent way, correct in every detail."

The best single lecture I have ever attended was a seminar by Mark Kač given at Columbia sometime in the early 1970s. Kač, a Polish-born expert in probability theory, is well known to both physicists and finance theorists for the eponymous Feynman-Kač method of solving the differential equations that occur both in quantum mechanics and in options theory. His seminar had the catchy title "Can you hear the shape of a drum?" In it he described the conditions under which an imaginary blind listener, endowed with a perfect ear capable of hearing all the frequencies of the sound waves emitted from a drum, would be able to mathematically determine the shape of the drum itself. This problem is part of the more general field of inverse scattering; years later at Goldman Sachs, Iraj Kani and I used a similar approach to show how an imaginary options market observer, having recorded the prices of all options on a stock, could then mathematically determine the shape of the surface that described all future stock volatilities.

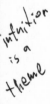

What was so impressive about Kač's presentation was his painstaking explanation of how he used his intuition to find his way out of the blind alleys he drifted into as he searched for a solution. He was also amusing. He recounted that in Amsterdam the same talk had mistakenly been advertised on campus with the title "Can you hear the shape of a dream?" and had consequently drawn a large and very different late-1960s audience. It reminded me of a similar story at Columbia about the curious crowd of medical students who showed up for an astrophysics seminar on stellar structure entitled "White Dwarfs and Red Giants."

To be one of T. D. Lee's graduate students was everyone's dream. The 1950s and '60s were the dawn of the age of symmetry in particle physics. Lee's theories and Columbia's experimenters—Lederman, Schwartz, Steinberger, and the one female professor in the department, Chien-Shiung Wu, whom everyone referred to as Madame Wu—were at the center of the search for symmetry and the discovery of its subtle violations.

Symmetry is the pattern that tells you how to generate one part of an object from another. It condenses information. Saying that a human face is symmetrical is another way of telling you that you do not need to draw both sides of it; instead, you can generate the left side from the right. Said differently, a truly symmetric human face is indistinguishable from its mirror image, which flips the left and right sides.

Before Lee and Yang, every physicist believed it to be obvious beyond question that the forces of nature are reflection-invariant, so that the mirror image of every natural event is itself an equally probable natural event. This assumed property of nature was called the law of parity conservation, because of the equality or parity between the mirror image and the actual event itself.

Physicists are familiar with four forces, the strong, the electromagnetic, the weak, and the gravitational force. The strong force binds together the protons and neutrons that make up the nucleus at the center of every atom. The electromagnetic force causes the electrons in atoms to orbit their nucleus and emit light. The weak force is responsible for "beta decay," the radioactive disintegration of nuclei by electron emission. Gravity, the oldest and most familiar force, governs the motions of falling apples, the earth and the moon, the planets, stars, and galaxies.

In the 1950s physicists knew that the strong and electromagnetic forces conserved parity. They unquestionably assumed that the weak force conserved parity, too. It seemed inconceivable that it shouldn't. No one could imagine that looking at nature in a mirror might yield a world that couldn't exist.

Then, two strange new and unstable particles, the *tau* and the *theta*, were discovered in cosmic rays. In most respects the two particles seemed almost identical; they had the same mass and electric charge, but they decayed differently. What could make two almost indistinguishable particles decay into two different final states? That was the famous *tau-theta puzzle* of the 1950s.

In 1956 Lee and his collaborator Chen-Ning Yang pointed out that the two particles might in fact be one and the same particle, which then, subject to the weak force, decayed in two different ways, but that this could only happen if the weak force responsible for its decay was *not* reflection-invariant. It was a preposterous suggestion that Lee and Yang took seriously and systematically. They analyzed all previous experiments that had studied the weak force in atoms and nuclei and found that, contrary to everyone's unquestioned belief, no previous experiment had ever truly tested the assumed symmetry between an event and its reflection. With further study, Lee and Yang suggested specific experiments to check for parity violation in nuclear weak decays.

Most physicists were skeptical. How, they wondered, could any of nature's laws not be symmetric under reflection? But within a few months, by early 1957, Madame Wu and her collaborators carried out the experiment Lee and Yang proposed, and showed that they were vindicated. Lee and Yang received their Nobel Prize that same year.

Lee and Yang's discovery that Nature was slightly asymmetric sparked a revolution. Slowly but inexorably, further experiments in the 1950s and 1960s revealed further subtle asymmetries of the weak interaction. T. D. was at the center of these investigations.

At Columbia and far beyond, T. D. was renowned and celebrated. At the weekly research seminars I attended on the eighth floor of Pupin, every speaker felt compelled to focus on him; as they spoke, their eyes fixated only on him, and he let no statement he did not fully agree with pass him by. No matter who lectured at the seminar, T. D. concentrated intensely on their argument, and interrupted at the first instant something was not satisfactory. At times he broke in on the initial sentence of the talk, refusing to let a speaker proceed until the point was clarified. Sometimes clarification never came; I once witnessed the humiliation of a visiting postdoc who was forced to defend the first sentence he uttered for the entire hour and a half allowed for his seminar. No one dared restrain T. D.

With his Moses-by-Michelangelo persona, beams of light emerging from his forehead, T. D. radiated an intense purity. At first I imagined that his rigorous questioning was the by product of a pure search for knowledge and truth. Later I began to detect a latent glee with which he savaged the imperfections in other people's talks. He enjoyed disorienting them. The only person I ever saw shake loose of his dogged grasp was the late Bram Pais, a small but feisty Dutch-born professor at Rockefeller University, who was able to half-playfully, half-ironically kid T. D. into loosening his jaws.

Brilliance seemed paramount in the Columbia physics department. T. D. was willing to supervise only the stellar *wunderkinder* who often went on to become inordinately young Columbia physics professors. The department developed an incestuous air; the pressure of his presence on his students-turned-faculty, like sons in their father's house, must have been fierce. Over time they seemed to gravitate towards research problems a little removed from the mainstream, as though searching for clear air to breathe. Unlike Rabi or Schwinger, who took on many more students and generated schools of disciples who propagated out into the world, T. D. never gave birth to anyone of his caliber.

Over time I noticed a darker side to Lee and Yang's genius. At an American Physical Society meeting I attended in the late 1960s, I observed that although they were both on the same panel, they avoided acknowledging each other's presence. In class at Columbia, I noticed that T. D.'s recounting of the insights central to their jointly published discoveries seemed to focus on his own feats. Finally, someone told me what most people in the field knew, that Lee and Yang had stopped working together several years earlier, and now no longer spoke to each other. Years later, after I left physics, I saw a copy of an angry reminiscence that T. D. had circulated in response to a published reminiscence of Yang's. It contained his vengeful version of how he and Yang had argued and then separated, and described how Yang had wept in his office.

I have no idea on whose side justice lay. I focus on T. D. here only because he was most visible to me, because he had made such enviable discoveries, and because he had such a powerful influence on the atmosphere we inhaled in Pupin Hall. It was disappointing to learn that even the Nobel Prize and almost eternal fame were not enough to overcome vanity and competition.

History takes strange turns. To Columbia students in the 1960s, Lee seemed to have the inside track in what we foolishly thought of as his race with Yang; I say "foolishly" because both of them had done outstanding work we could never realistically hope to emulate. Then in the 1970s, Yang's reputation accelerated. Two decades earlier, in what is now a classic paper, he had observed that Maxwell's theory of electromagnetism was the consequence of a subtle but powerful symmetry called _local gauge invariance_. Going out on a limb, Yang extended this symmetry to the strong and weak forces, too. The idea lay fallow for a decade or more. Then, suddenly, it provided the foundation for both the Glashow-Weinberg-Salam unified theory of weak and electromagnetic interactions and Gell-Mann's quantum chromodynamics theory of strong forces. Recently, some practicing physicists with an interest in finance have even begun to apply the same principle to the "trading force" between market participants that determines financial values. On this matter the jury has not even been assembled.

For current physics students, Lee and Yang are a part of history. For those of us who witnessed them, it was hard to resist the unfair urge to rank. The truth is that any one of us would be happy to have written just one the several remarkable papers they authored or coauthored. Yet when fellow Columbia physics students from those days meet up, they still argue about whether Lee or Yang was a better physicist, discussing the ancient epic feats of bygone heroes the way that the animals in the final chapter of _The Wind in the Willows_ reminisce about the fabled exploits of Mr. Toad and his friends.

I worked studiously throughout that first American academic year of 1966–67 and then, after a short trip home to South Africa, began my preparations for the September PhD qualifying exams.

The quals were extremely broad. They aimed to test one's general understanding of all of physics—classical mechanics, electromagnetic theory, optics, thermodynamics, solid-state, atomic and nuclear physics, and quantum mechanics—and probed your ability to explain all sorts of observed phenomena. One question, set by the constantly inventive Friedberg, described the denizens of a planet in a distant galaxy who recorded the risings, settings, and eclipses of their several suns and moons, and then demanded that you deduce their orbits from Kepler's seventeenth-century laws of planetary motion. For a brief but heady period after I finished studying, I felt that I had a good grasp of the whole of physics and would be able to come up with a reasoned answer to any question about the universe tossed at me.

I also took the theory section of the exam, in which an essay question asked for a description of some independent theoretical work. I wrote about the unified field theories of electromagnetism and gravitation that I had studied for my senior thesis two years earlier in Cape Town. I had been particularly attracted to a paper by Theodor Kaluza and Oskar Klein, two European physicists of the 1920s. Their paper had postulated that the universe we lived in was five- rather than four-dimensional, but that the extent of the fifth dimension was so small that we were unaware of it. They had then shown that if Einstein's general theory of relativity held in this larger five-dimensional world, with one dimension unobserved, we would experience the theory's forces as those of ordinary (four-dimensional) electromagnetic theory and gravitation. It was a platonically beautiful theory that seemed quaintly irrelevant to the pragmatic particle-hunting theorists and experimentalists at Columbia in the 1960s, but its day was to come again later in the 1980s and 1990s when string theories of particles and their interactions became fashionable.

I passed my qualifying exams easily and well enough to be admitted to the privileged class of people who were "allowed to do theoretical physics" at Columbia. But there was a caveat—I was required to complete two extra years of coursework before beginning my research. I was in for a long haul.

Although it was premature, I soon began to strategize about seeking a PhD advisor who would take me on as a student. I quickly but regretfully discarded any idea of working for T. D. Even the thought of approaching him was too daunting; he accepted only one exceptional student every few years.

Then I hit on the idea of working for Gerald Feinberg, the earliest of T. D.'s *wunderkinder*. Feinberg was a tall, skinny, stiff-looking man with a flattop haircut that always reminded me of someone I had once seen in an *Archie* comic book. Every day he wore a very small conservative bow tie and a belt whose gold buckle proclaimed "GF." The whole effect was very Fifties.

Feinberg was renowned as one of the earliest people to propose that the muon particle, to all initial appearances simply a sort of heavy electron, carried a special sort of quantum-mechanical flavor, a sort of "mu-ness" that differentiated it from the electron. He had attended the Bronx High School of Science, where he had been a classmate and friend of both Glashow and Weinberg, the physicists who later won the Nobel Prize for their unification of weak and electromagnetic interactions. Perhaps in order to avoid competing on T. D.'s turf, he had drifted out of the center field of particle physics and was then developing his own esoteric theories of hypothetical faster-than-light particles that he named *tachyons*. Physicists usually conjecture the existence of new particles in order to make a flawed or incomplete theory consistent, but Feinberg seemed to have had no really good reason for suggesting the existence of tachyons. Gell-Mann had once wittily suggested that Nature operated on the Totalitarian Principle that states, "Everything not forbidden is compulsory." So, perhaps, Feinberg's logic wasn't as frivolous as it seemed. In any event, it was a risky wager; if tachyons were found it would be staggering, but if they were not, nothing would change and no one would care. Anyone can speculate.

I wanted to be Feinberg's student, but I didn't know how to go about it. Since it was premature for formal arrangements and since I was naturally reticent and shy, I simply began to greet him very politely whenever our paths crossed.

Graduate school was a small community. In corridors and elevators and on campus, I was soon running into Feinberg several times a day, always giving him a polite hello and a nice smile. He would reciprocate similarly with a sort of nervous curling of the lips. As time passed, this limbo of flirtatious foreplay continued unabated. I could never find the courage to broach the question of being his student; I suppose I must have hoped it would just happen wordlessly. Every time I saw him I smiled; every time I smiled he bared his lips back at me with greater awkwardness. Our facial manipulations bore increasingly less resemblance to anything like a real smile; each of our reciprocated gestures was a caricature, a Greek theatrical mask signaling friendliness. One day, on about the fifth intersection of our paths on that particular day, I could stand it no longer. I saw him heading towards me down one of the long dark, old-fashioned, Pupin corridors, and immediately turned towards the nearest stairwell and went up one floor to avoid him. Having succeeded at this once, I was compelled to do it repeatedly. Soon I was moving upstairs or downstairs to another floor as soon as I saw him approaching, like the protagonist in some ghastly version of the video game *Lode Runner*.

My courtship of Feinberg, now badly out of control, ended abruptly one discomforting morning when we both entered the same elevator and rode up eight floors without looking at each other, pretending to be absorbed in reading the elevator inspection certificate. The end was a great relief.

I watched Feinberg from a distance afterwards. At the weekly coffee hour in Pupin, I noticed his vaguely Strangelovian bent for carrying logic to extremes, a weakness I later came to associate with many graduates of the University of Chicago business school. He had created an organization called the Prometheus Project, which aimed to plan for humanity's future. I observed long discussions between Feinberg and Milton Friedman's son David, then a physics postdoc at Columbia, about the application of hard-nosed rationality to society. I once heard Feinberg suggest that many of Manhattan's 1970s social problems could be solved by forbidding anyone who earned less than, say, $10,000 per year to live there. It had not occurred to him, apparently, that this excluded many of the people who worked at the university. Several years later we heard that he intended to be cryogenically frozen when he died, in anticipation of being reheated and resuscitated at a later time when whatever would cause his death would be curable. Sadly, he died of cancer in 1992. I recently found hundreds of Internet references to both Feinberg and the New York Cryonics Society, lamenting the fact that despite his advocacy of the Society, he ultimately left no instructions for his own bodily preservation.

Late in 1968, still searching for a thesis advisor, I ran into one last temptation to avoid becoming a particle theorist. My American cousin in Manhattan introduced me to Robert Herman, his old City College student friend from the 1930s. Herman, a physicist, had abandoned academia for family reasons and was now working at General Motors, analyzing vehicular traffic flow. Academic particle physicists looked down on this kind of applied physics as pedestrian work, so to speak, but Herman had done outstanding fundamental research before that. In the 1940s he had coauthored the first paper to suggest that the Big Bang that created our universe would have filled all of space with microwave radiation. Arno Penzias and Robert Wilson at Bell Laboratories later fortuitously detected this background radiation and won the Nobel Prize. Then in the 1950s, Herman and Robert Hofstadter, another City College friend of my cousin's, became the first physicists to probe the internal structure of the proton by shooting fast electrons at it and then watching them bounce off. If the proton were a hard, small object—like a miniature billiard ball—one would expect to see the electron occasionally recoil at a very large angle to the line of fire; if, however, the proton were spongy, there would be very few sharp collisions. Surprisingly, Hofstadter and Herman observed very few dramatic recoils; they concluded that the proton was a cotton-candy sphere with a soft interior rather than the small, hard, elementary object everyone had imagined. Hofstadter alone won the Nobel Prize for this work. My cousin claimed that Herman was deprived of his share of the Prize because of the selection committee's prejudice against scientists outside academia.

When we spoke, Herman suggested that I work in applied physics and sent me some papers on traffic flow he had written, but I was still a stranger to compromise and I declined. Coincidentally, though, my future PhD thesis would turn out to be closely related to the Hofstadter-Herman electron-proton scattering experiment.

I spent my second and third years at Columbia taking the myriad of required courses, all the while continuing my quest for a particle physics thesis advisor. Finally, in early 1969 I reached an agreement to work for Norman Christ. He was the most recent in the long line of T. D.'s *wunderkinder*, a polite and enthusiastically perky young man who was just about my age, but who had received his PhD under T. D.'s tutelage in record time two years earlier, before I had even arrived at Columbia. After two years as a postdoc at the Institute for Advanced Study in Princeton, he had returned to Columbia as a tenured associate professor. In terms of a career, he seemed to have everything one could hope for. It must have been a heavy burden, however, to carry the weight of so many expectations of precociousness. I was relieved, many years later, to hear him uncharacteristically comment that a physicist spends about half of his or her time enthralled and the other half in depression, an observation that corresponded closely to my own experience.

I was Norman's first PhD student and, perhaps because he had been a student so recently himself, our relations were stilted. During the four years I worked for him he never succeeded in finding a comfortable mode of addressing me. I suppose that the difficulty arose from the tension between the parity of our ages and the disparity of our relative positions. He could not bring himself to simply call me "Emanuel" and so he eventually resorted to addressing me as "Mr. Derman," uttered between invisible quote marks in a manner intended to imply ironic jocosity. I, in turn, could never manage to call him "Norman." It was only with my father- and mother-in-law that I ever again experienced a similar sort of naming difficulty: The first names they told me to use seemed to connote too much familiarity, "Dr." and "Mrs." seemed too formal, and the Slovak analogs of "Mom" and "Dad" that my wife used were too unnatural. In the end, with them though not with Norman, first names prevailed.

In the fall of 1968, I moved out of I. House to share an apartment with a friend on Amsterdam Avenue and 120th Street, just across the street from where I now teach financial engineering. With most of my foreign friends from the previous two years back in their home countries, I spent much time alone. One evening I experienced my first mugging at the hands of a group of teenagers, with two more muggings to follow over the next few years. But, on the plus side, sometime in the spring of 1969, I noticed a new and exotic foreign female student in the physics department library. Since women in physics were rare, a new arrival attracted everyone's attention. Though I hadn't yet contrived to meet her, I watched from a distance her laughter-filled gesticulating conversations with some of the other graduate students. Then, one Saturday evening, I saw her at a fellow student's party on 119th Street. I approached her and learned that her name was Eva. She had left Czechoslovakia for a summer job in Germany during the Prague Spring of 1968 and, after the Russian invasion, had not returned. Her English was charmingly limited; I felt sad to see the skimpy physics lecture notes she had jotted down in Slovak during physics classes that were delivered in English. When I walked her home from the party we discovered that we both lived in the same apartment building on 120th Street. Soon we were spending much of our time together.

I spent the summer of 1969 at a particle physics summer school at Brookhaven National Laboratories in Upton, Long Island. Most weekends I headed back into the city to see Eva; sometimes she came out to Brookhaven to visit me. We went swimming in the rough surf off Smith Point, in Atlantic Ocean waves of a size I hadn't seen since I had left Cape Town. But mostly the summer weeks dragged by slowly and yet unquietly on dreary Long Island, until finally, at summer's end, I went home to Cape Town to visit my family.

I was restless there, too. Three years had passed since I had left, and one day, confused about my future on all fronts, I visited an Afrikaner psychiatrist named Jannie Louw at the recommendation of my elder sister. He listened to my account of distant loneliness and uncertainty, and then half-pleased and half-displeased me by avoiding specific advice and instead suggesting a philosophical approach to my suffering. I went to see him once more, and when I left, he recommended that I read two books: Victor Frankl's *Man's Search for Meaning* and Rudolf Steiner's *Knowledge of the Higher Worlds.* I found some solace in Frankl, but never bothered with Steiner until years later.

One person who made a strong impression on me during that Brookhaven summer was Mike Green, a graduate student in particle physics at Cambridge. Mike was far ahead of me academically, already working on research for his thesis. Everything went enviably faster in British graduate schools. In subsequent years I ran into him regularly at summer research institutes in Aspen and Stanford, and at university seminars at Oxford and Cambridge. Always, he was single-mindedly working away on his beloved string theory, a model that treats elementary particles as tiny, one-dimensional, rubber-band-like, vibrating strings that wiggle and move at relativistic speeds. I always admired Mike's tenacity, his capacity for banging away at the same problem for years until it yielded. Fifteen years later, when I had already left physics, Mike became famous for proving that string theories could be mathematically consistent only if the universe had either 10 or 26 dimensions. Uncharacteristically, I didn't feel the smallest pinch of envy or competition at his deserved success. Like the Kaluza-Klein theories I had studied as an undergraduate, Mike's model of particles was viable only in a large-dimensioned universe, which could be mapped to our apparently four-dimensional universe only if its extent in each of those extra dimensions was so small as to be unobservable. String theory is so arcane that physicists sometimes describe it as "a little bit of twenty-first–century physics that accidentally fell into the twentieth century."

The physics department was home to more passionate clashes. Several professors, among them Leon Lederman, Malvin Ruderman, and Richard Garwin, worked part-time for the Jason Division of the Institute for Defense Analysis, a group of elite scientists from elite universities who studied defense-related problems. Norman Christ, my young PhD advisor, was a member, too. During the height of the Vietnam protests, Columbia antiwar student groups picketed these professors at their homes and in their seminars. Though the contents of the Jason reports were presumably secret, the antiwar activists circulated their titles. I recall one, "Interdiction of Trucks by Night," which we assumed to be about methods of bombing the Ho Chi Minh trail. One fall we heard that antiwar protesters had picketed Ruderman's home in his suburban neighborhood on the eve of Yom Kippur, pointing out the conflict they perceived between observing the Jewish day of atonement and writing military-related advisory papers. I recall Ruderman responding with great and somewhat disingenuous indignation at the invasion of his personal life. I was most impressed by Richard Garwin. Whereas most of the other professors tried to dodge the moral responsibilities of their military-related activities with a mixture of righteous outrage, wry charm, and vague ramblings about working from within the system, Garwin simply asserted that there was a role for force in the world, and that he believed in what he was doing.

Jason still exists, though a March 23, 2002, *New York Times* article reported that the Pentagon has withdrawn its budgetary support. Jason, the article jokingly noted, is rumored to be an acronym for Junior Achiever, Somewhat Older Now—English for *ex-wunderkind*, I guess.

In late 1969 I finally began my PhD thesis. Just at that time, the particle physics world I was entering was agog over two momentous new developments. First, experimentalists were discovering the earliest hints of the actual existence of quarks, and second, theorists were beginning to understand the origin of the subtle similarity between the weak and electromagnetic forces.

Gell-Mann's version of the Eightfold Way had predicted that the proton, the neutron, and all the other thus-far observed strongly interacting particles could in principle be made out of three smaller subparticles called quarks. Quarks, if they existed, had to be almost unbelievably peculiar; they had to carry a fractional electric charge of either one-third or two-thirds the charge of the proton, but no one had *ever* seen a particle of fractional charge. Although the Eightfold Way implied their existence, physicists were reluctant to take them seriously. Instead, avoiding the reality behind their mathematics, they had come to think of quarks as mathematically consistent but fictitious components that could never be observed. It was as though the only coins you had ever seen in circulation were nickels, dimes, and quarters, and you had concluded that somewhere there had to be a one-cent coin.

If a proton really contained three hard little quarks deep inside it, one should be able to "see" them experimentally by shooting a fast electron at a proton and observing it recoil sharply when it struck a quark head-on. The method is a little like looking for bits of eggshell in a sponge cake—once in a while, as you chew, you hear a sharp crack as your teeth hit a fragment of shell.

Robert Hofstadter, my cousin's City College friend of the 1930s, had observed no such sharp recoils, and everyone had concluded that the proton was pure sponge and no eggshell. Hofstadter's experiments, however, were limited. He had kept an eye only on the so-called *elastic* collisions, those in which the target proton remained intact as it recoiled like a struck billiard ball. Now, in the late 1960s, a later generation of physicists at the Stanford Linear Accelerator Center (SLAC) began to watch so-called *inelastic* electron-proton collisions in which the proton disintegrated rather than recoiled after being struck. Amazingly, in these collisions, many of the electrons did in fact recoil sharply, as though they had struck something very hard and small. Somewhere deep inside there truly were bits of eggshell.

Feynman, from his base at Caltech in Pasadena, had developed a simple phenomenological picture of the proton as a closed bag of hard little quark-like constituents which he called its "partons." In Feynman's picture, the energetic electrons that scattered off the protons at SLAC provided a metaphorical X-ray view of the partons inside the proton, much as an ordinary X-ray or a CAT scan uses high-frequency radiation to provide a view of our internal organs. Using the information from the SLAC X-ray of the partons, one could calculate many other properties of the proton itself.

More and more, we began to believe that protons, long thought of as unsplittable, might be composite—they might contain quarks. But this was not all that excited us; we were also increasingly becoming aware of the similarity between the weak and electromagnetic forces. Since the 1930s, physicists had been aware of an intriguing analogy between Maxwell's 1873 theory of electricity and magnetism and Fermi's 1934 theory of the weak force. However, no one had yet been able to extend this analogy into a consistent theory of the two forces. Then, in the 1960s, Glashow, Weinberg, and Salam, all working independently, accomplished this unification by creating what is now called the "standard model." They based their theory on Yang's symmetry principle of local gauge invariance.

The standard model related nature's forces to each other much like Mendeleyev's periodic table had connected the diverse chemical elements.

Mendeleyev had detected a hint of order in the properties of elements and then deduced the existence of other as yet-undiscovered elements necessary to complete the pattern. Similarly, Glashow, Weinberg, and Salam had detected a pattern in both the weak and electromagnetic forces, and then deduced the existence of other previously undiscovered weak forces necessary to complete their picture. The sum total of all these forces comprised the standard model. It was an ambitious but compelling theory; when it was verified, its creators won the Nobel Prize. Much of theoretical particle physics works in this way: You hear a few isolated bars of a beautiful song and try to figure out the whole piece by generalizing the pattern in the fragments.

My thesis work over the next three years employed both the theory of quarks and the Weinberg-Salam standard model which predicted new weak forces between electrons and quarks. One of these new forces, the so-called _weak neutral current_, would cause a small violation of parity in the collisions of electrons and quarks. If protons were bags of quarks, one should also be able to observe a small violation of parity in electron-proton collisions. The effect would be small and subtle, for the most part masked by the much stronger electromagnetic force between electrons and quarks.

In my thesis I proposed a new test of the standard model. In particular I suggested that experimentalists at SLAC try to observe the effects of the standard model's parity-violating weak force in the inelastic collisions of electrons with protons. In order to estimate the size of the signal, I made use of many of the skills I had gained during the past few years. I employed Lee and Yang's framework for analyzing parity violation and I used Feynman's parton-model description of the proton as a bag of quarks. In this way I calculated how much of a parity-violating asymmetry would be seen if the standard model were indeed correct.

I began my research in 1970. Slowly, I read the multitude of papers that explained how to use the parton model, repeating their published calculations on my own and checking that I could reproduce their results. Step by step, I learned the mechanics of the model and how to use it. Then I began my own work.

My first task was to carry out the long mathematical calculations that predicted the distribution of electrons recoiling after a collision with a quark. I did each calculation using "Feynman diagrams," the cartoon-like representation invented by Feynman to systematize the ways in

which particles interacted during collisions. I drew all the possible diagrams that could occur in a theory, and then, using Feynman's rules,
translated each picture into a mathematical formula and evaluated it.
The calculations, carried out with pen and paper, took up tens of pages.
I repeated each calculation at least twice to check for consistency. When
successive calculations didn't match, I searched each one for errors and
eliminated them until I found agreement. Today, however, much of the
repetitive algebraic manipulation would be done with symbolic mathematical programs like Mathematica™.

Feynman's diagrams and rules were a sort of bookkeeping-by-picture
process that miraculously captured all the details of the standard model
in a series of diagrams; they allowed people less talented than Feynman
to perform the most complex calculations carefully and correctly. Many
of the great advances in physics are like this; they codify and make routine what was formerly almost impossible to think about. Whenever I
have a new problem to work on—in physics or options theory—the first
major struggle is to gain some intuition about how to proceed; the
second struggle is to transform this intuition into something more for-
mulaic, a set of rules anyone can follow, rules that no longer require the
original insight itself. In this way, one person's breakthrough becomes
everybody's possession.

After several months I completed the calculations for electrons scattering off quarks. But in the real world electrons scatter off protons—
that is, bags of quarks. My next task was therefore to calculate what
happened when an electron hit a bag. I embarked on extensive numerical computations using old-fashioned, punched card programs that I
submitted to the university computer center to run overnight on their
IBM mainframe. It was tedious: In those days we had no interactive
terminals or PCs; one typographical mistake in punching the cards
could lose you a full day's work.

It was then that I learned never to trust any new formula I had
derived without thoroughly cross-checking it for consistency from all
angles. Usually, anything new and complex is an extension of some
older, simpler, and more familiar calculation. The first check is therefore
to switch off the complexity and verify that you obtain the familiar
results. I found it so easy to make mistakes in my calculations that I
began to wonder about the safety of flying—how could engineers possibly trust their calculations when they designed airplanes, where life
and death rather than theories and reputations were at stake?

It took me seven years in graduate school to get my PhD, an astonishing ten percent of a lifetime. There were three preparatory years of coursework, one subsequent warm-up year in the area of my research, and two more years of my actual thesis research. Finally, I spent a half-year writing the thesis, composing a paper for publication, and preparing for my thesis defense. A small number of my friends got out of Columbia in five years, but many took eight or nine.

Sometimes we tried to save others from our fate. In the early 1970s Doug Hofstadter came by our office in Pupin. He was still unknown, a PhD student in physics at Eugene, Oregon, and not yet the famous author of *Gödel, Escher, Bach*. It took some time before I realized that he was the son of my cousin's friend Robert Hofstadter of electron–proton scattering fame. Doug was contemplating a switch to Columbia from the University of Oregon where he was in graduate school. Though it felt deliciously like biting the hand that fed us, we tried to warn him away from Pupin.

Most of us grew to hate our stay in the physics department. We spent the better part of our twenties shuttered there. For the most part we were ignored, receiving little attention from the people to whom we were apprenticed. My friend Chang-Li Yiu spent more than six months working on a thesis problem without conversing with his advisor, only to discover that his advisor had solved the same problem a few months earlier. Then he had to begin again. Though I was better off—Norman Christ was responsible and I met with him weekly—I often thought I might never complete my degree. You could coast from year to year, receiving your Department of Energy research grant, while no one seemed to care when or whether you finished, or what you would do afterwards.

In defiance, I struggled to look unbeaten during the final few years. I remember walking hand-in-hand with my wife down Broadway and passing a crowd of Columbia professors strolling up Broadway on the way back from lunch at the Moon Palace. As our paths crossed, I tried hard to look nonchalantly happy and carefree, talking animatedly, pretending to myself and to the professors passing by that they had no effect on the other parts of my life.

But of course they did. One summer in the early seventies, during the student protests against the American invasion of Cambodia, Eva and I went camping in the Catskills mountains with Chang-Li and his wife. After several days in a tent, cut off from any news, we went to meet my in-laws who were vacationing in a nearby hotel. As we arrived, my father-in-law somberly announced to us that a small bomb had exploded in one of the physics department's bathrooms. Without a moment's hesitation Chang-Li and I leapt in the air for joy, whooping and cheering. My in-laws looked at us in bewilderment, and I suddenly realized how far beyond the elastic limit we had been stretched.

I had waited four years to begin my thesis work, but once I knew enough to get going, I progressed steadily. Halfway through the research I gave a seminar on some of my early results to T. D. and the rest of the departmental faculty. In early 1972 I finally published my first paper, in which I used Feynman's parton model to try to explain the results of a recent Columbia experiment carried out by Leon Lederman and collaborators. My calculation was simply a warm-up exercise for the thesis work to come, but its publication and the sight of my name in print after so many years of waiting exhilarated me briefly. I completed my thesis research by late 1972 and, at long last, in the spring of 1973, formally defended my work in front of a committee consisting of T. D. himself, Christ, and Lederman. I answered their questions and then I was done.

My thesis, *Tests for a Weak Neutral Current in* $l^{\pm} + N \rightarrow l^{\pm} + Anything$, was published in 1973 in the *Physical Review*. It was a competent piece of work that analyzed how the then-unverified standard model of weak and electromagnetic forces would uniquely manifest itself through parity violation in electron-proton scattering. In 1978, a collaboration led by Charles Prescott and Richard Taylor at SLAC published the results of an elegant and careful experiment that confirmed a level of parity violation consistent with the standard model. A recent book on the history of twentieth-century particle physics[1] refers to the audience's prolonged applause after Prescott's first presentation of their experimental results as "the long elegiac salute given to the end of an age." Their experiment put the final stamp of approval on the standard model of Glashow, Weinberg, and Salam. I was pleased to note that my 1973 paper was one of the first papers they referenced.

[1]Crease, R. P., and C. C. Mann, *The Second Creation*, Rutgers University Press, Revised Edition (1996).

Despite the amount of time it took to finish my thesis, I have no real regrets; in a way, I am proud of the struggle. What I learned in those years—perseverance as much as mathematics—has stood me in good stead on Wall Street as well as in academia. When trying to discover something new in any field, one has to spend many years thinking, making false starts, wandering down blind alleys and stumbling into ditches, only to emerge again and keep going. For this, a PhD is a good, if painful, training.

Years later on Wall Street I was horrified to notice quant résumés listing the nonexistent degree A.B.D. That, I soon discovered, was a common business-world acronym for "All But Dissertation," a way of describing those who had tried to obtain a PhD but left academia before they had completed their dissertation. Since a PhD is by definition a research degree, the main achievement of which is the completion of a piece of original research described in a dissertation, I looked at A.B.D. as a kind of "Wayne's World" PhD (not!). I resented the way it devalued the innovation and effort involved in doing research.

I then began the search for a postdoctoral position, a two-year, low-paying research appointment that was the standard first step towards an academic career in science. I mailed out scores of letters with my *curriculum vitae* to physicists whose names I knew. I gave research seminars at any of the schools that invited me. But academic jobs were scarce—the universities were filled to the brim with young, tenured faculty hired during the past decade; I might well have to wait for a generation of physicists to die.

As in most endeavors, it helps to have someone pulling for you. At Goldman Sachs, people like to say that you need a "rabbi" to become a partner, and the Columbia physics department was definitely short on rabbis. In the end, because my work was topical and I was lucky, I received a two-year postdoctoral position at the University of Pennsylvania in Philadelphia, set to commence in September 1973.

I did not attend Columbia's May graduation, held outdoors on the giant plaza in front of Low Library where only a few years earlier I had watched New York City policemen chase students with truncheons during the nights of the 1968 student occupation. None of my graduate school friends seemed to bother with the ceremony either.

I spent one month that summer in Erice, a beautiful town high above Trapani in western Sicily, where I attended the annual Ettore Majorana particle physics summer school. Up on the mountain I had a tantalizing glimpse of the life of successful physicists on the conference circuit, who visited exotic places each summer. I sat with some of them in the town plaza, smoking cigarettes and sipping Italian aperitifs. One morning I had a hot shave at the local barber shop, where I lay tilted back in a heavy leather chair while the barber sharpened his razor on a strop. Years later I met corporate lawyers and Wall Street salesmen who touted the fringe benefits of their jobs—first-class flights, expensive meals, and fancy hotels. I silently scorned their focus on the material benefits of work. In physics, I thought, the life itself was the benefit; talking about physics to interesting people in interesting places was the main dish, not the cutlery.

In Erice I observed with slight envy another attendee, Frank Wilczek. He had just graduated from Princeton and was already the coauthor of a famous paper in field theory. Yet a large part of me was exhausted with physics and the seven-year struggle to shine. I consoled myself with a few sentences Einstein wrote in his autobiographical notes, composed at the age of 67, about the aftereffects of his final examinations: "This coercion had such a deterring effect [upon me] that, after I had passed the final examination, I found the consideration of any scientific problems distasteful to me for an entire year."

2 currencies

Chapter 3

Ph.D's seeking postdocs ⇒ full faculties.

A Sort of Life

■ *The priesthood of itinerant postdocs* ■ *Research isn't easy*
■ *Almost perishing, then publishing* ■ *The delirious
thrill of collaboration and discovery* ■

O n Labor Day of 1973 I hired a friend of a friend who ran a small part-time moving business to transport me and my belongings to Philadelphia. In order to gain respect and imply responsibility, I had told my landlord that I was "Dr. Derman," feeling only a slight twinge of guilt at exploiting my title and trying to pass for a "real" doctor. Our mover, who drove my wife and me down the turnpike from New York, told us that he routinely rolled back the odometer on the van he rented before returning it to Hertz, a common 1960s-style view of the legitimacy of stealing from large impersonal companies.

At the end of that weekend I began trying to settle into solitary Philadelphia while Eva returned to our familiar Columbia graduate-student apartment overlooking Tom's Restaurant at Broadway and 112th Street, a location later made famous beyond the Columbia community by Suzanne Vega and the television show "Seinfeld." Eva still had several years to go on her PhD in molecular biology. I had hoped she could move to Philadelphia with me, but it was impossible for her to change schools and PhD advisors. She had only recently switched from physics to biology, and as a condition of entry into the biology PhD program, she had needed to promise that she would complete her doctorate in the department. In making the move to biology she had asked for a recommendation from Madame Wu, who herself lived in Morningside Heights near Columbia, 50 miles apart from *her* physicist husband at Brookhaven National Laboratories. Madame Wu had met with Eva and lectured her on the need for sacrifice, making it plain that, since they knew she was married to me and that I would graduate before her, she would not be admitted to the biology doctoral program unless she gave her word that she would stay on there when I graduated. In an era when no one had yet invented the notion of political correctness, it was quite permissible for faculty to gauge a woman's seriousness before admitting her to graduate school. A few years later, when I went to work in industry, we heard stories of interviewers in business who asked women whether they would have an abortion if they unintentionally became pregnant and thought that childbearing would interfere with their work.

For the next two years Eva and I saw each other only on weekends and during parts of the summer. The tension of living like this was to be a perennial feature of my future years in academia.

I had imagined postdoctoral life as a sort of priesthood, the blissful apotheosis of a life dedicated to knowledge. In top-notch universities, a postdoc in theoretical physics had no mundane obligations—no teaching, no administration, no fixed hours. What remained was transcendental. You were hired for your research talent. All you had to do was find something conceptually worthwhile that interested you and then work on it. All that mattered was what you achieved. It was simple, but the stakes were high. No one I knew thought much about getting rich or about what they would earn. Everyone hoped to achieve something numinously great and was willing to work an entire lifetime at it. We looked down on professors who ceased "doing physics" once they achieved tenure. As we got older, we took solace in the stories of people who made great discoveries after the age of thirty. It was very different from Wall Street, where I heard twenty-something traders talk about "their number," the amount of money they figured they needed to be able to quit, certain that they would never have to work again.

Reality, of course, was different. I was friendless at Penn, surrounded by married nine-to-fivers, a sharp change from the casual gregariousness of the graduate-student life that I had grown accustomed to. Philadelphia was disagreeably unsafe and deserted compared to Morningside Heights. I was a married person unaccompanied by his spouse, a little too old and attached for the company of single graduate students and a little too young and uncoupled for the domesticity of the married faculty. I had little social life and spent most of my time alone.

Postdoc life was an atavism, a relic of a time long past. Postdoctoral research positions had been created to provide a brief interlude between being a graduate student and becoming a professor. But Americans' post-Sputnik view of science as the moral equivalent of war had produced a bubble of young scientists that, now tenured, occupied all the available faculty positions; they would not retire in less than thirty years. Faculty need students, and so aspiring physicists continued to enter the head of the PhD pipeline, but when they emerged at the tail, there was almost nowhere to go. Postdoc positions temporarily filled the void. They lasted about two years and paid little. They worked well for universities, though, for they got to sample a new bunch of young research physicists each year, and could pick an exceptional one for the rare faculty position that became available.

It was less pleasant for the average postdoc. You started each two-year position in the fall with a one-year grace period, during which time you tried to begin, complete, and publish some interesting research, so that by the fall of the second year you could apply for another postdoc position in another lab or department somewhere else in the world. Mitchell Feigenbaum, famous for his contributions to chaos theory, described it aptly: "These two-year positions made serious work almost impossible. After one year you had to start worrying about where you could go next." If you were unlucky enough to have only a one-year postdoc position, which was not uncommon, then you had no respite; you had to start applying for your next job as soon as you began the current one. The only way out—other than abandoning academic physics entirely—was to write a paper so acclaimed that you would be offered one of the few faculty positions available.

Some of my PhD friends, passionate and desperate enough to stay in physics even if they were paid nothing, became "freebies," people who had found no job anywhere and then asked for and received a desk and rudimentary research facilities with no pay at a top-ranked institution. Their aim was to get into a stimulating environment, make good contacts, and then do a piece of work that would get them a paying job. One friend went so far as to turn down a paid postdoc job at a second-tier institution in order to become a freebie at Harvard, where he then pulled off some research that landed him a subsequent paid position at a first-rate place, SLAC.

At the University of Pennsylvania, now without a PhD advisor, I had to take my own road, and so I began to look for something new to work on. I had spent most my graduate student years working on high-energy phenomenology, comparing other people's theories with other people's experiments. It was useful and interesting, but not as visionary as the physics I had imagined doing. Trying to be ambitious, I began to study the so-called Lee model, an idealized and therefore analytically soluble theory of particle interactions that was the subject of an early paper by T. D. himself. I hoped that it would form the basis for a deeper under-standing of quark forces. I spent most of my first semester at Penn try-ing vainly to master the field. But I found it difficult to concentrate; I was restless from the lack of friends, tense from the strains of a geo-graphically divided marital life, and tired from all the back-and-forth driving—I would go to New York on Friday nights and return to Phil-adelphia early on Monday mornings. Some weekends I was just too weary to make the trip and remained alone in Philadelphia, killing time and feeling half-resentful.

My first semester passed without much significant progress. The ten-ured professor who had hired me had his own problems, and provided ambivalent encouragement. He seemed dispirited by the competitive-ness of physics. Once, inviting me over to his home for dinner, he spoke about how "we" had to resign ourselves to not having achieved some-thing great. His wife quickly pointed out to him that it was still prema-ture to include me in that "we."

I felt time racing by. The same professor tried to guide me into work-ing on a problem in his area, the algebra of weak and electromagnetic currents, but it was so far from my interests that it became almost repel-lent to me. What was the point of being in physics if you could not pick your own problems? By May 1974, at the close of my first academic year, I was heading for trouble. In three months I would have to start my next job search, and I had not published a paper; worse, I was not even involved in anything that could conceivably lead to a publication. I developed a visceral understanding of the meaning of "publish or per-ish," and made darkly foreboding comments to my friends and acquain-tances about where I was headed.

Life wasn't all bad, though. Three good things did happen that year, all extracurricular. I spent many evening hours in my Philadelphia bedroom learning to juggle three tennis balls. I started running more seriously than I had before, tagging on to a cadre of dedicated graduate-student long distance runners who trained every day at noon on the university's famous Tartan track, site of the Penn Relays. I remembered when Roger Bannister broke the four-minute mile, and now, temperamentally overenthusiastic to the point of stupidity, I ran a single mile against my stopwatch as fast as I could, several times a week, determined to remain ignorant of the benefits of warming up or running longer distances more slowly. Every few weeks I stopped to let my shin splints heal, and it took me several more years to acquire the patience to train rather than simply run as quickly as I could. Finally, I learned to play the recorder in a small group at a West Philadelphia arts center, enjoying my capacity to make even low-grade music in harmony with others.

My first academic year of employment passed, and Eva and I spent a month together in the summer of 1974 at the Aspen Center for Physics, where I was awed by the casual proximity of so many famous physicists. Aspen was popular; research space and apartments were in such short supply that some of the senior physicists had bought houses there in which they could spend the entire summer. The junior postdocs were allotted only a few weeks. We hiked in the mountains once or twice a week and swam at the Hotel Jerome pool where the women all seemed to have crocheted their own bikini tops—tops that they removed as soon as they sat by the pool. Each day I tried systematically to learn more about the theoretical structure of the increasingly topical Yang-Mills gauge theories of weak and electromagnetic interactions. I carefully worked my way through *New Yorker* writer and physicist Jeremy Bernstein's pedagogic introductory article in the *Reviews of Modern Physics* and, since he was an Aspen regular, I sometimes wandered over to ask him questions. Working, hiking, talking physics, listening to music at the Aspen Music Center, playing volleyball to let off steam—this was what academic physics was supposed to be like, but my enjoyment was tempered by my year without publication, which made me feel that regular summers in Aspen and the partaking of its pleasures would not be part of my destiny.

June passed quickly, and in July I traveled to Cape Town. My mother, like Stephen Hawking, had been ill with amyotrophic lateral sclerosis for several years, and each year I went home to see her. But while Hawking miraculously seemed to stabilize, my mother went steadily downhill in the 1970s, growing worse each year, first losing the ability to move her arms, her hands, and then her legs, until she finally began to have difficulty holding her head up or swallowing. It was a perpetual mystery to her that no one knew how to cure her ailment. In August I returned to New York for one month, continuing to read about gauge theories in our apartment or in the Columbia library while Eva continued her thesis work. As an academic, you could work (or not work) wherever you liked. It was freedom, but now, with one year as a postdoc gone and the future looming, it sometimes felt like the freedom to fail.

In September 1974 I returned to dreary Philadelphia, where I could no longer avoid pondering whether to try to seek another postdoctoral position for the fall of 1975, I had no new accomplishments to report on my résumé, something which was going to make job applications difficult. I began to think seriously of ceasing to "do physics,"[1] and to steel myself for the shame it involved. It seemed like my time had come. Then suddenly something good happened: A really interesting physics puzzle came along, and the techniques necessary to resolve it were closely related to those I had used in my PhD thesis.

Al Mann, one of the senior experimentalists at Penn, had been part of an international collaboration to scatter high-energy, muon-type neutrinos off protons at the CERN[2] particle accelerator in Geneva. Mann's experiment was very similar to the deep inelastic electron–proton scattering I had analyzed for my thesis, the difference being that he fired neutrinos rather than electrons at the proton target. According to what was then known about weak interactions, one expected the incoming neutrino to turn into a *single* negatively charged muon[3] when it collided with the proton. The proton would in turn then shatter into a debris consisting of many other protonlike particles, as illustrated in Figure 3.1(a). This was not exactly what happened, however. Searching through their data, Al and his collaborators discovered a number of so-called *dimuon* events in which there were two muons, one negatively and one positively charged, among the final products of the collision. These were

---

[1]My physicist friends and I spoke of what we did as "doing physics." My wife's molecular biology colleagues, strangely, never spoke of "doing biology," but rather of "doing science," a broader name for what seemed to me an equally narrow field.
[2]The European Center for Nuclear Research.
[3]A sort of electron, with the same charge but about 200 times the mass.

just the sort of "Swiss watch" collisions that Feynman had described, in which experimental anomalies could lead to the discovery of new particles or the new forces that produce them.

The puzzle was the cause of the two muons. There were (at least) two possible explanations, each involving the production of a hypothetical

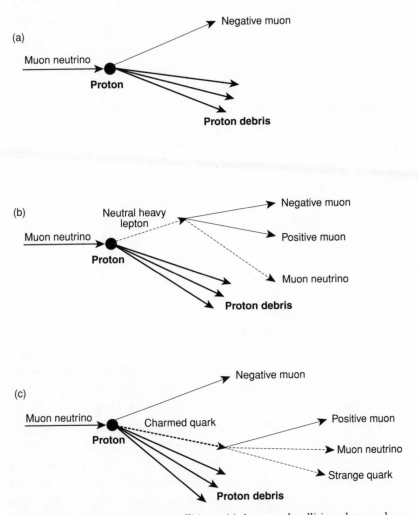

Figure 3.1   Neutrino-proton collisions. (a) A normal collision that produces a single negatively charged muon. (b) A hypothetical collision that produces a neutral heavy lepton, which in turn decays into two muons and a muon neutrino. (c) A hypothetical collision that produces a single negatively charged muon plus a charmed quark, which in turn decays into a positively charged muon, a neutrino, and a strange quark.

new particle. The first hypothesis was that the incoming neutrino had turned into a new *neutral heavy lepton*,[4] which then, because of the weak force, decayed into the two muons observed by Mann and his collaborators. This is illustrated in Figure 3.1(b). The second hypothesis was that the incoming neutrino had, as is normal, turned into the one negatively charged muon, but that among the proton debris was a new so-called *charmed* quark that was required to exist in the standard theory of weak and electromagnetic interactions, and that this charmed quark then decayed via the weak force to produce a second positively charged muon, as illustrated in Figure 3.1(c).

Which of these new particles—the hypothetical neutral heavy lepton or the hypothetical charmed quark—was the progenitor of the dimuons? The test would lie in the distribution of their speeds. The relative speeds of the positively and negatively charged muons would depend on whether the heavy lepton or the charmed quark had been their parent. In the former case, both muons arose from the decay of the heavy lepton and, because both had a similar origin, they tended to emerge with similar speeds; in the latter, the positively charged muon arose from the decay of a charmed quark and would have a very different speed. Much as each brand of water gun produces its own characteristic spray of water, so the different particles, when they decay, produce their own characteristic dimuon distribution.

Together with my colleagues Lay Nam Chang and John Ng, I began to investigate the properties of the dimuon distribution that resulted from heavy lepton production in order to compare it with the muon speeds reported by Mann and his collaborators. It was a classic phenomenology problem, the comparison of theory and experiment, closely related to my thesis work, and so I knew how to calculate the distributions of the final speeds and angles of muons. Lay Nam, John, and I checked each other's analytical calculations, and I wrote the computer program to evaluate the distribution of the muons. Suddenly I was involved again, and it was simply thrilling to be working on something new and relevant in close proximity to the experimentalists. I entered a period of great mental stimulation which resuscitated me. Spontane-

---

[4]An even heavier sort of electron, but neutral, that is, carrying no charge. There was no good reason why one should not exist, and so, according to Gell-Mann's totalitarian principle, it had to be there.

ously, I began to rise early in the morning; as soon as I awoke I rushed into work to calculate and program. I participated in long, intoxicatingly buoyant arguments and discussions on blackboards, where Lay Nam, John, and I took turns scribbling and talking, one of us seizing the chalk from the other. Rivalries and self-doubt disappeared as we pushed forward, working keenly late into the night.

The exact nature of the hypothetical weak force responsible for the decay of the putative heavy lepton was not known—it had to be conjectured, and there were a variety of forms it could reasonably take. Lay Nam, John, and I calculated the relative speeds of the muons for a wide (but not exhaustive) range of forces. We showed that for all the cases we considered, the predicted disparity between the speeds of the positive and negative muon, when both were produced by the decay of a heavy lepton, was much smaller than the disparity observed by Mann and his collaborators. Therefore, we claimed, it was highly unlikely that the dimuon events signaled the production of a new heavy neutral lepton.

We circulated our work as a "preprint," a mimeographed prepublication report sent out to other physicists in the field, and it drew a gratifying spurt of attention. Now, almost down to the wire, I had completed a piece of research that would get me my next postdoc position, just as my two-year stint at Penn trailed off into its last few months. I sent out my letters of application and, late in the spring of 1975, in the nick of time, I received postdoctoral offers from the University of Wisconsin at Madison and from Oxford University in England. Eva, who still needed one more year in New York to complete her PhD was obliged to stay at Columbia. If I was going to spend one more year on my own, I preferred European Oxford rather than ur-American Madison. I had had enough of empty-streeted Philadelphia.

The work we did on heavy leptons was topical and timely, but not quite thorough enough. Though we had shown that it was *unlikely* that a heavy lepton had produced the dimuons, we had not proved it truly impossible—we had not calculated the asymmetry for every possible form of the hypothetical weak force that caused its decay. A few months later, Bram Pais (one of the few Columbia seminar speakers I had seen stand up to T. D. Lee) and his long-time collaborator, Sam Treiman of Princeton, entered the scene. Both of them old hands at analyzing weak interactions, they derived a very general upper bound to the asymmetry between the speeds of the positive and negative muons produced in the decay of a heavy lepton, no matter what the form of its still unknown weak force. They showed that the maximum value of the asymmetry under any circumstances was smaller than the one observed by Mann and his collaborators, and so truly excluded heavy leptons as a source of the dimuons. What we had shown to be unlikely Pais and Treiman had then demonstrated to be impossible. More experienced and professional than Lay Nam, John, and me, they received the lion's share of the credit, but we got a little, too; it was more than enough to get me that second postdoc offer from Oxford.

I was through with Philadelphia, although I had survived and eventually prospered. I spent one month that summer in Cape Town visiting my mother, and another month at a theoretical physics summer institute at SLAC, where I renewed my acquaintance with Doug Hofstadter, now living at home with his family. He invited me to their house on campus, where I finally met his father Robert and his electron-scattering colleague Robert Herman, the two ex-City College physicists my cousin had told me so much about during my first years in New York.

A s I prepared to leave for England, once again invigorated by physics but now slightly fearful of moving to a new country on my own until Eva could eventually join me, I looked back at my nine years in America.

Physics was filled with so many extraordinary talents, old gods from the past as well as budding stars preparing to dominate the future. In those first few years, I saw and sometimes met many of them.

At Columbia, I had taken classes in statistical mechanics from T. D. Lee. I had listened to his many seminars and discussed my thesis with him. I had taught problem sessions in electromagnetic theory for Polykarp Kusch, watching him on campus in his late fifties as he bent over stiffly to play with his small son from a second marriage. I had drunk coffee and eaten cookies at countless departmental coffee hours in the company of Leon Lederman, Jack Steinberger, and Jim Cronin, all future Nobel Prize–winners then on the Columbia faculty. I had given lectures on my thesis work to theorists and experimentalists and had been questioned by many of them. I had heard colloquia delivered by the legendary Dirac and Heisenberg. I had heard Feynman, too, an enormously charismatic performer who spoke like a Brooklyn-born taxi driver, so much more casually charming than the Columbia faculty, and yet so aware of the charm he radiated. One Friday I listened to Edward Teller, the notorious cocreator of the hydrogen bomb and destroyer of Oppenheimer's reputation, as he lectured in the Columbia theatre while a crowd of antiwar protesters picketed him with posters and then silently walked out as he spoke. Later we flocked to watch a seminar on Uri Geller, the Israeli spoon bender, presented by two scientists from the Stanford Research Institute who were investigating his psychic skills. They were invited, of course, by Gary Feinberg.

At Penn, the physics department starred Bob Schrieffer, who had just won the Nobel Prize for his role in developing the theory of superconductivity. His white gull-wing Mercedes, reportedly bought with Nobel Prize money, lent a glamorous touch to the physics parking lot, as did the glimpses of his elegant, Scandinavian-looking wife. In 1976 our department hosted the international Neutrino Conference in the Amish countryside of Pennsylvania, and I again heard Feynman lecture. Later I summoned the courage to join a conversation of his in the bathroom. Seminar speakers came to Penn from all over the country. One fall Victor Weisskopf, a hero from the early days of quantum theory and one of the leaders of the Manhattan Project, came down for a visit from MIT. Another week brought a seminar by Steven Weinberg, whose standard theory of weak and electromagnetic interactions was just beginning to be vindicated. Among the pile of résumés that flowed into the department from postdocs in search of jobs, I remember one from Alan Guth, then a relatively run-of-the-mill applicant but soon to become the inventor of the theory of the inflationary universe.

I was beginning to become very aware of my limitations. There were people you met in physics who were simply off any scale you could imagine. When I read classic papers by Einstein or Feynman, I realized that though I could understand and utilize their framework, I could never have created it. My wife, having left physics for biology, knew something about both areas, and said that even the smartest biologists didn't leave you feeling that they were out of your league. Physics was different.

I have a friend who liked to point out the obviousness of various great discoveries in physics and finance. The obviousness is a delusion. Many things seem clear only once they have been taught to you in a historical context, with all the prejudices, confusion, and competing theories omitted. Every iota of discovery, in finance or theoretical physics,

Like Nikhil Jain,
this guy
loves
Blake

comes at the cost of long immersion, hard labor, and struggle. "Improvement makes straight roads, but the crooked roads without improvement are the roads of genius," wrote the English Romantic poet William Blake. Most of us in physics were lucky to be improvers, and knew we could never negotiate the crooked roads at all, though we had occasional glimpses, during sudden epiphanies in our work, of what it might feel like to stumble onto one.

Although I now sensed my limitations, I was nevertheless happily astonished at the recent reversal of my fortune. Only a few months earlier I had been morose and ready to quit; now, with one successful bit of work behind me, I was again thrilled by the hunt and longed to figure out some puzzle no one had solved before. Ever since, through ups and downs, I have tried to remember that no matter how low you get, about work or life, you can take some solace from the fact that the future is unpredictable. Even in the midst of misery, unexpectedly good things can happen without warning.

Chapter 4

A Sentimental Education

■ *Oxford's civilized charms* ■ *One physics paper leads to another*
■ *English idiosyncrasies* ■ *The anthroposophists* ■

From October 1975 to August 1977, I spent my days happily doing physics at Oxford. Once again, I arrived there alone; my wife arrived seven months later to begin her first postdoc. Once again, predictably, I found it difficult to be alone in a strange city, just as I had during my first few solitary weeks in New York nine years earlier; the same intense feelings recurred.

It didn't help that social life at Oxford revolved around the autonomous and distinct colleges that comprised the university, and I didn't belong to one. I had been hired directly by the Department of Theoretical Physics, which was housed in two old, single-family brownstones that had been joined together. The Anglo-Irish novelist Joyce Cary had lived in one of them before he died of amyotrophic lateral sclerosis, my mother's disease. While faculty colleagues went off to eat lunch or dinner with port and walnuts at their exclusive High Table at the head of the college dining hall and to then smoke their postprandial cigars, and while graduate students joked together at their much lower tables in the same dining halls, my uncollegial postdoc friends and I (Indians, Pakistanis, Cypriots, Australians, and a few Americans) sought out one of the few Indian restaurants in the nongown section of the city.

I felt naively proud to be at Oxford. Coming from Anglophile South Africa, I saw Oxford as the epitome of academic life. And doing physics when I got there was suddenly much easier; I had struggled through the valley of the shadow in my first year at Penn, but now I knew how to find suitable problems on which to work. I had learned how to complete a piece of research or, failing that, how to at least salvage something publishable and interesting. I learned to let one piece of work flow into the next. I finally knew how to treat research a little more like a business.

At Oxford I continued working on the theory of dimuon production. Heavy neutral leptons were dead, as my colleagues and I had suggested and as Pais and Treiman had proved. The dimuon events could instead signal the production and subsequent decay of a short-lived charmed quark, an equally interesting possibility. I set about calculating the distribution of dimuons that would correspond to the decay of newly produced charmed quarks. It was useful work, professionally done. I did more theoretical calculations, wrote more FORTRAN programs to compute dimuon distributions, documented the work, circulated the preprints I wrote to other physics departments, and published the papers. I still remember the excitement of working late into the night, hurrying to debug programs and then submit them to the computer center. I recall best the unspoiled joy of spontaneously waking early, tired but driven, and then rushing off to work because I *wanted* to go to work and couldn't sleep any more. I was excited to see what came next.

Meanwhile, back in Philadelphia, Lay Nam and John continued on their related but independent work. We had no email or ten-cent-per-minute telephone calls to link us. Collaboration across the Atlantic was cost-prohibitive and communication was viscous in those pre-Internet days. Not only did we think it unrealistic to telephone to discuss research, but even airmail postage and xeroxing were expensive. The Department of Theoretical Physics at Oxford, itself on a limited budget, restricted each of its postdocs to 40 free photocopies a month. After that we paid for copies of articles we wanted. Computation was more difficult, too. There were no PCs and no Matlab™ or Mathematica™ programs. I used to crosscheck my Monte Carlo computer programs, written in FORTRAN 66, by programming similar but simpler calculations for special cases on the latest Hewlett-Packard 25 programmable pocket calculator I had bought before I left New York.

I spent that whole year working on the phenomenology of charm production. It was a good life. I felt adult because I was earning a living, yet I was often fancy-free in the way that I imagined a life spent on acquiring knowledge should be. Eva finally arrived in early 1976 and we settled into the habits of Oxford. We saw exhibitions and art performances at the Oxford Museum of Modern Art, and took in old movies at the bitterly freezing Penultimate Picture Palace in working-class Cowley. Once I saw Iris Murdoch at a College garden party. Eva and I went for long walks on Port Meadow next to Jericho, where we lived, and drove to the Vale of the White Horse and the Cotswolds, where the skies could become menacingly grey in just a few minutes. We watched touring boats wait patiently for locks to slowly fill and empty in the nearby canals of the Thames. We took picnics with graduate students in punts on the Cherwell River in the late afternoon. The northern summer evenings were so long that I could first have supper and then still have time to go for a late bare-foot run on the trimmed grass cricket fields and tennis courts that tiled the University Parks next to the Department of Theoretical Physics. I was invited to give seminars in Cambridge, London, and Paris. I attended another neutrino conference in Aachen, Germany, where at midsummer the western sky still continued to glow slightly as the eastern sky began to lighten. We drove down to London to visit friends on weekends; we went to Crete on vacation. It was idyllic.

I made one tactical mistake in my research. Though I had been hired by Chris Llewellyn Smith, a well-known theorist who later became the head of CERN, I worked alone most of the time that first year. When I completed my study of charmed quark production and decay, and was ready to write it up for publication, I thought I sensed a small unspoken expectation on Chris's part that we should write the paper jointly. Like the little red hen, I felt that I had done the work, and so I should publish it. In retrospect, I was wrong. He had hired me and I had benefited from his advice; there would have been nothing seriously amiss in working together on a joint paper. More to the point, it would have been good for my career. Chris was a much better known (and a better) physicist than I was, and with his name on the paper, it would have been more widely read and perhaps would have led to further collaboration. But my pride stood in the way. Later that year, when another physicist carried out a similar analysis and received broader attention, Chris pointed out to me that I would have been better off if I had written the article with him. He was right. Years later, working on financial models at Goldman Sachs, I became much less compulsive about such strict authorial cost accounting.

The world of theoretical particle physics in the 1970s was filled with antediluvian inefficiencies and oddities. Authors circulated their work as "preprints" before they published them in refereed physics journals. Preprints, which had started out as informal research notes to be circulated among colleagues, had become institutionalized; physicists all over the world sent their preprints to anyone they thought might be interested or influential. They also sent a copy to the library at SLAC, which then compiled a fortnightly list of newly received preprints to its subscribers, who could then request a copy from the original author. The Oxford department of physics was relatively poor.[1] When I or anyone else wrote a new paper, Oxford shipped the preprints by surface mail. As a result, physicists in the United States first received new work four to six weeks after it came out, a significant delay if competitors were working on similar problems. Correspondingly, most physics departments in the United States sent their preprints by surface mail; this doubled the delay. The playing field was thus decisively tilted against small or foreign institutions—their lower budgets meant that they were the last to receive written word of new work. On one occasion, eager to communicate my results and assure my future, I paid to xerox, collate, and airmail 60 copies of a preprint at my own expense. Nowadays, all new research is posted on the Web, itself an invention of physicists at CERN, and can be downloaded at virtually no cost by anyone.

Oxford was proudly old-fashioned. One student I knew carefully peeled his dessert banana and then ate it as though it were a sausage, delicately pinning it down on the plate with his fork while he cut off slices with his knife. I met a fiercely Anglophile Canadian who began to smoke pipes and wear tweed jackets and cavalry twill trousers with handsomely heavy hand-sewn English shoes, all actually ideal (I had to admit) for walking on the muddy footpaths in the mild but perpetually damp climate. Within six months his adopted British accent became indistinguishable from the real thing. Another friend, a Junior Fellow at his College, took me for dinner at High Table. All the dons were

---

[1]Back in academic life after years on Wall Street, I now sometimes feel I have been spoiled by the resources available at investment banks in the 1990s, where offices were plush, the costs of research journals were unquestioned, the latest color printers abounded and you simply called System Administration when you had a computer problem.

overwhelmingly courteous, leaning over to chat with me whenever my friend, the most junior Fellow, was obliged to leave the table in order to pass around the port and walnuts.

While some of the colleges were exorbitantly rich and had Fellows who lived really well, the academic departments in the university were less well off. I shared a crowded office in the Department of Theoretical Physics on South Parks Road with Don Sinclair, a gruffly likeable but difficult Australian who was an early developer of lattice-gauge theories of strong interactions. He worked late into the night, using his vast array of colored felt-tip pens to cover his desk with foot-high reams of paper filled with lattice computation diagrams that looked like Tinkertoy models. Because the university provided no heating on winter evenings when the temperature dropped rapidly in the thinly insulated house that contained our office, Don stubbornly turned up the heat to maximum during the day in a futile attempt to amass warmth for the evening. Our office became virtually uninhabitable, a smelly sauna by day and too cold to hold a pencil without gloves at night, with only a brief transition between the two. Once, when he was having a hard time with a woman, he became much more communicative and commented to me, sadly but accurately, that he was one of those people who became much nicer when they had troubles.

I found the English naturally xenophobic. In America it had been a slight advantage to be South African; foreigners were welcome and considered interesting. In England, you were just another inferior colonial. Eva's Slovak friend Zuza, who like her had left Czechoslovakia when the Russians invaded, had attended Oxford and now taught at a nearby high school. One day, speaking about an English colleague, she commented: "You know, he's really awfully clever, and should be headmaster, but he'll never manage it because his wife is Swedish." This seemed to require no explanation. I felt similarly discomfited about being Jewish. A graduate student friend asked why we gave our son, Joshua, born at the end of our stay in Oxford, "such a Jewish name." In response I vainly cited Joshua Nkomo as part of my African heritage. Another student told me how "Jewish" the computer center was about the amount of time they gave you on its machines. One day, my banana-slicing friend informed me that his department would soon be hosting "some Jews from the Weizmann Institute;" he was clearly quite confused about the difference between Jews and Israelis. None of these people was trying to be offensive but, after a year of this, I found myself unthinkingly hesitant to say anything that would reveal my roots.

Many of the foreigners I knew had similar experiences. Savas, a Cypriot friend who had lived in England since the Turkish invasion of Cyprus, had a specially restricted British passport that would expire if he spent more than three years out of the country. Soon I realized that any bias against foreigners seemed vaguely plausible. When an Indian postdoc friend bought a slightly battered secondhand car and parked it on South Parks Road near the Clarendon Labs, I teased him by leaving him a note in which I purported to be the head of the department; I informed him that the shabby appearance of his car diminished the dignity of the grounds, and asked him to therefore refrain from parking it so close to the laboratory. He took this in dead earnest and ran off to speak to the head of the department before I could catch him.

The university itself was stuffily bureaucratic, and when you angered them they resorted to reporting you to your superiors. After two years in Oxford and just two months before I was to return to New York, the chief medical officer sent me a letter demanding that I be X-rayed to exclude the possibility of tuberculosis. I wrote back to point out that if they were seriously concerned about my putative tuberculosis, they should have X-rayed me when I first arrived. He forwarded my response to the head of the physics department, adding the following handwritten annotation: "Dear Prof. ——, What charming people you have in your department!" I was astonished that the professor himself then took the trouble to rebuke me.

Some experiences left lasting impressions. At one of my wife's department parties I was introduced to a Swedish woman who turned out to be the daughter of the late Oskar Klein, the codiscoverer of the Kaluza-Klein theories I had studied as an undergraduate in South Africa. Klein was also the master builder of some of the pillars of particle theory, the eponymous Klein-Gordon equation that described spinless quantum particles and the Klein-Nishina formula for Compton (photon-electron) scattering.

Another visiting postdoc, Predrag Cvitanovic, lingered in my mind for years afterwards as someone who seemed to do exactly what he liked, and liked what he did. He was a darkly handsome Croatian who had left

Yugoslavia for the United States when he was a teenager. Predrag always spoke as though he had lived a life of enviable independence, free of other people's conventions. He went cycling around the United Kingdom, danced in Oxford night clubs, and acted in a production of Blake's "Songs of Innocence and Experience" that I watched at the University Parks one evening. He wore tobacco-colored Adidas sneakers and blue denim farmer's dungarees over a checked shirt. When his mother visited him briefly, he spoke about her as though she were just another of his fun-loving acquaintances. I was always a little awed by his apparent self-sufficiency. I recall suffering his scorn once at a very-Oxford garden party. I had uttered some sentence that contained the phrases "my wife" and "my car," and Predrag issued a loud denunciation of people in the world who went around talking about "my this and my that." I accepted his display of extreme independence at face value, never asking about the difficulties that must have led to it. James Gleick, in his book *Chaos: Making a New Science*, mentions that at precisely the time I knew him, Predrag was working on an aspect of chaos theory that was critical to Mitchell Feigenbaum's subsequent breakthrough in the field. Gleick writes that Predrag was so captivated by the field that he chose to work on it without telling anyone that he was doing so, even though he had been hired to do particle theory. Particle physicists, the ultimate reductionists, might well have looked down on chaos theory, a field that ostensibly had nothing to do with the fundamental nature of matter and could have been invented fifty years earlier. When our son Joshua was born in 1977, shortly before we left Oxford for New York, Predrag brought over a bottle of wine to celebrate, and that was the last time I saw him at any length. I ran into him once more in 1984, shortly after the birth of our daughter Sonya, when I was pushing her in a stroller near the Great Lawn in Central Park. I always remembered him as someone who seemed to be captain of his fate.

Sometime in 1976 Chris Llewellyn Smith brought Stephen Wolfram to the department. A precocious Eton high school student of about sixteen, Stephen was already writing his own research preprints on particle physics. Those early papers were unexceptional, but the mere fact that he could produce them at his tender age justifiably intimidated the Oxford graduate students. I, luckily, was too old to be seriously threatened; he belonged to another generation. Stephen attended Oxford and eventually became the head of Wolfram Research and the cre-

ator of Mathematica™, a system for doing symbolic mathematics on a
computer that has become widely used by physicists, mathematicians,
and quants.

One afternoon I saw an advertisement in the Oxford papers for the
Anthroposophical Society, an organization of devotees of the late German guru Rudolf Steiner, whose books had been recommended to me
by Dr. Louw in Cape Town eight years earlier. I had taken a glance or
two at them over the years and had been left cold. During a lonely day
in my first few months at Oxford I walked into the little Steiner bookstore and picked up his *Knowledge of the Higher Worlds*. That night in bed
I started to read it, and was astounded and exhilarated to experience in
the first few sentences the clear and authoritative pronunciations on the
complexity and confusion of life. I never became more than a dabbler
in the field, but the anthroposophists' books left a strong and uplifting
impression on me, despite their turgid, Germanically flavored English.

The anthroposophists didn't reject the scientific approach approach
to knowledge, but they rejected the naive and arrogant materialism
espoused by so many scientists. Instead, as I understood it, they advocated the reliance on careful external and *internal* scientific observation
in the style of Goethe. I liked the fact that Steiner referred to the soul
as directly as other people referred to material objects. He attributed a
primacy to one's inner perceptions, regarding the interior world to be
just as much a part of reality as the exterior. I was pleased, a few years
later, to read Bruno Bettelheim's *Freud and Man's Soul*, in which he
pointed out that Freud's original German texts had used simple, direct
terms to describe the psyche (the Greek word for *soul*). According to
Bettelheim, it was James Strachey, Freud's English translator, who had
replaced Freud's resonant and easily accessible *Ich, Es,* and *Über-Ich*, the
German for "I," "It," and "Above-I", with the faux-medical, Latinized *id,
ego,* and *superego*. It was also Strachey who, referring to slips of the tongue,
replaced the German "Fehlleistung" with the pseudoscientific *parapraxis*.

My interest in the late Steiner intensified following the publicity he
and his disciple Owen Barfield received when Saul Bellow—then a
Steiner devotee, too—won the 1976 Nobel Prize for literature. The
narrator in his novel *Humboldt's Gift* studies Steinerian meditation in
Chicago, and Bellow alluded to Steiner and Barfield in several articles
and interviews. I went on to read Barfield's *History in English Words*,
an enthralling account of his theory of the development of human

consciousness as extracted from the parallel development of English vocabulary.

Steiner's views were descended from even stranger turn-of-the-century mystics, Madame Blavatsky and the Theosophists, and perhaps Gurdjieff, too. He combined German romanticism with Eastern mysticism. He had theories about everything—from childhood, education and teaching the mentally retarded to art and organic gardening, and I liked whatever I was able to understand. Mostly, whenever I tried to tell my friends about him, I was met with scorn. Over the years, however, I discovered that other people I admired had been influenced by Steiner and his school, in particular several early twentieth-century painters, among them Vassily Kandinsky, Arshile Gorky, and Arthur Dove, who drew on his lectures and sketches of the higher worlds. While at an exhibition in a Soho New York gallery in the late 1990s, I saw large photographs of the colored-chalk illustrations Steiner had scrawled on a blackboard during his philosophical lectures. Later, visiting clients of Goldman's in Madrid, I dropped into the Thyssen Museum, where I stumbled across several Dove paintings whose resemblance to those illustrations was immediately apparent. In The Hague, too, after a Euronext options conference, I saw early Mondrian paintings of lilies that were influenced by Steiner's attempts to portray the spiritual essence of living beings. More recently, I reread Gleick's book on chaos and was intrigued by his description of the influence of Goethe, Steiner, and Schwenk (another Steinerian artist and observer) on the early chaos investigators Feigenbaum and Libchard. All of them, as he told it, were proponents of the same ideal: Careful independent observation and a reliance on all of one's own senses.

A year passed and I spent most of the summer of 1976 at the theoretical physics institute at SLAC, returning to the United States in order to keep my green card valid. Then, in my last year at Oxford, I began to work on more fundamental theoretical topics with Tim Jones, a fellow postdoc. We developed a theory that tried to explain the near similarity of the electron and the heavier muon by postulating that Nature imposed an additional permutation symmetry between the two particles. Our model was a simple extension of the now popular standard model of weak and electromagnetic interactions that, in addition, linked

the electron to the muon. Over the next few years I continued working on this class of models, extending the permutation symmetry to
include the newly observed *tau lepton,* an even more massive sibling of
the electron and muon. If our model was right, it predicted that the
muon, the tau lepton, and the b quark should all decay in peculiar and
previously unobserved ways.

Just as beauty in art and music often emerges from the tension of creating something new within the limitations of an accepted framework,
so it is that many of the deep truths of theoretical physics emerge from
the attempt to describe Nature's laws within the confines of very general guiding principles. If one is lucky as well as clever, the principles
will rule out everything except the one true theory. The extensions to
the standard theory Tim and I worked on were not particularly profound, yet it was exciting to be guessing at the existence of new sym-
metries and new particles—and to dream of being right. I felt a hint of
the potentially deeper joy that came from trying to divine God's laws,
which was quite different from the everyday happiness that came from
the workmanlike comparison of other peoples' theories against other
peoples' experiments. I also sensed, however, the potential of a much
greater disappointment: One was most likely to be wrong.

Thinking back, I am reminded of reading about Feynman's excitement at being one of several physicists to first guess the correct form of
the parity-violating weak interaction initially observed by Madame Wu
and her collaborators in 1957. Feynman's more technical and singular
work on the renormalizability of quantum electrodynamics in the late
forties was a *tour de force* that created the formalism used by physicists for
years afterwards. Yet he was apparently more excited by his joint discovery of the true form of the parity-violating weak interaction, because,
for a brief period before he communicated his results, he felt he knew
something about the nature of the universe that no one else did. This
was the attraction of working on new theories.[2]

Then, in the autumn of 1976, with one year at Oxford over and one
year remaining, it was time to begin searching for my next position.
Though the department told me I could stay on a third year, it was clear

---

[2]In the end, the fairly pedestrian theory Tim and I developed was not right. But an ex-
physicist I hired at Goldman, who had searched the academic citation databases to see
with whom he was coming to work, told me that there are still occasional contemporary references in the literature to the papers I wrote then.

to both Eva and me that Oxford was only a temporary stopping point. A few weeks later at a conference at the Rutherford Laboratories near Oxford, I was introduced to Bram Pais, a professor at the Rockefeller University in New York. He knew of my work on dimuons, which he and Treiman had so clearly trumped. I knew interesting things about him, too. I recalled that years earlier, during an invited seminar at Columbia, I had seen him casually and charmingly deflect an intellectual attack by T. D. Lee. Chris Llewellyn Smith had told me that Pais had been in hiding during World War II in Holland, much like Anne Frank. Finally, I had coincidentally read bits of his doctoral thesis. As a student at Columbia ten years earlier, I had been required to demonstrate translation proficiency in two foreign languages used by scientists. Even as long ago as 1967 that was an already archaic requirement, a relic of the prewar era when many original physics papers were still written in German, French, or Russian. Since I had studied Afrikaans, itself a sort of kitchen Dutch, at school in South Africa, I decided to demonstrate my proficiency at Dutch translation. Searching through the Columbia physics library for Dutch papers to practice on, I stumbled across Pais's PhD thesis on Finsler spaces in differential geometry; he had written it in Dutch before he emigrated to the United States in the late 1940s. I recalled it well, not only because I had studied Finsler spaces in South Africa when I worked on unified field theories, but also because he had dedicated his thesis "Aan Mammie en Pappie" (To Mommy and Daddy). Speaking with him in Oxford, I found it difficult to reconcile this childlike dedication with his aggressively urbane persona, part New York street smarts and part European suavity. Nevertheless, with a job at stake, I tried to be charming, too, and told him I had seen both his thesis and the reference to his parents.

A few months later, I sent off a hopeful application for my next postdoc to Pais at Rockefeller. I thought a position there would be perfect for my wife and me: Our first child was on the way, we thought of New York as home, and there were plenty of academic opportunities for Eva in New York. But I could not count on a job where I wanted one, and so I applied to many other schools. Then I waited.

A high school friend in the corporate world passed through Oxford that spring and asked me pointedly where I would be in the fall. I said I was still waiting to hear who would offer me a job. "You mean you really might have no work at all?" he asked, demanding of me a degree of uncomfortable explicitness that made me doubt his benevolent intent.

My nonacademic friends could not understand the code we postdocs lived by. I once proudly told a South African friend that an article of mine had been accepted in *Physical Review Letters*, one of the most prestigious journals in the physics community. He asked me how much they paid me to publish there. I was embarrassed to explain that it worked the other way: My physics department had to pay the American Physical Society several hundred dollars in page charges to see the paper into print. This was beyond his understanding; he thought I was indulging in vanity publishing.

I was lucky that year. In the spring of 1977 I received a letter offering me a two-year position at the Weizmann Institute in Israel. It was tempting, but I wanted to go back to the States. A few weeks later, to my relief, a postdoc offer from Rockefeller arrived and, since Eva could get work there too, I immediately accepted. I was safe for a couple of years.

The summer of 1977 was England's hottest for many years—each weekend the pubs ran out of ice. We spent the long clear days punting, picnicking, and working, until our son Joshua was born on August 1. Because he was born abroad, Joshua was British, and was obliged to endure an extended interview about his political beliefs and jail record at the American Embassy in London a week later. I answered for him and he was given his own green card. It had been a good two years, and a week later we returned to New York, confident and happy.

■ *Chapter 5* ■

The Mandarins

■ *Research and parenthood on New York's Upper East Side* ■ *A*
good life, but . . . the tensions of twin careers ■

The Rockefeller University was a little pocket of privilege. Its faculty and postdocs lived on their academic salaries in elegant sub-
sidized apartments near Sutton Place on New York's Upper East
Side. Rockefeller was not so much a university as it was a large research
organization. Established in 1901 as a medical research institute, it
evolved in the boom years of American research funding into a luxuri-
ously equipped and accredited university that awarded only graduate
degrees. In the expansion of the 1960s, Rockefeller hired not only biologists but also mathematicians, logicians, philosophers, psychologists,
linguists, and physicists. Then, in the late 1970s, as the good times
receded, they slowly rolled the odometer back until they once again
focused predominantly on biomedical work.

It was gratifying to tell people you worked at Rockefeller; it had a
sort of elitist ring because of the famous biologists and logicians who
had worked there. At Rockefeller in 1944, Avery, MacLeod, and
McCarty discovered that genes were made of DNA. The famous analytical philosopher Saul Kripke worked there in the early 1960s. In the
elevator of the Tower Building where I worked, I used to see Mark
Kaç, the stocky, red-faced, bald, and charmingly accented Polish-Jewish
mathematician whose masterly lecture on drum shapes I had heard as a
student at Columbia. At that time I knew little about the Feynman-Kaç

77

theorem that linked Feynman's view of quantum mechanical evolution to the solution of the partial differential equations of quantum mechanics, statistical physics, and options theory. Years later I read Kač's short, fascinating intellectual autobiography; I discovered how much work he had done on defining the nature of randomness. On the wall outside his office he had pinned a large American Mathematical Society photoposter of the attractively regal-looking Polish mathematician Sonya Kovalevskaya. When I once commented on it, he told me in his heavily accented English that she was "certainly the best looking mathematician of either sex."

Rockefeller seemed luxurious and aristocratic, an enclave of gardens, auditoriums, high-rises, and labs peopled by intellectuals devoted to the pursuit of knowledge. No teaching, no courses, no undergraduates—just research. You felt like a philosopher-king in the middle of grimy 1970s Manhattan. We lived in a university-owned high rise on York Ave., near New York Hospital and only one block from my office and Eva's lab. I had a private office larger than any I have had before or since, with at long last more than enough bookshelves, all wood-paneled and adjustable. My office and our apartment both looked out on the East River, a heliport and the FDR Drive. Looking through the windows at any time of the day or night, one saw helicopters bearing presidential candidates or trauma victims while cars snaked up and down the Drive and large boats cruised along the river. If you narrowed your field of vision just enough to see only the traffic, it resembled nothing so much as a 1950s comic strip about life in the city of the future that my father used to read to me as a child.

In homage to Oxbridge, Rockefeller had no traditional departments of study. Instead, individual professors ran their "labs." There were several senior professors of theoretical particle physics. Pais, a tiny man and the most renowned professor, had hired me into his lab; his former collaborator Mirza Abdul Baqi Bég, a burly Pakistani with a Pancho Villa mustache who always cited the famous German-Jewish physicist Rudolf Peierls as his mentor, ran another lab. In a much more low-stakes version of the Lee–Yang quarrel, Pais was rumored to be at war with Bég, and we heard reports of prolonged shouting matches. We also heard that Pais had made a bitter enemy of Murray Gell-Mann, his 1950s collaborator, who, according to George Johnson's biography of Gell-Mann, always referred to Pais as "the evil dwarf." After what I had seen of Lee and Yang, I was not overly surprised by these feuds.

How hard and how long you appeared to work at Rockefeller was irrelevant; what counted was what you accomplished (and, perhaps, the aura you radiated of how much you might accomplish). I went in to work in the late morning and sometimes worked late into the evening, and spent much time with Josh at both ends of the day.

I was happy at Rockefeller. Josh would wake very early and I would take him out for long walks in his stroller through East Side neighborhoods, stopping for early morning bagels or Egg McMuffins. We had long conversations; I was always tired, but it was immensely satisfying. I was ecstatic about child rearing, open to all sorts of only half-plausible Steinerian theories of education. Steiner advocated talking to children above their level of understanding, since, he argued, every word you said to them when they first entered the world was above their level, and yet they learned to understand. I did this naturally. What counted in the end was the time spent with Josh. Watching him through his first two or three years, I developed a great appreciation for the mystery of life and the strange abstractness of time. He learned and remembered locations in space, the names of objects, even adjectives and adverbs, without visible effort and much more easily than locations in time (*yesterday, tomorrow*) or states of color (*red, green*). Long after he could make sophisticated statements ("I'm mad at myself!" he once exclaimed when he broke a toy), he would still confuse *yesterday* with *tomorrow* and *red* with *green*. I began to half-believe the theory that time and color were not as self-evident as they seem, but rather inventions or discoveries made at some earlier point in human history, like the discovery of farming, and then internalized and transmitted to us through the generations. Perhaps, when a child remarks that both a leaf and a sweater are green, he or she is isolating some immensely abstract quality of two vastly different objects that was once beyond human comprehension.

One of the more interesting Rockefeller physics faculty members was Heinz Pagels, the author of *The Cosmic Code*, a popular book on quantum mechanics. Heinz was the first person I ever saw combine a business suit with white Adidas Country sneakers. He was charming and easy to like, with a penchant for trying to impress people by referring to his rich social life outside of physics. He was a humorously compulsive name dropper. He could not simply remark "I had dinner with McNamara last night in Aspen;" he felt obliged to add " . . . you know, Johnson's Secretary of Defense." He was preternaturally attuned to conversational trends, with an uncanny knack for anticipating the future trajectory of someone else's sentence, especially someone politically more powerful. Speaking with Pais, Heinz could quickly complete a remark that Pais had just begun, first grabbing hold of Pais's train of thought in mid-sentence by echoing it softly, and then, growing louder and bolder and swifter, taking ownership of the sentence and running it to its conclusion as though it had been entirely his idea. I liked talking to him. Sadly, he fell and died a few years later while hiking in the mountains near Aspen where he and his family spent most summers.

Heinz was friendly with Jeremy Bernstein, the physicist and *New Yorker* writer whom I admired because he, too, seemed to be living a more rounded life than most physicists I knew. Bernstein had written a paper or two with Feinberg and T. D. Lee, and I had once been amazed to see T. D. harass him during colloquium at Columbia. Bernstein had been writing books and *New Yorker* articles on physics for the general public since the 1960s, starting with a profile of Lee and Yang after they won the Nobel Prize. He wrote honestly and clearly, trying hard to demystify the subtleties; as a result, I think, his books never sold as well as those of the more sensational popularizers of quantum mechanics and cosmology.

One of the great pleasures of academic life was that, after you had fulfilled your teaching duties—and there were none at Rockefeller!—your time and space belonged to you alone. I could work when and where I liked; I could decide to take an afternoon off to run six miles in the park or to see an exhibition at a museum, and then work that evening. Heinz and I went to see *Close Encounters of the Third Kind* the weekday afternoon it opened. Such small freedoms, together with the long vacations spent doing physics in interesting places, gave one the sensation of being nonmonetarily rich, and compensated for the low noncorporate salaries. My office was sacred territory; no one walked in after knocking unless I shouted "Come in!" If I locked the door from the inside, wanting to concentrate or be alone, people behaved as though I were not there. I thought that this kind of privacy was a right, but it was a privilege, much rarer than I realized. I was naively shocked, a few years later at Bell Labs, to apprehend that both my time and my office belonged to AT&T, and could be invaded at any moment without apology or warning knock from my boss, my colleagues, or the mail deliverer. Wall Street, of course, would lay claim to even more of my personal space and time. Soon this academic freedom would end for me. But in the meanwhile I did physics, joined the New York Road Runners Club, ran along the East River Drive and around Central Park, and played with Joshua mornings and evenings. It was a good life.

As my two years at Rockefeller rushed by, I grew increasingly uncomfortably with Pais and sensed his disapproval. Perhaps he disliked my relative lack of talent, or my lack of deference on subjects outside of physics, something that he may have perceived as disrespect. I admitted to myself that Pais was a much better physicist than I was, but I could not make myself unquestioningly play second fiddle in conversations on novels, movies, or world affairs. I felt obliged to behave as though my opinions had as much right to be heard as anyone else's, and it probably was not a good idea. At the end of my first year at Rockefeller, Pais's secretary began putting job advertisements for other schools' postdoc positions in my pigeonhole in the departmental office, and I knew I was not going to get a third year in his lab.

Eva, Josh, and I spent one month that summer at the Aspen Center for Physics. Then, in September 1978, I took Pais's hints to heart and started to evaluate my situation. I was 33 years old and halfway through my third postdoc; where was this peregrination going to end? I concluded I either had to find a position as an assistant professor with a good chance of tenure, or else get out of physics.

One day in 1978 I suddenly found myself flirting with the idea of going to medical school and becoming a genuine doctor. My thoughts went pretty much as follows: Physics is a harsh meritocracy. Most of the merit is concentrated in a small number of legendary figures at the top. If you aren't Feynman, you're no one. A competent, but not brilliant, research physicist had little to feel good about; who needs what you provide? You could try to get one of the rare full-time teaching positions in a small college somewhere, but you had to like teaching more than I did to do it that many hours a week. So, though it *was* good to think that

I was dedicating my life to what I thought of as transcendental pursuits, it had begun to feel insufficient. In medicine, in contrast, I imagined that I could so some palpable good merely by being competent.

I was not the only person who thought this way. Several medical schools had recently begun to accept applicants with PhDs in the natural sciences but no premed degree into their program. The University of Miami at Coral Gables would transform you from a PhD to an MD in two years, summers included, but in order to apply you need to have passed the Graduate Record Exam (GRE). Now I had never taken the GRE; it was not even administered in South Africa when I applied to Columbia in 1966. I closeted myself in my don't-come-in-without-knocking Rockefeller office, telling no one what I was doing, and spent a week or two taking practice GRE exams. I refreshed my undergraduate physics knowledge, learning the values of natural constants and atomic physics energy levels by heart. I revisited all the topics that I had not studied since my first year in graduate school. Finally, after a sleepless night because Josh was ill and feverish, I took the general and physics sections of the exam one entire Saturday on the Columbia campus; I did well. Coral Gables sent one of their graduates, an intern at Sloan Kettering near Rockefeller, to interview me, and I was accepted.

I couldn't do it—I simply lacked the courage to continue down this path. I would have had to move to Florida for two years, and Eva, whose parents lived in New York and whose career as a biologist seemed to have more promise than mine as a physicist, had no reason to disrupt her work by relocating to Florida. Though I paid the registration fee to keep my place in the program, I knew I would probably renege. Indeed, a few weeks later, pleading family difficulties, I called Coral Gables to back out. I would have had a very different life had I become a practicing physician, and I still envy people whose work does visible good.

During my last year at Rockefeller, I applied only for "real" physics jobs, those tenure-track assistant professorships at schools that took research seriously, or the few longer-term postdoc jobs that promised some semblance of stability. I spent much of the winter traveling around the country giving seminars at whichever department or national laboratory would consider me seriously enough to invite me, and eventually landed two assistant professorships. The first was at Illinois Institute of Technology in Chicago, attractive mostly because of its proximity to Fermilab, which had a giant high-energy particle accelerator and an excellent theory group, too. The second was at the University of Colorado at Boulder, a good school with a physics department of reasonable quality that had received over one hundred applications for their one job in theoretical particle physics. I interviewed there in December 1978 and then waited. After several months, I heard I was third on their list. As time went by, first the female postdoc at the top of their list obtained a better offer elsewhere; then the second choice, a male postdoc with a wife in academia who had already obtained a permanent position on the East Coast, declined in order to stay near his family. The next offer came to me.

I liked Boulder much more than Chicago—I had the chance of a good position in a beautiful town. Eva, however, had no immediate possibility of her own long-term job there, and it made little sense for her to accompany me there without one. So, knowing that I would likely go to Boulder on my own that fall, I shut my eyes and accepted their offer. Though it wasn't ideal for her, Eva agreed to investigate academic opportunities in the Boulder area. I hoped that some way or other she would soon find a reasonably permanent position there or in one of the nearby Denver research hospitals.

This was the start of several difficult years. Despite Eva's own career demands, a part of me expected her to move to Boulder, and I was resentful that she did not. In the meanwhile, the State of Colorado declared a faculty hiring freeze, so that no permanent positions for her could materialize soon. I had moved to new jobs in new cities and countries on my own with regularity the past six years, but this time I would be leaving behind not only a wife, but a son, too. I had been as much a part of his upbringing as anyone over the past two years. At times I proposed that I should take Josh with me to Boulder. Eva and I fought and scrambled. In July the three of us left for a week-long vacation to Abaco, a small and isolated out-island in the Bahamas. On our second day there, returning from an uncomfortable trip on a rented motor boat to a nearby island, I found messages instructing me to call both my home in South Africa and Eva's parents in New York. For years I had always left a vacation phone number with my family in South Africa in case of emergency, so I knew immediately the significance of the call: My mother had just died of amyotrophic lateral sclerosis, ten years after she first became ill. Isolated on Abaco, we had to charter a small plane to fly from Palm Beach and then take us to the mainland.

From there we quickly returned to New York, and I flew off to Cape Town for the funeral.

At the end of that summer I packed up my office at Rockefeller. On the Friday at the start of the long Labor Day weekend, I flew out to begin my work in Boulder. Eva was going to stay on at her postdoc job at Rockefeller while she tried to find a faculty position in Colorado.

I had explained to Joshua that I *had* to leave for a while, but that I would phone and write. In retrospect, I am not sure why I thought I "had to"; I left because I felt compelled to continue doing physics. With the precocity of a two-year old who had spent much of his first two years talking to adults, Josh seemed to understand. Eva brought him down to the taxicab to say goodbye to me as I left for Kennedy. As I got into the taxi, I saw him in Eva's arms; he leaned towards me and shouted urgently "Daddy, don't go!" On the flight I drew a picture of myself on the back of an airplane postcard to send to him, and as soon as I landed in Denver I called him. I felt bitter at having left and resentful about my situation.

Chapter 6

Knowledge of the Higher Worlds

■ *A two-city family* ■ *New age meditations*
■ *Karma* ■ *Goodbye to physics* ■

In 1979 Boulder's downtown consisted of a pedestrian mall about six blocks long and a couple of blocks wide, lined with hip clothing and hiking stores and natural-food cafes. The summer weather was hot but dry; unlike humid New York, you could feel the cool of the shade as soon as you stepped into it. Winter was crisp. The canyons twisting out of the town and into the foothills of the Rockies beckoned weekend hikers, and Frank Shorter's store was a mecca for long-distance runners. (It was Mecca without the mosque—there was no Tartan running track anywhere in Boulder, although there were many nice runs along the outskirts of the town.) I had a clean white office in the Gamow physics building, and lived a short downhill walk across the campus in a low-rise, dark, dingily wood-paneled and linoleum-floored apartment in faculty housing. It was dated and dusty, but perfectly okay.

Boulder was also home to the Naropa Institute, the trendy center for Tibetan Buddhism in America headed by Chogyam Trungpa, Rinpoche, whose final appellation signified something like the Venerable One. In the summers, Alan Ginsberg ran their Jack Kerouac School of Disembodied Poetics. In parallel, the back streets of the town were filled with a ragtag bunch of small cults and their gurus; I particularly remember seeing the recruiting center of the Guru Maharaj Ji, the smug-looking, twelve-year-old Perfect Master who wore a Rolex. Mo Siegel had created Red Zinger and founded the Celestial Seasonings Tea Company in Boulder; it was one of the local legends of commercially successful hippiedom, eventually bought by Hain for about $380 million in March 2000. The campus bulletin boards and the local newspapers were filled with personals for neighborhood masseurs, self-help, the Alexander method, and all sorts of other hope-granting institutions of self-improvement. I had to admit I liked it.

Before moving to Boulder I had received a Department of Energy Young Investigator Award in High Energy Physics Research. As a result, I had no courses to teach that year, only some undergraduate problem sessions to tutor. I was used to rising late, but Boulder ran on an early schedule. Many restaurants opened only for breakfast and lunch, shutting down completely by early afternoon, something I had never seen in New York. Every Tuesday morning I had to start teaching at 8 A.M., one identical problem session after another for about four hours. It shocked my unworldly system. A late riser until then, I never succeeded in going to bed early the night before, and I more or less wearily wasted the Wednesday of every week, trying to get back to my normal working schedule.

The rest of the time I came into my office each day and tried to work on various extensions of one of my models. But I was separated from family and friends and miserable about having left Josh behind, so I worked with a heavy heart. No one in the department spoke to me much during the day. The graduate students were busy with their own lives, and the faculty members, mostly married, worked hard from early in the day and then went home. As time went by, I hit an impasse in the problem I was working on, and there were no colleagues with similar enough interests off whom I could bounce ideas. For months, every new attempt I made to circumvent the sticking point failed; I needed hope most of all. If, early on a given day, I had a sudden idea for a strategy that might solve my problem, I would quit work immediately and go home. In this way I postponed disappointment for one more day. I preferred to do nothing for a little while, and then go to bed savoring the little dollop of optimism that my new strategy would work the following day. Usually, my joy lasted only a few hours; each new method failed pretty quickly.

When I had first arrived in New York, I appreciated the city's street life and diners as an antidote to loneliness. There were always people you could watch coming towards you as you drifted in the ambient currents of people along Broadway until all hours of the night: animated Spanish speakers, bums, people cursing furiously to themselves. Boulder wasn't quite as lively, but the outdoor mall I discovered on my first night there was filled with students and locals and not yet lined with the upscale chain stores that came later. Instead, the mall had a small-scale, local-commerce aura. Hippies with backpacks and sleeping bags slept outdoors in the small park. Every block of the mall teemed with crowds centered around amateur magicians, folk singers, guitarists, belly dancers, jugglers and acrobats, all performing till 10 or 11 P.M. I went there almost every evening, strolling up its length and down again ceaselessly, always alone, stopping for a snack, eyeing the people and watching the shows. Much of the time, I liked standing in the crowd around a hip-looking, mustachioed, good-humored, short, dark guy who juggled, ate fire, swallowed swords, and often used the word *mojo*. He never failed to cheer me up. Saturdays and Sundays, after a run or a movie, I always returned there. Eventually, I began to be embarrassed about being seen, over and over again, by the same storekeepers, waiters, and waitresses. I was always solitary, always reading a book. I had no alternative.

During the week I spoke little to anyone in the department. From Monday through Wednesday or Thursday, I was able to do some physics. Then, as Friday approached, I grew dread-filled, apprehensive about another weekend with my own company; my capacity to work tailed off as I began to scan the local papers and make obsessive plans for what I would do in each segment of the day: pancakes at the communal center table at The Good Earth, then a run, a little work, a walk on the mall, a foreign movie in the evening.

My solitary personal life amplified the lonely activities of a theoretical physicist and an academic. You were always banging your head against a wall, trying to quell the need for company in order to keep studying or calculating. I hated the solitude and envied people whose daily work involved dealing with other people. Years later, I found daily life as a quant to be richer and less isolated than life as an accademic. On any given day you might speak to other quants, read theory, interact with traders, write software, speak with clients, give talks and explain difficult concepts to smart but relatively innumerate traders. Until I experienced it, I wouldn't have believed that an investment bank could be more collegial than a college.

Shortly after I arrived in Boulder I went to the Buddhist center. Once I had become fond of Steiner's *Knowledge of the Higher Worlds*, I kept the book around as a talisman, reading bits of it but only occasionally doing some of the spiritual exercises it recommended. I had never managed to be really rigorous about it, and grew to understand that you needed a community and a school to keep you conscientious. Now I decided to attend a few introductory lectures on Tibetan Buddhism given at the Dharmadhattu.

The classes were given by followers of the Rinpoche who were not hip at all, but rather businesslike and regular-looking; part of their spiel was that their practice was consistent with living *in* the world rather than retreating from it. As far as I understood it, the meditation required sitting cross-legged and then simply watching your thoughts as they bubbled up, as though you were dispassionately watching someone else in a movie. You paid unsentimental attention to your own fantasies, obsessions, worries, desires, passions, and disappointments with the detachment of hearing someone else's problems. I liked it, but it was very difficult to do: In no time at all you could suddenly find yourself worrying and strategizing rather than watching. If you caught yourself getting involved, you weren't supposed to grieve or fight it, but simply recognize that distraction itself as just another distraction to be observed. I started attending the Dharmadhattu to meditate on some Sunday mornings, sitting for as long as I could. Their regular session was three hours; someone walked silently around the flamboyantly decorated Tibetan-style room, wordlessly correcting an occasional case of bad posture; once an hour a gong rang, and everyone followed the leader in walking silently around the room for a few minutes, easing cramped muscles. I never looked at my watch; time was on someone else's hands.

The teachers warned you that sometimes, while meditating, you might see strange visions or experience eerily supernatural sensations. Should that happen, you were not to pay undue attention or to regard the vision as a sign of spiritual progress. Instead, you were supposed to acknowledge these as natural occurrences, similar to the other thoughts or feelings bubbling out of your mind. Sometimes, indeed, the walls of the room seemed to shimmer and glow for me, and I couldn't resist feeling naively pleased and vain, despite my teachers' warnings.

At one of the introductory lectures I heard a man in the front of the room ask a question that reminded me of my Steiner dabblings. His name was Roy Hershey and he, like me, was relatively new to Boulder. My instincts were correct; he had trained as a landscape gardener in Europe with the Anthroposophists who, like Steiner himself, thought of plants as the living hair on a living earth. I liked Roy and we had occasional dinners together. Thin and lively and, unlike my physicist colleagues, not career-oriented, he ate more slowly than anyone I have ever seen. He took his time, unperturbed by hurried waiters and unapologetic about it; Roy could easily spend an hour over a plate of pasta. Sometimes he harangued me about the spiritual benefits of buying and preparing one's own meals rather than eating out, but most evenings I still succumbed to the temptation to eat in a restaurant while reading a book rather than go home alone. One evening I invited Roy over and cooked pork chops with orange sauce out of Pierre Franey's Sixty-Minute Gourmet; then we sat on my carpet and meditated for half an hour. Roy claimed to meditate every day in his room in the house he shared with a crowd of people. I envied his free time; he had no job for most of the time I knew him.

Boulder had many spiritual groups "doing the work" together. Roy attended one that met once a week, run by Francesca, a quietly tough woman in her early thirties. She charged about ten or fifteen dollars per person for the weekly group meeting in her house that Roy invited me to attend, and I went along, despite my skepticism.

Before allowing me to join, Francesca required that I first have a private consultation with her. On the appointed afternoon I left my office and went to her house. I answered her questions and remember telling her about my difficulties with living so far from my wife and child; I also told her about my resentments. Then I started attending her meetings.

The group consisted of a range of people, from college kids to dropouts to one middle-aged married man, each obviously there because of some personal difficulties. Francesca had little money. She was nice-looking, but had an unsettlingly bright yellow skin that, she said, was the consequence of a diet rich in homemade carrot juice. At her meetings, she spoke about attitudes to life, read to us from self-help books, elicited discussion, and ended the evening by playing relaxation tapes. It was corny, but not complete nonsense. In the matter of being happy, I could see, both sophisticated and unsophisticated people need the same simple help. It was humbling to be given what looked like trashy paperback self-help books (*The Mystic Path to Cosmic Power* was the title of one, I recall), and see through the clichéd style to the biblically simple truths of some of the statements inside. Francesca worked hard at people. There was something confrontational and unfair about the way she operated, bringing up private facts she knew about you in front of everyone at the meeting, forcing you to publicly confront unpleasant problems and your own contribution to them. I wondered whether she enjoyed provoking these embarrassments, or whether she did it because she thought it was good for you. It reminded me of a verse in Blake's *Auguries of Innocence*: "A truth that's told with bad intent beats all the lies you can invent." Occasionally, an evening would end with someone feeling really bad about something she had said, and she would offer to stay up all night with the person involved and talk it through.

We knew little about Francesca's personal life. Sometime in the spring of 1980 she left Boulder, to follow some man or perhaps to get married, according to Roy, and then the meetings ceased. I had an uncomfortable lunch with her at a vegetarian restaurant shortly before she left. As usual, she was positive but hurtful. "What's it like being a physicist?" she asked. I started to bemoan the difficulty of being ambitious, the smart people in the field, the struggle, the political battles, the need to move, the weariness. "No, not your complaints, tell me about the good things, the positive parts!" she insisted. It was sensible. I never saw her again.

The academic year that started in September 1979 sped by rapidly. In late October Eva's mother took a week off work to help us and brought Joshua to visit me. He was two years and two months old, and I was immensely grateful to her for visiting with him. Always foolishly scared of disappointing Josh, I was quick to explain to him that this was only a temporary visit, and that he would have to leave in a week. As usual he seemed to understand everything. We spent a week visiting playgrounds and the almost fabulous Grand Rabbit toy store, where, on his last day in Boulder, I bought a Lone Ranger figure; I gave it to him as a gift and distraction just before he and his grandmother left me and boarded the plane. Then I was alone again. Eva's mother called me from New York when they arrived, knowing that I would be upset at their departure.

At Thanksgiving I went back to New York for the long weekend. As soon as I arrived I anxiously explained to Josh that in three days I would soon depart again. Our babysitter Helga, who looked after Joshua all day long, told me that sometimes, as she wheeled him through the streets in his stroller, he would point to some stranger who must have resembled me and ask her "Is that my Daddy?" I had no knowledge of his inner mental states, but I hurt to think that they might encompass a world in which I could live in his neighborhood and yet not visit him.

At Christmas I returned to New York for a tense winter semester break. In January I flew back to Boulder. Having to take care of Joshua on her own, Eva developed back trouble and had to spend a week in the hospital, prone. On weekends in Boulder I read Spinoza, taking some comfort from his rigorous and unsentimental look at the logic of life's unhappinesses. In May 1980 I returned to New York for the summer. As I began planning for the course I would teach in the fall, I also began to consider that I might not return there.

I spent the summer working in an office kindly provided by the Rockefeller University, in whose postdoc apartment Eva, Josh, and I still lived. I considered applying for physics assistant professorships in the New York area, but there were too few of them and I was exhausted at the thought of more comprehensive job searches. As midsummer approached, I realized that I had no intention of going back to Boulder to live another year like the one I had just endured.

Karma is the mechanical expiation of sin, according to Tolstoy, and at that time I thought I understood its meaning. The universe wanted you to renounce vanity, ambition, and pride, and embrace God. To do it voluntarily would be best. But if you didn't, then karma, the everyday workings of the universe, would slowly and mechanically grind away at your vanities, flaying off your skin of pride and self-importance, like potatoes in an automated peeler, until you submitted.

What was I to do instead? The oil crisis and commodity inflation of the late 1970s and early 1980s had pushed interest rates up and had driven down the value of the Treasury and corporate bonds that had long been a staple of investment portfolios. The world of fixed-income investors longed for the old days of price-stable products. Investment banks responded with the financial-products boom of the late 1980s— Treasury bond futures, bond options, CMOs, swaps, and swaptions, whose increasing mathematical complexities ultimately led to good employment opportunities for physicists in finance. If I had left Boulder and physics in 1984, Wall Street would have beckoned clearly.

But in 1980, the early days of the energy crisis, the sirens that sang to weary physicists as they sailed from postdoc position to postdoc position were the energy and communications companies: Exxon Labs in Newark, Schlumberger in Ridgefield, Connecticut, the Solar Energy Research Institute (SERI) in Golden, Colorado, and Bell Laboratories at locations throughout New Jersey. They were the Wall Streets of the 1980 physics community.

The smallest deformation of my life in pure physics would have been a job in applied physics, at SERI or Exxon or Schlumberger, working on the physics of oil extraction or solar energy heating. But I was disappointed and ashamed to leave physics, and arrogantly snobbish about its subfields. "If I can't do pure physics," I thought to myself, "I'll be damned if I do applied!" If they expelled me from the monastery, I didn't intend to worship God in the world. I would rather quit religion forever.

Looking back, I was quite clearly wrong (although in the end fate took care of me anyway). Everything is interesting when you examine it closely enough to be able to reconcile its quality and its quantity; every field is fascinating when you have sufficient familiarity with its nuances and begin to try to bridge the gap between its form and its implementation. Applied physics can provide an assortment of tasks, a mix of long-range and short-term problems, a chance to instruct and entertain—in short, a refreshing alternation between the obsessive world of solitary research and the lively world of dealing with people.

"*You can do what you want, but you cannot want what you want*," wrote Schopenhauer in his *Essays and Aphorisms*, which I had started reading. This was true, I thought. I could no longer want to do physics, much as I would have liked to. In the struggle with myself, I got to savor Schopenhauer's hard, cynical view of the universe and its driving forces, all phrased and condensed so beautifully that it read like poetry. I never forgot it. His crystal analysis and elegant style far transcended Steiner's clumsy pronouncements of the truth given without explanation, but they gave a much colder comfort.

In entering physics almost twenty years earlier and now in leaving it, I was not alone; I was in part a follower of fashion and a slave of circumstance. Despite my sensation of free will, I had been part of the largest-ever graduating physics class at Cape Town in 1965 and the largest-ever entering physics class at Columbia in 1966. Similarly now, I was part of the tidal efflux. Several people I had known as students or postdocs in physics had already left the field and were now working at Bell Labs. Furthermore, a molecular biologist acquaintance of Eva's, Lucy Shapiro, had a husband, Harley McAdams, who worked at Bell Laboratories in Murray Hill, New Jersey. Lucy suggested to Eva that I interview with him. Reluctantly, I went out to spend a day there in the summer. I gave a half-hour talk on an introduction to gauge theories and the research I had done, trying hard to be qualitative and entertaining, and soon I had an offer from them. According to my future friend Mark Koenigsberg, an applied mathematician from MIT who was already working there but had been away the day I interviewed, they liked me a lot. Mark had a penchant for scientific metaphors and used to tease and flatter me for years afterwards that since my interview they rated everyone else they questioned in milliDermans.

After thinking about their offer, I decided to go back and learn more. So, in the late summer of 1980 I again drove down the New Jersey turnpike and turned west on the Route 22. Harley was a Department Head at Murray Hill in the Business Analysis Systems Center, a group of genuine ex-rocket scientists and engineers who had converted themselves into business analysts in order to extend their careers when the space program funding at Bell Labs had died out. He had broad interests and liked working there; it gave you the chance, Harley told me, to delve into all sorts of things you could never have studied otherwise. Personally, I wasn't sure I was interested in learning for the sake of learning; I was still ambitious for achievement.

Though they offered me much more money than the University of Colorado, I still yearned for physics, and asked Harley if I could work three days per week, pro rata, and continue to do physics at Rockefeller the remaining two days. He declined, sensibly explaining that it was an arrangement that wouldn't really work for them. In the end, I accepted the job with the deepest misgivings and guilt. I was committing treason.

When I told a South African physicist friend that I was going to work for AT&T's Bell Laboratories, he uncharitably reminded me that eleven years earlier, at the annual Washington, D.C., meeting of the American Physical Society in 1969, we had marched to protest the antiballistic missile system being built by AT&T. Now, he pointed out, I was going to work for them.

I wrote a letter to the chairman of the physics department in Boulder to apologize for my decision not to return. A few weeks later, at the very end of summer, Eva, Joshua, and I flew out to Boulder to pack up all my belongings. Eva, perhaps fearful that I would hold her responsible for my situation, spoke to the senior professor in the particle theory group, who encouraged me to change my mind and stay on. But I was too far gone, and could no longer even imagine preparing to teach particle physics that fall. We took a brief, tense holiday in Steamboat Springs, where we watched a real rodeo to Joshua's great delight, and then returned to New York. I took Josh to visit my family in Cape Town in October, and returned to start work at the Labs at the start of November.

Chapter 7

In the Penal Colony

■ *The world of industry—working for money rather than love*
■ *The Business Analysis Systems Center at*
Bell Labs ■ *A small part of a giant hierarchy*
■ *Creating software is beautiful* ■

Every morning I had to be at my desk at 9:00 A.M. Now, after seventeen years on Wall Street, this sounds comfortably late; it seemed remarkably early then. I woke up around 7 A.M., if Josh hadn't woken me earlier. I ate breakfast, skimmed the *New York Times*, took my car out of the garage beneath our Rockefeller University apartment building, drove crosstown to the Lincoln Tunnel, shot down the New Jersey Turnpike, turned west on Route 24 at Newark, and headed for Murray Hill. It was a reverse commute, and took about an hour. Coming back, even against the evening traffic, required anywhere between one and two hours. The first morning, uncertain of how long it would take to drive there, I arrived early and stopped at the local McDonald's for an Egg McMuffin, feeling romantically proletarian in a Hopperish sort of way.

I had never commuted to work before. I had always worked at what I wanted to work at. Now, I was like almost everyone else, doing what my *boss* wanted me to do, for money. This was the real world.

For the first few weeks, as I drove down the turnpike, I nursed my sad thoughts like a late-night whisky, taking small slow sips, trying to savor the taste of my plight, seeking some perspective. At first,

I attempted to treat the entire commute as a meditative exercise. Then, after a few weeks, I gave that up entirely and instead listened to news and music. What I liked most was talk radio, then still in its infancy in 1980s New York. My favorite driving station was WBAI, 1960s-style alternative radio that teemed with opinionated underdog people who spoke for an hour about anything that bothered them. I listened to Mike Feder, an Upper West sider who, once a week, in Spalding Gray-style monologues, spoke ceaselessly and amusingly about the more harrowing episodes in his life, and also about his occasional epiphanic moments of happiness. Years later he worked at the Shakespeare and Co. bookstore on West 81st and Broadway, now long since squeezed to death by superstores and the Internet. I listened to Margot Adler talk about women's issues, and about her life as a Wiccan before it became fashionable. A gay guy ran an hour of sentimental show music where I first heard Karen Akers sing German-style cabaret. Sometimes, I listened to classic novels as "Books on Tape." But talk shows suited me best, particularly talk by unhappy, oppressed people. I also enjoyed self-help shows, especially Toni Grant on WABC in the late afternoon when I drove home, who, with her beautifully enunciated liquid American accent, told callers with problems to begin by taking "baby steps." Those five years at Bell Labs were the only period during which I ever listened to the radio for longer than a few minutes.

People who had always worked to make a living told me that Bell Labs was an ivory tower. To me, it was working for money. I had earned about $18,000 dollars at Boulder. I started at $42,000 at the Labs, moving up to $49,000 within half a year. But it felt like much less in New York, and the extra pay did little to relieve my loss of direction in the world, though I tried to pretend otherwise.

Ever worried and compulsive, I took AT&T's manifold rules much more seriously than they did. I was supposed to be there each morning by 9 A.M. One day a faulty gas pump caused my car to falter en route, and I could see I was going to be at least ten or fifteen minutes late. Panicked, I stopped at a public phone near the highway at 8:45 A.M. and called my boss's secretary to warn her of my delayed arrival. When I got there only half an hour later, she scathingly told me I was insane to think anyone cared. But I had been paid to pipe, so I felt I must play every note of the tune they called. I resented this so pathologically that I paid more attention to the letter than the spirit of their rules. Once, I needed a morning off to go to Joshua's nursery school and tried to explain it to Harley. He was kind enough to tell me that he didn't even want to know about this sort of stuff. But I was too literal and immature to take advantage of these sensible freedoms. Years later, after I left, I realized that I could have done whatever I liked there, and for a very long time too, before anyone would even have noticed. My friend Mark Koenigsberg, shortly before he left for Salomon Brothers in late 1986, spent a good part of his time studying books on options theory, trying to find a closed-form solution for the value of the American put. I doubt anyone fully knew what he was doing. While it would have been a great discovery, it would have brought no direct commercial value to the Business Analysis Systems Center. But then, what would have?

The Business Analysis Systems Center. Or was it the Business Systems Analysis Center? I truly cannot remember. It consisted of about a hundred people in Building 5, all of us ex-scientists of various kinds, now thinly retreaded to provide internal consultation on various AT&T business problems that might be amenable to mathematics. We were ruled over by our director, Jim Downs, a former applied mathematician in his late forties who had by some latter-day miracle of loaves and fish come to lead this fiefdom.

Everyone was disproportionately fearful of Downs. He seemed to regard social intercourse as a competitive Olympic event, perfecting his own jiu-jitsu style of conversation that aimed to quickly unbalance his opponent. He accomplished this by making aggressively oracular and cryptic statements on whatever topic was under discussion. To my chagrin, his senior employees evangelized about his mysterious wisdom. I recently heard Roger Lowenstein, a reporter for the *Wall Street Journal* and author of *When Genius Failed*, comment that John Meriwether "never played unless he had an edge." Downs believed he had an edge everywhere. He had to dominate every exchange. Any fact you knew, any interest you had, was a glove slap that required him to retaliate and outduel you. If Mark Koenigsberg made a remark about solving a boundary-value problem in heat conduction, Downs responded with a Southern drawl about something clever (but unrelated) he claimed to have done with Fourier analysis twenty years earlier. When he saw a group of us preparing to depart on a lunchtime long-distance run, he joined us at once, despite having just completed his lunch. He pushed ahead at a furious pace, determined to subdue every young or empty-stomached one of us, until he faded out with cramps. I felt uncomfortable around him and kept my distance, but once, when we got involved in a pretentious conversation about meditation as a route to achieving selflessness and humility, he more or less insisted that he was more humble than the rest of us. The irony in this argument almost escaped me, and certainly ran far ahead of him. I suppose that all he really suffered from was an exaggerated form of the insecure competitiveness that afflicts many scientists and academics, but it made him a disquieting manager.

My assigned supervisor was Ron Sherman, one of four supervisors beneath Department Head Harley. Ron was a rotundly genial PhD in Engineering who had coauthored an important Lab study on EMP (Electro-Magnetic Pulse), the sudden surge of Faraday electrical currents and heat that would occur in the wires of the national telephone network as a result of the intense magnetic fields induced by nuclear explosions. A nuclear attack might therefore melt and destroy the network, even if it left people unharmed. Ron was one of the gentler people in our center, good-humored and kind despite an earlier family tragedy that left him a single parent of two young sons, one of whom was already writing well-received plays. Ron seemed to me to lead an enviably charmed life at the Labs, setting his own arrival and departure schedule imperturbably. He had broad interests, and year by year accumulated more degrees: first a PhD in Engineering, then an Executive MBA, and finally, I think, a law degree. Clerical and secretarial help were sparse at the Labs, and Ron seemed to take some small amount of glee in occasionally giving me long documents to xerox for everyone in our group, late in the day when I was preparing to leave. Sometimes he asked me to take minutes at group meetings, complimenting me on my handwriting; sad to say, it succeeded in making me feel simultaneously important and infantile.

Ron and I were but two nodes in a very large hierarchy that contained not only the whole Labs, but also AT&T, Western Electric, and God-knows-what-else that belonged to the Bell System in those previstiture days. There were roughly four MTS (Members of Technical Staff, like me) under each supervisor; there were four or five supervisors (like Ron) under each department head like Harley, and four Harleys under each Jim Downs. From there the tree branched upwards to higher and higher levels, eventually encompassing the whole company. If they extended the organization by only four more levels, I used to think, they could employ every adult in the United States.

Every new employee grew to be instinctively aware of these reporting levels. When you first joined the organization, someone quickly explained to you that the Bell Labs level structure was shifted up by half a level from the more or less parallel structure at AT&T, and that, therefore, we lowly MTS at the bottom of the Labs totem pole were actually *almost supervisors on the AT&T scale!* Often, in the five years I spent there, I heard someone proudly say "I just came back from a four-level meeting!" I never found out whether this meant that the meeting was important enough to have been graced by the presence of someone from exalted Level 4, or whether it meant that the meeting was so diverse that there had been people from four different levels there simultaneously. Levels with low numbers were more auspicious, and you trembled at their mysterious splendor. Jim Downs used to say that you could never comprehend the activities of someone more than one level above you; the activities of someone two levels higher were destined to be forever a mystery, unless you got promoted. It sounded very Kafkaesque. What especially impressed me about Wall Street in general and Goldman Sachs in particular, when I came to work there five years later, was the absence of reverential fear. At Goldman, at that time, it was relatively easy to approach important (and wealthy) people if the business seemed to require it. As an example, I spoke to Bob Rubin a couple of times in my first years at Goldman, when he was head of Fixed Income.

The Bell System was a massive bureaucracy of about one million workers, linesmen to lawyers. It had its own enormous encyclopedia of rules and regulations. I once watched one of my supervisors search through the book of appropriate practice to find out what to do about my call to New York City jury duty. Like the army, Bell stripped you of all external trappings of merit, status or honor, and then imposed its own—Supervisor, Department Head, Director, and so on. Somehow, one understood that business cards could carry no external academic credentials; Andy Salthouse, an ex-physicist and passionate amateur astronomer and asteroid hunter who joined the Labs a little before me, explained that this was necessary in order to avoid the tension that might otherwise occurs when an MTS with a PhD reported to a supervisor with only a master's degree.[1]

In physical space, the Business Analysis Systems Center was located in prefabricated barracks at the upper edge of the prestigious Murray Hill campus, the most interesting and academic part of the Labs. In logical space, we were part of Area 90, Network Systems. Area 10, the lowest number, was the crown jewel, a pure research center where first-rate scientists and engineers carried out advanced research without the burden of having to seek government funding. As a regulated monopoly in those precompetitive days, AT&T could charge its consumers whatever it needed to pay the bills.

Area 10 was absolutely world-class in computer science and physics. Brian Kernighan, Dennis Ritchie, and their coworkers had invented the now legendary C programming language and the UNIX operating system there, and then built the entire suite of programming utilities that carried nerdily cute names like *awk, ed, sed, finger, lex,* and *yacc.* Area 10 had played a large role in evangelizing the dual view of programs as both tools and text, written not only to control electronic machines but also to to be understood and manipulated by people. At the labs people were proud of programming and viewed it as an art. In physics and engineering the Labs was an experimental and theoretical powerhouse, producing research in electronics and information theory that made possible many of the subsequent advances in communications. Bardeen, Brattain, and Shockley had invented the transistor there in 1947, and Claude Shannon published his landmark paper "A Mathematical Theory of Communication" in the *Bell System Technical Journal* in 1948. There were fundamental discoveries made, too—Penzias and Wilson won the Nobel Prize for discovering the cosmic radiation left behind by the Big Bang, as predicted by Robert Herman. Even during the period I worked there, Horst Stormer, now at Columbia University, did the research on the quantum Hall effect that recently won him a share of the Nobel Prize. Near the end of my stay there, in 1984, Feynman came to give a

[1]On Wall Street until the late 1990s, PhDs s rarely listed their degrees on their business cards, because to do so would have outed them immediately as nonbusiness people. For the same reason, it took a long time before quants and programmers routinely put their email addresses on their business cards. A rise in the prestige of PhD degrees occurred slowly but steadily between 1996 and 1999 as dot-coms prospered.

talk on the theory of quantum computing, a technology then just emerging into infancy. The economics research group in Area 10, later disbanded, was also renowned; Robert Merton had published his definitive paper "Theory of Rational Option Pricing" in the 1973 *Bell Journal of Economics and Management Science.*

I envied anyone and everyone in Area 10 their apparent freedom, and rued my self-perceived lack thereof. For several years I commuted in a shared minivan from Manhattan to Murray Hill and back, and met a number of other Members of Technical Staff who, like me, worked in the applied areas of the Labs. I noticed that engineers who had come to the Labs straight from graduate school became rapidly accustomed to the corporate bureaucracy and pettiness; they had known nothing better. But those of us who had previously been independent scientists always chafed at the civil service atmosphere, and many of us ultimately left.

Bill Toy, with whom I collaborated a few years later at Goldman, had been a particle experimentalist whose PhD advisor, Jerome Friedman, later won the Nobel Prize for discovering the quark structure in the deep-inelastic electron–nucleus scattering experiments that had stimulated my PhD thesis work. Bill had also worked at the Labs prior to coming to Goldman and had experienced similar frustrations to mine. Our trouble was that we wanted to get things done. The Labs could be fun if you were the kind of person who was simply happy to tinker away with expensive up-to-date equipment, but we didn't function that way. I wanted the satisfaction that comes from creating something. But in Building 5, so many of the projects I worked on ended in a confused impasse. You did some work; you wrote some internal document; Harley told Jim Downs about it; he then pronounced it a failure or a success for some cryptically inarticulate reason you couldn't understand. We were forbidden from publishing it because it was proprietary; yet often, no one inside the company had any real use for it. I was increasingly sympathetic to whomever coined the slogan "information wants to be free."

I detested the cult of manageriality at the Labs. I was thirty-five years old when I arrived there, and very quickly realized that you got no respect in Area 90 unless you were a manager. In my previous life in physics, talent and skill were everything—you felt sorry for people who ceased creating in order to become administrators. But at the Labs, talent seemed to be a commodity, fodder for managers to buy and redistribute. Supervisors were actually forbidden from doing "technical work" on the grounds that competing with their employees in this way was demoralizing. Instead, managers became experts at intracorporate maneuvering. They seemed to have forsaken their abilities for an incestuous familiarity with the system which was valuable only in that organization, at that time.

I felt old at the Labs. My colleagues treated all forty-year old MTS as over the hill. Against my best intentions, I began to look at them and myself in the same way. I could not imagine living like that for the next twenty years. When I eventually went to work at Goldman, I was relieved and exhilarated to discover that the firm appreciated solid skill and talent. Traders, salespeople, programmers, options experts—they all worked with their own hands and made a very good living.

It was also at the Labs that I first witnessed political correctness. It was only 1981, but once a year we were compelled to attend a day-long, off-site, group therapy-style meeting run by external consultants. There, we were trained in color and gender sensitivity. We played group games in which you had to declare in public what kind of animal you identified with, and why. (The otherwise meek woman who became my supervisor a year later said she identified with lions, because it was the females in the pride who killed.) We listened to music and described the feelings it evoked. We acted out skits representing hypothetical crises in the workplace. In one episode, for example, we were told that a crowd of male and female MTS had gone for lunch to a nearby offsite restaurant, without their supervisor. While there, one of the male MTS told a dirty joke. A woman MTS felt demeaned. Should she have (a) kept quiet, (b) confronted the male, or (c) spilled the beans to her supervisor on their return to the Labs? I don't recall the correct answer.

You were supposed to bare your soul about your prejudices in these extracurricular sessions in front of your colleagues and supervisors, and then return to work with them again the next day. The apparent justification for this invasion of privacy was that your personality and prejudices could affect the quality of your work and were therefore a legitimate corporate concern. I detested this conflation of the personal and the corporate. Just because I worked for them didn't mean I had to discuss my internal hang-ups in public one day a year. Nor did I especially want to hear about theirs. At the tail end of the dot-com bubble, twenty years later, I was dismayed that for a brief period even Goldman Sachs ran rife with consultants successfully peddling their quackishly trendy prescriptions for team building.

Meanwhile, in Building 5, conformity of ambition ran wild. Several of the women there, ex-scientists like the rest of us, were avidly reading *Dress for Success* and following its precepts. They began wearing mannish suits with padded shoulders and silk neckties. One female MTS warned me never to wear a brown suit, speaking with an earnestness so great that I have never been able to buy a brown suit since, for fear that she really knew something significant. One day, nevertheless, she cried in my office while telling me about her personal problems. No one seemed to know whether to be businesslike or empathetic. At some time in the middle of my stay there, Bell Labs itself was rent apart by the breakup of the Bell System and the divestiture of the Baby Bells. I remained with AT&T, while some of my colleagues were sent off to Bellcore, the newly formed telecommunications laboratory of the Bell Telephone Companies.

The inefficiencies and irritations of working at the Labs could fill a book, but the stupidity that most illustrates the picayune nature of the bureaucracy was the command, from somewhere above, sometime in 1984, to enter our overtime hours (at work or at home) onto the time cards we filled out each week, even though there was no pay for overtime at all. This was simply an inducement to suck up to your management by lying to them about how much work you did above and beyond the call of duty. It was an irrationality worthy of the "Dilbert" cartoon, whose creator Scott Adams, unsurprisingly, spent several of his working years at Pacific Bell.

But there were some good points to life there, too. The Center was filled with ex-physicists and mathematicians, part of the late-1970s *zeitgeist* that caused scientists to stream out of academic life and into corporations. Many of them were particle physicists I had known before. I grew friendly with Mark Koenigsberg, who loved puzzles of any kind. He was absent the day I first came to interview, but soon after I started work we bonded over a mutual dislike of many of the same things. Six months after I left the Labs for Goldman, he followed me out the door to Salomon Brothers. Mark and I became friendly with Larry Kegeles, a physicist about my age whom I had met a few years earlier when he was a PhD student in general relativity at the University of Pennsylvania. Steve Blaha, another former particle physicist I had met at various conferences over the previous seven years, had come to work in the Center, too, giving up his academic post at Williams College. He too left the Labs a few years later to become a software consultant and author in the Boston area.

Mark, Larry, and I banded together. Once I dragged them to the Ethical Culture Society in New York to listen to a talk by Chogyam Trungpa himself. Larry, like me, had an affinity for the offbeat, and he became interested in Reichian analysis. Years before, I had seen Dusan Makeveyev's funny movie about Reich, *W.R.: Mysteries of the Organism*, and enjoyed its Slavic sensibility and clever equation of sexual and political repression. Now I read Myron Sharaf's *Fury on Earth*, a biography of Reich's strange brave life.

Life at the Labs was lax, and we went out to eat long lunches at low-quality Jersey restaurants on Route 22. When we occasionally took visiting interviewees out to dinner, the rendezvous of choice was L'Affaire, whose pretentiously sophisticated name told you everything about the people who ran it, the food they provided, and the people who took us there. Once, sitting in my car in the parking lot outside Building 5 during a prolonged downpour after a long lunch off premises, Mark, Larry, and I pondered the famous two-condom combinatorial problem that spread through the Center:

> Two (heterosexual) couples decide to have group sex with each other in all possible male-female combinations. They have only two condoms, and everyone is scared of catching some venereal disease. How can they manage four couplings with only two condoms? The first man puts on two condoms, one over the other, and then sleeps with the first woman. Only the outer surface of the outer condom and the inner surface of the inner one has had contact with any potentially infectious surface. The man removes the outer condom and sleeps with the second woman. The second man then dons the removed outer condom whose inner surface has until now had no contact with anyone's skin, and sleeps with the first woman, whose only contact has thus far been with the outside of the same condom. Finally, the second man dons the second condom over the one he is already wearing, and sleeps with the second woman, who again only experiences a condom she has already touched.

It was impossible to resist the temptation to generalize to N couples.

Larry was a serious marathoner, and he and I went running together several times a week at lunchtime, part of a small crowd of avidly compulsive runners at the Labs. We would walk down to the small shower room that belonged to the Building and Grounds staff, change, warm up on the grass, run for 30 to 45 minutes, warm down, stretch, shower and change, and then eat lunch in the cafeteria. It took close to two hours, and put a sizeable dent in the workday, especially if you worked nine to five, but no one seemed to care. I have never before or since been that fit or that fast.

We held an occasional educational seminar in our group and once, early in 1981, Larry gave a talk on the Black-Scholes theory, which I had never heard of up to that point. I became briefly fascinated by the fact that options payoffs involved the algebra and calculus of Heaviside (indicator) functions, which I had used in particle physics; later I came across an early paper by Mark Garman of Berkeley, who exploited these same relationships. But options theory was largely irrelevant to what we did at the Labs, and my temporary interest quickly faded. I understood nothing about hedging or risk-neutrality, and I paid no attention to the stock market.

Several years later, Larry, Mark, and I were sent to a two-week MIT executive summer session on finance, taught by Stuart Myers from his textbook with Brealey. We lived in a campus dorm and luxuriated in our freedom from corporate life, running on the MIT track in the late afternoons and eating in Cambridge in the evenings. Myers's course focused on the Capital Asset Pricing Model, and I was captivated by the apparent similarity between financial theory and thermodynamics. I saw a perhaps-too-facile correspondence between heat and money, temperature and risk, and entropy and the Sharpe ratio, but have never since figured out how to exploit it. The course was brief and intense and required more work than we put into it. One of the lecturers was Terry Marsh, now a Professor at Berkeley and a founding partner of the financial software firm Quantal. At that time he was just beginning to make his reputation, and I was always happy to run into him years later at professional finance meetings or when I gave a seminar at the Haas business school at Berkeley.

I viewed AT&T as a job, and a disappointing one at that, but Larry had a strong spiritual streak, and believed that we were all playing a part in improving human communication. I thought that laughable then, but perhaps on some level he was right. Nevertheless, he, Mark and I—all stifled—were gone within five years.

What I did like above all else at the Labs was the beauty of creating software. Ignorant people called it "coding," as though there was something mechanical about it, the mere uncomprehending translation from one set of symbols to another. People who liked it unabashedly called themselves "programmers." Whatever you called it, I discovered that programming was one of the purest activities; it was truly architecture with words. By some strange unanimity of opposites, both my scientist and business-world friends were condescending about programming—they thought it inferior to doing physics or making money. But I fell in love with it.

When you program well, you are trying to design a machine to perform a task. You design with a man-made programming language—FORTRAN, Lisp, C++ or Java, for example. Programming is not that different from instructing a friend to perform a task for you. The big difference is that the computer is much more literal than any friend, and so every detail of the task must be specified as though the computer knows nothing about the world.

Until I arrived at the Labs in 1980, I had never realized how elegant and challenging programming could be. I had never used a computer terminal. During my student and postdoc years, all my programs had aimed merely to obtain the numerical values of complicated mathematical formulae, over and over again; I thought of the computer as a glorified adding machine. My only exception had been at the University of Cape Town, in 1965, when I used punched cards to enter a vocabulary into the machine and then created randomly generated short poems. I had always thought of that effort as a childish lark.

But at AT&T in 1980, the whole firm was embracing C, the simultaneously graceful and yet practical language invented by Dennis Ritchie about ten years earlier at Murray Hill. He had devised C to be a high-level tool with which to write portable versions of UNIX, the operating system also invented there by Ken Thompson and Ritchie.[2] Now, everything from telephone switching systems to word-processing

---

[2]Writing operating systems in a high-level language like C was a new idea. Operating systems used to be written from scratch, arduously, in the idiosyncratic, low-level, hard-to-read, and primitive *assembler* or *machine code* that came native on each new machine. By using standard C rather than each machine's particular machine code to write the operating system, you could quickly create a version of UNIX and all its tools to run any newly manufactured computer, simply, by first getting C itself to run on that machine.

software was being written in C, on UNIX, all with amazing style. Eventually, even physicists, who are generally interested only in the number of digits after a decimal point, began to forsake ugly utilitarian FORTRAN for poetically stylish C. Programming was in the late stages of a revolution about which I was just beginning to learn.

The revolution's credo demanded that programs be humanly comprehensible texts of information. This had not always been the case; because programs had to be stored in expensive and limited computer memory, programmers had traditionally concentrated on making them as concise as possible. They bragged about writing "tight" code that was terse, condensed, and cryptic, even confusing. It was OK as long as it ran fast, the thinking went; style was almost irrelevant and content was king. Programs were therefore error-prone as well as hard for humans to understand and modify—implicitly, they were written for the computers that would mechanically execute their commands. Hard to create, programs tended to have surprisingly long subsequent lifetimes during which they required expensive maintenance, modification, and enhancement. This was the set of circumstances that caused the anxiety behind Y2K.

What are you doing when you program? You are trying to use a language to specify an imagined world and its details as accurately as possible. You are trying to create this world on a machine that can understand and execute only simple commands. You do this solely by writing precise instructions, often many hundreds of thousands of lines long. Your sequence of instructions must be executed without ambiguity, by an uncomprehending automaton, the computer, and yet, in parallel, must be read, comprehended, remembered and modified by you and other programmers. Just as poetry strives to resolve the tension between form and meaning, so programming must resolve the conflict between intelligibility and concision. In this endeavor, the language you employ is critically important.

At the Labs, one regarded code-writing itself as a task in need of tools. They encouraged programmers to view each specific program they tackled as an instance of a class of more generally useful programs, and then to use the computer to create that class. They devised programs to write part or all of their programs. The UNIX community at the Labs had created, out of love rather than duty, a suite of editorial and analytical tools to help write, examine, and modify their programs. Thompson and Ritchie's UNIX programming environment used the computer not merely as the automaton to execute the program, but, just as importantly, as the tool to create it. The computer was not just the hammer, but also the forge with which to create the next-generation hammer.

Bell Labs Members of Technical Staff didn't just churn out programs; instead, they thought about the subtasks (reading input, solving equations, formatting output, for example) that the program needed to do. Then, they wrote little, special-purpose programming languages that could be used to generate these subunits of the larger program. Finally, they used these little languages to create the entire program itself. They were always generalizing from tasks to tools.

Because AT&T was a regulated utility, forbidden from making a profit by selling software in competition with IBM and Digital, the Labs distributed these tools freely to universities. This dissemination produced an entire generation of programmers who thought of programming not as a chore, but as a literary endeavor with the computer as medium. How lucid, elegant and structured your program looked was as important as how efficiently it ran.

Kernighan and Plauger wrote a famous and influential book in the 1970s called *The Elements of Programming Style*, its title a homage to Strunk and White's classic monograph on writing well, *The Elements of Style*. They were part of a movement that perceived programming and code development as art.

This culture was already widespread when I arrived at the Business Analysis Systems Center. All new employees learned UNIX and its Bourne-shell scripting language, as well as C for programming, the S language for statistics, and the line-formatting text editor *ed*. I remember the excitement of learning to use Bill Joy's visual text editor *vi* shortly after it was released. To their credit, the Center organized a sequence of master's-equivalent courses on computer science, taught mostly by professors from Columbia University in New York City. I learned software design and algorithms from John Kender, a mild-mannered, low-key expert on vision software; we learned database theory from David Shaw, who later founded the investment boutique D. E. Shaw & Co., as well as the first free email service, Juno. At D. E. Shaw, David employed Jeff Bezos, who later left to found Amazon.com.

David was already a free-wheeling entrepreneur. He had run a software company while studying computer science at Stanford; when I met him he still radiated a sloppy academic demeanor that didn't completely jibe with his business-oriented self-assurance. He was an early incarnation of the now ubiquitous capitalist academic. In his back trousers pocket he carried his appointments in a small leather DayTimer that had conformed to the shape of his body. The book had been manufactured in Pennsylvania and was very American middle manager, with its one-month spiral-bound inserts with space for lists of Appointments and Things To Do. It looked very unprofessorally businesslike, an early precursor of soon-to-arrive European Filofaxes and, a decade later, American Palm Pilots.

David clearly thought big. In those days he was planning what he called "NonVon," a parallel-processing computer comprised of many small processors and memory units. It was to be the antithesis of the standard computer with one large central processor, a design that had prevailed since John von Neumann and the ENIAC computer of the 1940s. David's confidence inspired fear and envy. John Kender complained half-jokingly to me that while he and the other assistant professors in the tenure race at Columbia were trying to get modest government grants to do their work, David was always talking about ambitious proposals on a much larger scale, with plans for NonVon eventually to require a staff of tens to hundreds. John thought he and his colleagues had no chance of tenure in comparison with David's broad vision and unquestioning self-confidence that bordered on braggadocio.

John was right about David's capacious *weltanschaung*, but wrong about his exact path to glory. David left Columbia soon afterwards and went to work in Nunzio Tartaglia's fabled group at Morgan Stanley, doing pairs trading.[3] When that effort eventually ended, he created D. E. Shaw & Co. His new firm touted itself as specializing in the interaction between technology and finance, nurturing their reputation as secretive

---

[3]Pairs trading is the search for statistically significant oscillatory patterns in the spread between pairs of similar stocks. If you believe you have detected such a phenomenon, you short the expensive stock and buy the cheap one when the spread is large, and then reverse the trade when/if the spread narrows. Since Tartaglia's renowned but temporary successes at Morgan Stanley, trading houses, hedge funds, and the scientists they employ have regularly and hopefully attempted to build model-driven, so-called "statistical arbitrage" money machines of this type.

builders of high-powered computer systems used to seek out trading opportunities. *Fortune* magazine in 1996 referred to it as "the most intriguing and mysterious force on Wall Street today." I knew hiring managers on Wall Street who interviewed anyone from D. E. Shaw, if only to find out what went on in its obscure depths. But most Shaw employees you interviewed didn't know much about how things worked there. In 1997, when I was invited to introduce David as the luncheon speaker at a conference, I said that ". . . you could think of D. E. Shaw & Co. as the Batcave, with David as Batman, watching the world, himself visible only through a glass, darkly." But building a riskless money machine, especially on a large scale, is not that easy. There are not that many riskless profits to be harvested in the world. Eventually the struggle to make the same return on larger amounts of capital makes ever-riskier strategies tempting. In 1998 D. E. Shaw & Co., in partnership with the Bank of America, reportedly lost close to a billion dollars on the same sorts of strategies that decapitated Long Term Capital Management and took appreciable pounds of flesh out of many other hedge funds and investment banks.

M eanwhile, in 1981, I attended the computer science courses offered by the Labs and learned the practical art of programming. I was especially entranced by language design and compiler writing, and spent most of my time creating specific little languages that allowed users to solve specialized problems.

In high-level languages like Java, C, or even ancient and despised FORTRAN, you can easily write brief, sophisticated commands that instruct the computer to carry out complex operations. You can program in a style that corresponds rather closely to the way an educated person thinks or talks about mathematics. But a computer's central processing unit, the primitive brain that actually performs the logical and mathematical operations, is an *idiot savant* that has been engineered to "understand" and respond only to simple babytalk. It is as though you want to tell a small child who grasps only baby talk (but has a very good memory for long sequences of it) to take the dog for a walk. You cannot just say "Take the dog for a walk!" This assumes too much knowledge of the world. Instead, you must translate that high-level, big-picture command into a corresponding list of very elementary sequential actions, each describable in baby talk. You must say something like:

Fetch the dog;
find the leash;
tie the leash to the dog's collar;
hold the leash tightly;
open the front door;
follow the dog for five minutes;
if the dog steps off the sidewalk, pull him back using the leash;
. . .
return to the front door;
enter through the door;
unleash the dog.

If you design a high-level language that allows its users to issue sophisticated commands such as "Walk the dog," you must provide a compiler that translates these commands into the baby talk machine code that the central processing unit can follow. Clearly, one mistake in translation, or just a little lack of specificity, and the dog and child will never return!

When John Backus and his team at IBM invented FORTRAN as a "FORmula TRANslation" language in the late 1950s, they wanted to allow programmers to manipulate complex mathematical formulas. Their compiler had to *automatically* translate any FORTRAN command into a sequence of the baby talk machine code that the simple logical computer circuits could follow. The compiler had to not only translate reasonable commands into baby talk; it also had to refuse to translate unreasonable or nonsensical ones. It had to to shout "Foul!" if you asked it to compile the command "Dog the! for take walk." In brief, it had to comprehend grammar.

Grammar is the set of rules that legitimate sentences must satisfy. Adults recognize grammar intuitively, without thinking, but computers must follow rules. Backus developed a mathematical formalism for describing and parsing grammars that facilitated the task of language translation. It worked well for simple programming grammars that are less complex and subtle than those expressing natural languages.

Backus's formalism, called BNF for Backus Normal Form, provided a methodology for creating grammatically consistent computer languages, and paralleled similar discoveries by Noam Chomsky on generative grammars. Working with this formalism, I learned how to design small grammatically consistent computer languages.

BNF helped you to define the grammar of your computer language. It allowed you to create a compiler that would parse sentences in your language and accept only the grammatically correct ones. This was half the battle. The other half was to write the part of the compiler that translated each grammatically correct sentence into baby talk. This was painstakingly tedious and difficult; a mistake in translation is potentially fatal in a program that people rely on to do mathematics or control spacecraft.

The UNIX operating system was a breathtakingly liberating environment for program writers. It contained two of the most beautiful tools I had ever seen: they were called *lex* and *yacc*, and they allowed me to create compilers almost effortlessly. *Lex* was an abbreviation for "lexical analyzer." *Yacc* stood for "Yet Another Compiler-Compiler," and was another of the cute acronyms that characterized many UNIX tools. You could use *lex* to create a subprogram that would recognize all the words in your language. You could use *yacc* to create another subprogram that would parse and recognize legitimate sentences, and then take the actions you deemed appropriate. *Lex* and *yacc* were "non-procedural" programs—you weren't required to write all the details of lexical analysis and parsing; instead, you simply told them *what* grammar you wanted to recognize, and they wrote a program to do it, using algorithms for matching patterns that went back to the computer pioneers Alan Turing and Stephen Kleene. With *lex* and *yacc* as aids, I learned to create my own computer languages.

A little like Feynman diagrams, which allowed workaday physicists to compute unthinkingly the detailed quantum mechanical probabilities that had formerly demanded the genius of Schwinger or Feynman, these parsing tools allowed regular programmers to prosaically create languages that would previously have required magnificent exertions.

I used to always equate computation with numerical evaluation. Now, having been exposed to the linguistic aspects of computing, I regretted I had not recognized them before. I fantasized about escaping the Business

Analysis Systems Center to become a true research computer scientist in Area 10, and made an attempt to transfer. But I had neither the credentials nor the background, so it was quite impossible.

Nevertheless, for most of my five years at the Labs, I worked on building compilers. I spent several years designing and implementing a language I named *HEQS*, a "Hierarchical EQuation Solver," an equation-solving language for businesspeople who knew enough to specify the equations they wanted to solve but lacked either the mathematical ability or the time to solve them. The name had the obligatory UNIX cuteness, but it was also a homonym of "hex," which succinctly reflected my secretly morbid view of life in Building 5.

Like *lex* or *yacc*, HEQS was a nonprocedural language—users could state what they wanted done ("Solve these equations!") without having to specify a procedure for accomplishing it. (FORTRAN and C, in contrast, are *procedural* languages that demand that the programmer specify, in excruciating detail, how to execute a task.) In its final incarnation, you could give HEQS a collection of thousands of algebraic equations (linear, nonlinear or simultaneous) and have it solve them or tell you why some error you had made in specifying the equations made a solution impossible. HEQS also provided tools for analyzing the set of equations; users could examine the relation between input and output, and understand the chain by which altering one variable's value affected other variables. In essence, it allowed business users at AT&T to spend their time specifying the relationships in their business or accounting model without worrying about how to solve it.

Six or seven years later, after the widespread advent of PCs, spreadsheets like Visicalc and Lotus provided tools for doing the same thing. Until then, various businesspeople at AT&T headquarters used HEQS for model solving, and programmers in our center employed it as an equation-solving engine in many of the applications we built. I was pleased to keep one foot in the research world by describing it in an issue of the *AT&T Technical Journal*.[4]

---

[4]At this time I also began attending various computer science research seminars and conferences, where I was always struck by the difference in quality between computer science research and physics research. In physics, seminar speakers described completed achievements. In computer science, however, the majority of the talks were about plans for systems, sketches of new languages, and unimplemented ideas. The hurdle for declaring accomplishment seemed much lower.

I developed HEQS on my own, delving into *lex* and *yacc* to design the language and build its compiler. Once users had entered the equations they wanted to solve, my program regrouped them into sequences of smaller sets of simultaneous equations, ordered so that the output from the solution of one set provided the input you needed to solve the next. Stimulated by the courses on computer science I had taken at the Labs, I realized that I could represent each variable in the set of equations by a node in a directed graph, and that reordering the equations was equivalent to decomposing the graph into its strongly connected components. I was naively proud to be doing real math.

There were helpful resources wherever I turned. I found that Chris Van Wyk, an MTS in Computer Science in Area 10, had written a set of UNIX tools for solving simultaneous equations. He had started this project while working on his PhD thesis at Stanford under Donald Knuth, the famous author of the four-volume *The Art of Computer Programming* and the inventor of *TeX*, a widely used language for mathematical typesetting and word processing that has become standard among scientists. Steve Blaha, my particle-physicist friend at the Labs, told me that Knuth had been his college roommate. As we worked together I was impressed by Chris's professional programming skills; I was an amateur, living by my wits, while Chris was the real thing, a researcher working in his area of expertise. I felt doomed to remain a mere dilettante.

HEQS was a good idea, and soon, as people in the Center started using it for solving larger sets of equations, it needed a more skillful and efficient implementation than I could provide. My version of HEQS allowed users only single numbers (scalars) and one-dimensional vectors to represent financial time series. A colleague, Ed Sheppard, was assigned to work with me, and we planned to rewrite the system to incorporate multidimensional array variables in order to represent more general financial time series. While I was away on a two-week beach vacation at Fire Island with my family, Ed suddenly threw himself into redesigning and then rewriting the entire system—without giving me advance notice. I returned to a *fait accompli*, a completely new, enhanced, and almost unrecognizable APL-flavored version of the language. Ed's version now incorporated vastly complex dynamically linked data structures, whose details I knew I would not live long enough to master. Ed had also cleverly modified HEQS so that, once you had used it interactively to develop and solve a financial model, you could then use it generate a C program that would solve your equations many times faster.

Programming came naturally to Ed in a way it never would to me, and his proficiency daunted me. Sometime in late 1984 he left to join Asymetrix, a Seattle-based company founded by Paul Allen. For the remainder of my stay at the Labs, I was a victim of our success: I often had to spend days at a time diving into his code to fix the residual bugs that showed up in algorithms I had never written and never fully understood.

It was around this time, seeing Ed write and design code, that I realized how many physicists misperceived the nature of jobs and careers in the nonacademic world. Physicists tended to think they were so smart that, once they descended to a job in the "outside world," their talent would allow them to work in a 9-to-5 mode and still outperform their colleagues. But, in any nonacademic job, there are people for whom that particular work is not a compromise but a passion and dedication, taken seriously. They, rather than the smart but coasting physicists, set the standards of excellence.

HEQS ended happily for me. Chris Van Wyk and I eventually wrote an article on HEQS that appeared in the software journal *Programming: Practice and Experience* in 1984. I was overjoyed to publish again rather than perish, to be "doing science." Even now, I get a small kick out of seeing occasional references to that paper on the Web, though most of them undoubtedly occur because Chris continues to work in the field of nonprocedural languages. I was pleased to discover recently that Lucent, the descendant of Bell Labs, still offers HEQS for sale at $89.00 on its website at https://www.lucentssg.com/heqs.html. In this era of Mathematica and Excel, however, I cannot imagine who buys it.

I learned almost nothing about business or finance in the Business Analysis Systems Center between 1980 and 1985. In contrast, the software engineering skills I learned there stood me in good stead, and formed the basis for much of the fixed-income financial modeling infrastructure I later built at Goldman Sachs in 1987.

Despite the excellent education, I always felt subservient and demeaned at the Labs. Only a month after starting work there I took Joshua, barely three years old, to play on the lawns at Rockefeller University where we still lived. He loved to take off his shoes and run barefoot through the grass. While he did so, I sat there ruminating about what I was doing. Suddenly, he came over, looked at me, and asked: "Daddy, why you sad?" I knew even then that my daily reverse commute to the Labs would be merely temporary. I just didn't know how I would find a way to end it.

■ *Chapter 8* ■

Stop-Time

■ *Wall Street beckons* ■ *Interviewing at investment banks* ■ *Leaving the Labs* ■

How to get out of the Labs? That was my daily obsession for five years. Meanwhile, always the complainer, I came home every day and droned on indignantly about my plight, burdening anyone willing to listen to my own Passover Seder, the story of how I came to leave the land of academic milk and honey and live under Pharoah in the land of the Business Analysis Systems Center. I recounted the heavy labors that were inflicted upon me and strategized about how to get free. Every day was *Paradise Lost* and *In Search of a Lost Time*. I know I drove my wife half crazy.

When I took three-year-old Josh to the Center's Christmas party, I worried that he would give me away—I had spent so many evenings at home disparagingly describing my frustration with bosses and coworkers within his earshot that I feared he would recognize someone's name when I introduced them and repeat one of my remarks. Before driving out to Murray Hill that morning, I cautioned him not to repeat anything I had said about anyone. Of course, he didn't.

At that party, Mark Koenigsberg told me about a date who had taken him to see a movie he hated intensely. We knew that our tastes in movies were diametric, and the more he described the plot, the more I was certain I would like it. As soon as the party was over, I drove back to New York and went to see the film—Louis Malle's *My Dinner With André*, with

André Gregory and Wallace Shawn. The self-indulgent dinner conversation about the contrast between a mystical search for fulfillment and the mundane pleasures and disappointments of everyday life resonated deeply in me. It reminded me of the sense of possibility about the future I had once experienced when I had first wanted to be a physicist; it also reminded me of the potentialities for happiness that I had sensed while meditating at the Dharmadhattu in Boulder. On that December afternoon, *My Dinner With André* imbued me with a such a vast sense of hope and salvation that I felt uplifted. Its aftereffects dissipated astonishingly slowly, trickling out of me for about a week. Two months later, wondering if its salutary effects had been merely a fluke, I went to see the movie once again, and once again felt better, though this time only for several days. Malle, Gregory, and Shawn depicted the middle ground between hope and despair so well; a few years ago I saw their *Vanya on Forty-Second Street* and felt similarly moved, at the first viewing and the second.

I was naive and felt demeaned by the "moneyness" that underpinned everything we were supposed to work on at the Labs. Despite the vicissitudes of life in physics, I had worked out of love, and now I was working for money. Though Bell Labs was ranked as one of the top 100 places to work in America in 1985, it was at the top of my own selfish list of the worst places I'd worked at. My karmic destiny, I suppose, was to have my vain illusions about life and work painfully sandpapered off me as I brushed against the rough surface of the world. Later, when that process was complete, I would be able to enjoy life at Goldman, Sachs and Co. Had I come to work at Goldman straight out of graduate school, I might well have hated it for its intensely pecuniary focus just as much as I hated the Labs.

Meanwhile, I obsessed about changing my life. There were a variety of excellent programmers who worked in a software research group within the Business Analysis Systems Center. Dave Korn worked a few offices down from me, busy creating the now ubiquitous UNIX Korn shell; Emden Gansner and Jonathan Shopiro were both enthusiastic contributors to object-oriented programming in general and to Stroustrup's C++ environment in particular. I tried to transfer into their group, but Downs insisted that it was narrow-minded of me to think that I had to be located with them to do interesting work. Perhaps it was just as well. Though I was envious of Emden's calm, undistracted ways, I was quite incapable of emulating his temperament. He never asked for help with debugging, but read whatever manuals were necessary and then patiently dug deeper, struggling for as long as it took to solve the problem. I simply ran for help at the first panicky opportunity.

Even when my managers graciously allowed me to telecommute from home one day a week, I chafed at my shackles. I yearned for academic life and considered retracing my steps, exploring how to become a long-term physics postdoc again with Baqi Bég at Rockefeller or Norman Christ at Columbia.

Then, in late 1983, Wall Street began to beckon.

The first hints of my life-to-be began with occasional calls from headhunters in New York City. Soon, we all knew their legendary names— Jory Marino, Rick Wastrom of Smith Hanley, Rita Raz of Analytics, Steve Markman of Pencom, to name just a few of those who preyed on Bell Labs. Many of them are still active now, still advertising in the Sunday *New York Times* or on the Internet. Out of the blue, someone you had never heard of would cold-call you at work and ask if you wanted a job that paid $150,000—a huge amount in those days for an ex-physicist making less than $50K—and then command you, urgently, to come to his or her office immediately, before it was too late. These recruiters might flatter you by saying they had heard of you; in fact some acquaintance at the Labs had simply given them your name, or they had found it in a Bell Labs internal directory wheedled from some disgruntled employee. A few times, at their behest, I would leave work early and drive back into Manhattan to meet one of them, putting on my rarely worn navy blazer and 1960s knitted tie in a poor effort to simulate business attire. I owned no suits. Headhunters could keep you waiting for hours, like God as the Puerto Rican janitor in Bruce Jay Friedman's *Steambath* I saw on PBS around that time. Many headhunters were imperious, high-handed and low-mannered, and none of us knew enough to doubt their implicit claim that they held the keys to the kingdom.

I had several mostly unpleasant interviews at Wall Street firms in late 1983. I knew nothing about options theory and regarded myself as a software person. In those days, information technology on Wall Street was a land of mainframers who were educated in COBOL or FORTRAN or MIS and you needed only one eye to be king. At the Labs I had learned to

design and maintain programs with a sophistication beyond that of most
of the renegade scientists and coders on the Street. On interviews, because of my experience with HEQS, I advertised myself as someone who
could design a computer language to match the Street's modeling needs.

One of my first interviews was with Zach Cobrinik, now an ex-
Goldman partner and then a very boyish member of the Goldman Sachs
Quantitative Strategies group that I headed seven years later. At that
time the group was run by David Weinberger, who shortly thereafter left
for O'Connor in Chicago. Zach seemed most interested in finding a
systems administrator for their VAX, a task of little interest to me, and
so I declined to continue the process.

Some months later, another headhunter sent me to Salomon Brothers
about a position whose nature was never explained. I spent no more
than ten minutes naively informing my interviewer about the benefits I
could bring them by solving financial models with simultaneous algebraic equations using HEQS. Then, in the middle of our conversation
he was interrupted by a colleague; he suddenly stood up, apologized
curtly, and left for something that he said had urgently arisen, promising
to resume our discussion at some future time. Neither he nor the headhunter ever called again. Despite repeated attempts, I could never get
through to the woman in Personnel who arranged the interview; she
was always unavailable. For a long time I thought they were simply very
busy; finally I realized that this was their way of brushing me off. I never
understood why it wouldn't have been easier to tell me that they simply weren't interested.

T hen, in late 1983, when Eva was pregnant with our daughter Sonya,
a headhunter I knew arranged an interview for me in Stan Diller's Financial Strategies Group (FSG) in the Fixed Income Division at Goldman
Sachs. There I met Ravi Dattatreya, a former PhD engineer from Bell
Labs who had himself migrated to the Street a short while earlier.

Stan's group addressed a new need for quantitative modeling at
Goldman. By tradition a gentlemanly equity house that concentrated on
IPOs and stock trading for large institutional clients, Goldman had
recently begun to step onto Salomon's turf, the hurly-burly and plebeian world of bonds and mortgages. Stock trading was a simple, gutsy,
risk-taking business that required little intellectual or technical capital.
Bonds were more complex; they involved numbers, arithmetic, algebra,

even calculus. As my trader friend said, there's no competitive edge to being smart in equities.

The trick in the stock market was to estimate the right price for a share of stock in one of several thousand different companies. The bond market comprised fewer securities, but each security was more complex, sometimes bewilderingly so. The 900-pound gorilla in the market was the American Government, the source of liquid, ever-flowing Treasury bills, notes, and bonds that sprang from the government's need to borrow. Government bonds were characterized by a wide choice of maturities and coupons and, since they were backed by the full faith and credit of the United States, they would never default. Foreign governments issued bonds, too, some of them more prone to default than others. Corporate bonds were even riskier; a company might run out of cash and then be unable to make their promised payments. Some bonds could be "called"—the corporation had the option to end its obligation to keep paying a high rate of interest on its loan after interest rates had dropped by prematurely repaying the amount they had borrowed. Mortgages sold by homeowners were among the most horrifically elaborate bonds; they too could be suddenly called (that is, prepaid) by homeowners who had either sold their houses and no longer needed the principal they had borrowed, or who had discovered that they could now get cheaper financing as interest rates dropped.

All this complexity made it difficult to decide where value lay, and thus opened the door to mathematically adept modelers on the Street. The Fixed Income division at Salomon relied for their mathematical analysis on Marty Liebowitz's renowned, large, and enviably experienced Bond Portfolio Analysis (BPA) group. Goldman was slowly realizing that they needed something similar. FSG and its leader, Stan Diller, a former Columbia University PhD in Economics and one of the earliest academics to cross over to the Street, was their solution.

The problem on everyone's mind was the sudden increase in the volatility of interest rates. Before the 1980s, investors used to apportion their investments between stocks and bonds in a fairly static sort of way. Traditionally, they viewed the bond portion as safe and the stock stake as risky. Then, in the late 1970s, about the time I was teaching physics at Boulder, American interest rates rocketed and gold and oil prices soared. Bonds, previously perceived as nonvolatile, became risky. While everyone knew that stock investors might have to stomach a 40 percent drop in a bear market, few investors had imagined something similar could happen to Treasury bonds. The trading desks at investment banks, which naturally carried large inventories of bonds with which to supply their customers, saw their portfolios abruptly decline in value. As the intrinsic riskiness of fixed-income securities became manifest, a new approach to managing interest-rate risk began to diffuse through the industry. Desks wanted to hedge their varied and complex bond portfolios with large offsetting trades in cheap liquid bond futures. Hedging and risk management became the new thing, crucial both for wholesalers like Goldman Sachs and for institutional investors, too.

In the universe of equities, arithmetic was enough to do business; you didn't have to worry about even the simplest algebra until you got involved with options. In fixed-income land, by contrast, investors measured a bond's value by its yield, the average percentage return you would earn over its lifetime if you bought it at its current market price and received all future payments of interest and principal. As soon as you began to contemplate the relation between a bond price and its yield, the storm clouds of algebra, sequences, series, and, finally, calculus loomed blackly in the appendices at the backs of textbooks. A stock is only a stock, but even the simplest bond is a derivative security whose value depends on interest rates.

Therefore, suddenly, bond traders in the early 1980s needed analytic and mathematical skills to understand a portfolio of hundreds or thousands of bonds and its characteristics. They also required computing power; paper and pencil, a book of yield tables, even a hand-held calculator, were too slow and inflexible to amalgamate all the angles. Only on a computer could you estimate the value, sensitivity, and risk of many different securities in real time.

You couldn't buy commercial risk-management systems in the late 1970s. Do-it-yourself tools like spreadsheets were not yet ubiquitous. Most of the programmers in information technology couldn't handle bond mathematics, and most of the traders on the desk were unable to program. A trading desk had to turn to some jack-of-all-trades who could build their risk management tools, from the low-level databases through the financial valuation models to the high-level user interface.

The jack-of-all-trades in that era was unlikely to be an MBA or a PhD in Finance—even if they knew enough quantitative finance, most of them looked down with disdain on programming and mathematics as cheap, geeky skills they could pay other people to do for them.

Mathematicians, too, tended to avoid programming, preferring analysis to computation. Computer scientists, though they knew discrete mathematics and Boolean algebra, were often uncomfortable with continuous-time mathematics.

PhDs in physics or engineering fit the jack-of-all-trades bill pretty well. First, the mathematics of finance closely resembles the mathematics of physics. Furthermore, physicists don't grow up wearing white gloves; they have no scruples about tackling tasks beneath their so-called dignity. They do their own math and programming; the willingness to do so is an essential part of graduate student and postdoc subculture.

This was probably why Stan's Financial Strategies Group consisted mostly of former physicists, applied mathematicians, and engineers, many with PhDs. All of Stan's hires came from a culture in which you did your own dirty work—you developed your own theory, did your own mathematics, and then wrote your own programs. It was a hiring model I tended to repeat a few years later, when I staffed the groups I led, not out of principle but rather because of a natural affinity for that intellectual style.

When I first started interviewing on the Street, Stan was among the most famous practitioner-quants. An article in *Forbes* about him in the early 1980s was titled "Diller's Dillies," a patronizingly flattering reference to the awkward, foreign quant-nerds the reporter met. Stan had a reputation for hiring foreigners; I had heard some people imply that he liked inarticulate technophiles so that he could manage their work and present their results, but I think that was unfair. Most quants, then and now, came from abroad because immigrants often see the quickest path to success in hands-on work. It's the next generation that prefers management and business school.

Stan wrote occasional lengthy research reports on his group's work, original and creative papers phrased in a distinctively unorthodox and inbred style.[1] They were insightful and intuitive, but hard to classify and always a touch off-center: too technical for early-1980s Wall Street, not

---

[1] Years later, I noticed that he was almost always the only author on his reports, thanking the people that worked for him in the acknowledgements, but never including them on the author byline. After my experiences in physics, I never again worried too much about sharing credit with collaborators. It almost never did you harm.

quite rigorous enough for real finance academics—and insufficiently hard-sell for a sales piece. As a consequence Stan gained less influence than he deserved. But his work on the options embedded in mortgage portfolios was prescient, foreshadowing the more formal and rigorous work of the growing number of finance academics already entering the field.

When I met them, Diller and Co. were already pulling together a team skilled in finance, mathematics, and programming, and they wanted me to join them. I think it was my software skills that appealed to them as much as my talents in physics. Stan was a true pioneer in embedding financial models in portfolio trading systems, and a good decade ahead of his time in understanding the importance of professional software engineering in this endeavor. Later, after leaving Goldman Sachs in 1985, he built AutoBond, an early mortgage portfolio valuation system at Bear Stearns. Today he runs Polypaths, a company that produces fixed-income portfolio analysis software.

Nowadays, the cosmos of trading systems is very different. PCs are ubiquitous, spreadsheets are easy to use, and risk management software is increasingly available from tens of companies selling everything from building blocks to turnkey systems. Nevertheless, the largest banks still build their own software in order to book, value, and hedge the latest products as soon as they come to market. Even today, though, risk systems are balkanized, each one focusing on one or two product classes at most. There is still room out there for a system or language which can handle all the classes of securities—mortgages, swaptions, currencies, equities, metals, energy derivatives, and so on—that a large firm trades.

I returned to Goldman for another inspection with no idea what to look for. An article in the *New York Times* about switching jobs suggested asking your potential employer what you would be doing ten years in the future. At the end of my second visit there I sat down again with Stan. He explained to me that Wall Street was one of the few places you could eventually make $150,000 a year without running your own small business like an accountant or a doctor.

"If I come here," I said, "What will I be doing ten years from now?"
Stan became instantaneously irate.

"In ten years," he proclaimed, "You'll be doing whatever the hell you'll be doing now, only making more money! I don't want to be jerked around by someone coming in here and thinking about doing something different!"

I couldn't comprehend then what infuriated him. Ten years later, I understood his frustration. After a few years on the job, quants in banking often grow envious of the better-paid traders and salespeople who sit in the driver's seat. He must have thought that I was applying to his Financial Strategies Group with the devious plan to insinuate myself into trading. The last thing Stan needed was a new employee who wanted to tunnel out of the quantitative group into the business area before even beginning his work.

Ten years later I found myself on Stan's side. Similarly but with more restraint, I deplored the ambitious maneuverers I often interviewed who tried to use the Quantitative Strategies Group I ran as a conduit into trading. "I'm willing to program for a while in order to pay my dues," was their standard refrain, and it put an end to all interest on my part. I was sympathetic to their aspirations, but I had my own responsibilities and needed people eager to do the hard detailed analytical work. This meant programming, too.

Nowadays, transitions are easier and many PhD's do succeed at getting positions directly on the "business side," especially in smaller banks and hedge funds. But then as now, quants who yearn to move to the business side often begin to scorn their former academic skills. Stan must have well understood this self-loathing, this need to become someone else, though he certainly never seemed to want to be a trader himself. The *Forbes* reporter asked him what academic degree he had. "A PhD," Stan retorted, "But don't tell the people I work for—they'll knock a half million off my pay!"

I agonized over Stan's offer during a skiing vacation with Eva—pregnant with our daughter Sonya—and Josh in frigid New Hampshire in late 1983. Always the obsessive, weighing every alternative, I called everyone in the world who knew someone who had worked at Goldman. I pondered repetitively. Still, I couldn't make up my mind.

Through my friend Don Weingarten at IBM I tracked down a scientist from Watson Labs who had worked for Stan for one year, developing an in-house computer language for manipulating financial time series. The people I had met at Goldman told me he had found Wall Street intolerable after a life in research.

"What was it like there?" I asked him.

"Don't go," he said tartly, trying to give me a feel for the environment, "Unless you're willing to be yelled at all day for something you didn't do."

Those few words settled it. I knew I would not accept the job. I needed to suffer a little more before I was ready to move.

I slogged through another year at the Business Analysis center, collaborating on a more advanced version of HEQS. Then, a year later, I resumed the job search with a few more interviews. Once, I visited Jeff Borror's IT group at First Boston and, on the day of the 1985 hurricane scare in New York, they offered me about the same money as I had made at Bell Labs. I declined. Another time, a headhunter sent me to a small midtown medical software company. When I showed up in my AT&T business uniform—the navy blazer, gray flannel pants, white shirt, and knitted tie—the door to the office suite was opened by a bunch of barefoot, twenty-something guys in shorts and T-shirts. They gave me a written test on C programming; I recall being asked to write a routine to merge two files, and also to disentangle a sequence of intentionally confusing nested *#define* C macros. I wasn't interested in working there.

By mid-1985 I was ready. I called the headhunting firm that had originally introduced me to Ravi Dattatreya and Goldman and said I was now interested in the job I had turned down eighteen months earlier. I got little response—the headhunter seemed to have lost his touch with personnel at Goldman, and was unable to get me an interview. Time passed. I grew impatient and one day I called Ravi in FSG directly. He remembered me and brought me in, and after a full day there I was once again offered a job to work on software. During the year-and-a-half that had passed, Stan had unfortunately left Goldman for Bear Stearns. This time I didn't agonize too much and accepted the job.

In November 1985 I left the Labs for Goldman. At my farewell party Larry and Mark gave warm speeches. My closest friends there, they were both secretly on their way out, too. Larry, like me close to 40 years old, was enviably in the midst of deciding that, after having been a physicist and an AT&T business analyst, he would rather be a medical doctor, and was taking biology courses in the evenings and preparing for the MCAT. A year or two later he was at Mt. Sinai Medical School, and is now a psychiatrist at Columbia doing brain research using positron emission tomography, a true combination of physics and medicine. Mark, less than a year later, took a job working for Bob Kopprasch, head of options research in the Salomon Brothers BPA group.

During the party, my first and most *sympatisch* supervisor, Ron, took me aside for a chat. He told me that I already knew more about computers than I would ever need to know on Wall Street. It seemed self-evident then, but the world was changing fast. When I got there, Wall St. was indeed backward, mainframed and undistributed. My Labs training in UNIX software development would keep me a little ahead of run-of-the-mill IT day laborers on Wall Street for only four or five years.

Chapter 9

Transformer

■ *The Financial Strategies Group at Goldman,*
Sachs & Co. ■ *Learning options theory* ■ *Becoming a quant* ■
Interacting with traders ■ *A new cast of characters* ■

s that *still* the same cold you had when you started here?" a woman in the crowded elevator asked brusquely as she peered down her dry nose at my wet one some time in January 1986.

The first day for new hires at Goldman is always a Monday, and mine had been December 2, 1985. That morning I attended orientation, listened to a brief description of the firm, chose my health and life insurance plans, got ID'd and fingerprinted, and, finally, used my free lunch voucher to eat in the cafeteria. Goldman had a mere 5,000 employees back then, and there was still an intimate feel to the place.

I had left Bell Labs in late November, with only a few days to decompress between jobs. The next day the weather turned suddenly chilly. On Friday, November 29, I went for a run on Riverside Drive, wondering how I was going to keep fit when I could no longer exercise at lunchtime. By Sunday morning I was coughing and feverish. Too embarrassed to postpone my first day at work, I went in for orientation.

For the next few months I simply couldn't get enough rest to recover. Our family had been stressed the prior two years: My father-in-law had died suddenly in early 1984, my father in 1985, and now, only a few months later, my mother-in-law was in the final stages of pancreatic cancer. While Eva tended to her mother and tried to still do some laboratory research, I looked after Sonya on evenings and weekends, bearing the brunt of a typical two-year-old's appreciable will. Nights consisted of short bursts of sleep interrupted by multiple bottle fillings and subsequent diaper changes. We were all weary and upset.

Six weeks later, the dreaded early-morning phone call came from an unexpectedly different source. My sister's husband in South Africa had suddenly died. The call about Eva's mother came several weeks later.

Over several weeks my "flu" transformed itself into a semipermanent cough and runny nose that prevented me from sleeping. One chilly winter's Friday night I drove Joshua and Sonya to spend the weekend with some friends in East Hampton so that Eva could have uninterrupted time with her mother. By 10 P.M. on Sunday night I was at the end of my tether. What I needed most was some rest and sleep. I abandoned our apartment at midnight, left a message at work that I was sick, and checked into the Empire Hotel at Lincoln Center. Then, I swallowed a Valium to ensure that I would sleep, and spent the next day and a half in bed. Miraculously, that minuscule amount of rest did the trick. My nose stopped dripping, my perpetual cough deliquesced, and by Wednesday morning I was back at work and more or less normal, at least as far as my physical health was concerned.

Despite my illness, I had been learning a vast amount rapidly. My supervisor, Ravi Dattatreya, had a combative sharp-edged personality, and he liked to take pointy little verbal jabs at people, feigning to see how they would respond. But he was an excellent mentor: He had deep intuition about financial theory, and he understood how the trading and sales businesses worked.

When I arrived at Goldman's Financial Strategies Group I had thought I was going to work on the software engineering aspects of bond trading. But in 1985 the over-the-counter bond options business was burgeoning, and Ravi managed their needs. Within a few days of my arrival he introduced me to the bond options desk and assigned me to work on its valuation models. One Friday he gave me a copy of the famous Cox-Ross-Rubinstein paper on the binomial options model and told me to read it over the weekend. It was an immensely lucky opportunity; I got to work on an interesting and very relevant unsolved business problem which eventually made my reputation, and, just as importantly, I developed a relationship with traders who had a genuine and practical interest in theories and models.

The bond options desk was run by Peter Freund, a thirtyish lawyer-turned-options trader. Peter had a deep and serviceable grasp of the subtleties of options theory, but was busy much of the time writing business memos to Bob Rubin, then the head of the Fixed Income Division and soon to become cohead of Goldman itself, before eventually moving to Washington as Clinton's Secretary of the Treasury. I enjoyed talking to Peter, who sometimes placed his outstretched hand on my shoulder as we spoke, resting the full weight of his arm there for a few minutes. It was my first experience of the tactile side of being an employee. At Bell Labs supervisors didn't touch you much; at Goldman senior people tended to squeeze your arm or shoulder in a paternal and yet patronizing sort of way, even if they were much younger than you.

The most striking and voluble member of Peter's group was David Garbasz, a former graduate student in geology who had become a trader of bond options. He befriended me late that December at the annual Christmas party thrown by the Fixed Income Division at the South Street Seaport. It was a fabulously raucous party, given during the heyday of Wall Street ostentation. Giant shrimp and bite-size chunks of steak lay heaped on tables; we danced to a rock band composed of a bunch of traders; it was quite unlike the child-friendly, brownies-on-paper-plates affairs at Bell Labs to which I was accustomed. David took me under his wing and, on that freezing December night, though I was still half sick, he dragged me to accompany him on the walk home. We strode several miles from the Seaport north through the Lower East Side, able to see our breath in the midnight darkness, until I eventually found a cab to take me the rest of the way home. David was hot-headed and lively, attractively impetuous and passionately sharp-tongued and cynical, always writing letters to Bob Rubin in which he reportedly threatened to leave for greener pastures because of some dissatisfaction or other. I was a novice, and he took it on himself to teach me the ropes. We had many lunches together at the Fledermaus, the "in" place on South Street for the traders.

Another member of Peter's team was Jacob Goldfield, a young, scruffily unshaven, lanky Harvard law graduate who never even bothered to take the Law Boards, but immediately joined Goldman as a trader. David took Jacob under his wing, too, and we got along well; Jacob had studied physics as an undergraduate, and was a hands-on programmer who wrote many of his own trading tools. A very smart kid, Jacob soon radiated a quietly impressive mystique, and colleagues began to defer to him. He held his cards close to chest, absorbing information from everyone while emitting none himself, the embodiment of a perfect trading temperament. Unlike the 1980s masters-of-the-universe-style traders, Jacob never used foul language.

Everyone knew that Jacob was a protégé of Bob Rubin and had his ear. It was clear he was on a fast track.

The problem Ravi had given me in my first week at Goldman was rooted in the economics of the early 1980s. Goldman was on the "sell side": We sold securities to the money managers, insurance companies, pension, and mutual funds that comprised the "buy side." Many of these buy-side firms bought bonds issued by corporations, municipalities, or governments, and in the late 1970s and early 1980s, when interest rates were high, they could earn a pretty good rate of return. As interest rates in the mid-1980s slid steadily downwards from the inflationary peak of the Carter era, bonds paid lower interest, and these funds could no longer earn the high yields of the past few years. In an attempt to pump up their declining returns, many funds began to generate revenue by the periodic selling of short-dated call options against the specific bonds they held. There was substantial money to be made supplying these calls, and so, in early 1986, the Treasury bond options business at Goldman accelerated.

Loosely speaking, a call option on a bond is a contractual bet between two parties that the bond price will end up above a prespecified strike price on some definite future expiration date. The buyer of the option pays the seller a premium, the cost of the call option. At expiration, if the bond price is above the strike price, so that the buyer has won the bet, he exercises his option to receive the payoff. The payoff of the call option is the difference between the market price of the bond at expiration and the strike price. Effectively, the seller of the call option has to deliver the bond to the owner of the call option in exchange for a payment equal to the strike price, even though it is worth more. The bottom line is that the owner of the call option receives any upside the bond brings over and above the strike price, but suffers none of the downside.

The buy-side funds sold call options to Goldman to generate extra income. A mutual fund owning a $100 Treasury bond could sell a one-year call option on that bond, struck at $100, for about $2, thus boosting their yield. As long as the $100 bond itself didn't appreciate, this $2 was pure gravy. But with options, every reward has a corresponding punishment. Suppose interest rates were to fall and the bond price were to rise to $106 a year later. In this case, Goldman would exercise its call option and force the fund to accept a price of only $100 for the $106 bond, leaving the fund with a gain of $2 from the option premium offset by a $6 loss on the bond—a net loss of $4. In essence, the fund was taking a bet against interest rates declining.

Goldman's role was that of custom tailor. The funds could have sold listed interest-rate options and bond futures contracts, available on the Chicago exchanges, to make their bets. But these listed instruments provided only a limited number of standardized strikes and expirations, too constrained to match the particular strikes and expirations of the bonds actually owned by a fund. To accommodate them, Goldman bought over-the-counter (OTC) call options from each fund, each option a privately negotiated contract written on the specific bonds held by that fund. The options contacts were chosen to expire close to the dates on which the funds had to report their quarterly earnings. If interest rates did not decline and the funds won their bet, they kept the premium and enhanced their reported return.

The enterprise of selling bond options, like many early-stage businesses, was particularly profitable. A trading desk could charge clients an extra fee for an option that was custom-tailored to fit a fund's exact needs. The bond options desk at Goldman offset the risk of the tailored option they had sold by buying a bundle of cheaper listed options and futures that approximately matched its payoff. There was some risk involved in hedging tailored options with listed ones; the mismatch in strikes and expirations made the hedge approximate rather than exact. You could think of the fee as our desk's compensation for being willing to accept and manage this risk.

To hedge one option with another, firms like Goldman needed a model that told you each option's value and its sensitivity to changes in interest rates. The renowned Black-Scholes model for stock options, which Ravi had told me to learn, did not strictly apply to bond options. Stocks are relatively simple; they guarantee no future dividend payments and have no natural termination date, so their future prices are unconstrained. Treasury bonds are much more intricate: Because they promise to repay their principal when they mature, their price on that date is constrained to be par. Furthermore, since all Treasury bonds can be decomposed into a sum of more primitive zero-coupon bonds of varying maturities, they are all interrelated.

My new boss Ravi had heuristically modified the Black-Scholes stock option model to make it work, at least approximately, for short-dated Treasury bond options. He had written a computer program to implement it, and the bond options desk now priced and hedged their options by means of it. As they got more experienced at using it, Peter Freund's desk discovered that Ravi's model was fine for short-term options but questionable for longer-term ones; it suffered from a variety of theoretical inconsistencies stemming from its inadequate modeling of the long-term behavior of bond prices. It was an ingenious first cut, quickly created to catapult the desk into doing business, but now both the model and its computer interface needed work. A few days after I arrived, Ravi directed me to extend the model and the program. It was a feet-first introduction to working with traders, and much of what I know about the need to be pragmatic and business-oriented as a quant I learned in those first few months working with Ravi and the desk.

From the desk's point of view, the greatest hindrance to exploiting the model for business was not the theory, but rather the lack of a graphical user interface. Each time a salesperson needed to value an option for a potential trade with a client, he or she had to type in, on one line after another, the bond's current price, maturity, and coupon as well as the option's expiration and strike; then the salesperson had to enter the current short-term interest rate and the bond's assumed future yield volatility. One more tap on the return key and the program computed the model's theoretical price and told you how to hedge it with the underlying Treasury bond. If you wanted to compute the option value for a variety of volatilities, expirations or strikes, you had to repeat the same sequence, entering items and hitting return keys all over again.

Setting up a trade could take several days—a typical client might get a quote from Goldman, hang up, call another dealer to get their price,

ponder a while, and then call us back the next day to continue the discussion. At that point someone on our desk would have to start running our model again by reentering all the terms of the deal. This slowed
down the interaction with clients, and was far too viscous for a growing business.

The software engineering was deficient, too. Ravi's program had
been written in FORTRAN, but the scientific and financial worlds
were rapidly moving towards C, which provided much better tools for
collaborative software development. Ravi instructed me to learn options
theory, rewrite the model in C, and construct a friendlier front end. It
was a perfect assignment since it immediately exposed me to theory,
implementation, and interaction with the business. I spent the next few
days making a rapid first pass through the theory of stock options as
described in the original Cox-Ross-Rubinstein binomial paper. Then,
I studied the FORTRAN version of Ravi's bond option model and set
about rewriting it in C on FSG's VAX computer.

Within a few weeks I was learning on many fronts and adjusting to
new social and computing environments. When I ran into hurdles, Ravi
grew impatient and irritable. One day, only three weeks or so after I had
arrived, he suggested that, since I was taking longer than he had
expected, he should perhaps give the work to someone else to do. Upon
returning home that evening I took some perverse pleasure in reporting my first taste of Wall Street brutality to Eva, and got some shocked
sympathy. I wanted to show her that, with my passage from the civil
groves of physics to the harsh engine rooms of capitalism, I had now
entered a world in which people ten or more years younger than me
found it necessary to crack the whip when I didn't trot fast enough. But
in truth, it wasn't that bad—Wall Street has been always meritocratically
discourteous. It never seemed to me that great an indignity. In the nine-
teen years that have elapsed since then, I have been ordered about by
young traders, had my back patted and my upper arm encouragingly
squeezed in elevators by newly minted partners, and, once, been pushed
across the trading floor and cursed in full view of everyone there by an
angry and foul-mouthed saleswoman. There is a general lack of respect
for age in all of this that makes you disregard your own age, and I like it.

I soon finished programming the model and began to think about
attaching a friendly front end to it. In those pre-Macintosh/pre-
Windows days, windowing packages were a rarity. Brought up on the

UNIX philosophy, I began building my own generic toolkit for data entry and display. I hurriedly force-marched myself through the manual for the UNIX "curses" library that allowed you to flexibly read and write 80-character-by-24-line screens of text, and designed an interface. In a month or so I had created *Bosco*, a new calculator named after an affectionate abbreviation for my son Joshua.

Though the new model was better, it was my new user interface that had the biggest impact. It made negotiating with clients easy. All the model's input and output were visible on one screen, with one field for each item of data to be entered (the bond coupon, maturity, and so on), and one field for each answer the model provided (the option price, its hedge ratio, and so on). There were also fields for storing information about the client and the trade. To run the model and obtain an option price, you simply hit the "Calculate!" key. To change an input field value, you moved the cursor to the relevant field, entered the data, and hit "Calculate!" again. This saved countless keystrokes compared to the command-line interface that drove the previous FORTRAN version. Best of all, at any instant you could save all the details of a potential trade to a computer file for future retrieval. If you used the calculator to value an option during a preliminary conversation with a client, you could store all the information in the file and then resume the discussion the next day exactly where you had left off.

Though primitive by today's standards, this was astonishingly better than what the desk had used before, and the traders and salespeople were overjoyed. By creating and saving the most common types of option trades as templates in files at the start of each day, they could respond rapidly to clients, accommodating many more requests much more efficiently. Ever since, it's been impossible for me to overlook the difference that a simple and well-designed piece of software can make to a business. Despite the genuine glories of quantitative modeling, quant groups often have the most dramatic effect by improving the ergonomics of trading and sales.

When I became head of the Quantitative Strategies Group in the Equities Division a few years later, I always tried to recreate for anyone new in the group my first fortuitous experience with a trading desk. I set them a problem whose solution was useful to traders, and which required both theoretical analysis and software implementation. In that way, I hoped, they would develop a relationship with their end users in the trading division, learn the jargon and style of the business, and combine both theory and practicality.

Like many organizations, Goldman's Financial Strategies Group into which Ravi inducted me that December was rife with politics. Stan Diller, who had left Goldman shortly before I arrived, had reportedly often kidded that his was the only second-rate mind on Wall Street. To replace him and grow the business, the partners in charge of the Fixed Income Division had brought in two finance professors from the midwest. One was tall and lean, fast-talking and confident; the other was much shorter and spoke slowly. Their arrival didn't displace Stan on the mind-ranking charts.

The new structure they imposed was very different from what I had seen of Diller's. Diller appeared to have led FSG autocratically, but with a vision of trading as science. He had accentuated a quantitative approach to financial research, with an emphasis on software development and trading systems. He had sought out PhDs—engineers, physicists, computer scientists, and mathematicians—most of whom arrived ignorant of finance and then learned theory and business on the job. He sought people who could simultaneously do finance, math, and computer science, and had an interdisciplinary view of the world to which I'm still partial.

The new hegemony placed more emphasis on management. They had been given *carte blanche* to grow and they went on a hiring spree that rapidly grew the Strategies group from fifteen or twenty ex-scientists to about a hundred people, many of them professional managers who claimed they knew how to "talk to traders." They certainly knew enough to realize that they were on to a good thing and wisely made the most of it while it lasted. Over time, the modeling and programming groups became inverted pyramids: one or two technically skilled people at the bottom, who could write programs or build models, supporting a larger number of human conduits above them who passed the results up to the trading desk and then passed the subsequent responses back down again. Having a PhD and being good at research or being able to program well was not an advantage in this structure.

David Garbasz, with his usual accurate eye and sharp tongue, took to calling the two new heads of FSG Mutt and Jeff, and sarcastically referred to the organization they now headed as the "Financial Tragedies Group." In 1986 Goldman was still getting used to managing quants.

Despite the politics, I loved Goldman and FSG, and made many new friends among the programmers and quants. Most of them were much younger than me—it was my second career and their first. Working away in my undistinguished cubicle—for the first year I had no seat in an office—I did occasionally feel incongruous. One day, as I mindlessly whistled a Beatles song to myself while I programmed my bond option model, I heard the 23-year old kid in the next cube turn around and exclaim astonishedly, "How do *you* know *that?*" In fact, though, age didn't matter that much if you had ability, and the turbulence in financial markets since then—the crashes of 1987 and 1989, the collapse of Long Term Capital Management and Russia's default in 1998—has made the appearance of maturity an advantage.

Among the new people I met was Roscoe, the amiable, cheerily disillusioned leader of a group of good-humored programmer malcontents who occupied the cubicles on what he called Dissident Row. Everyone on Dissident Row ate lunch early and then took a constitutional up to the Brooklyn Bridge and back again. Roscoe's real name was William Dumas and he was rumored to be related to Alexandre Dumas, *père*. He had little respect for the new regime in FSG, and referred caustically to one of the new MIS managers who circulated ancient corporate memos on good programming style from his previous employer as the "Master of the Do-Loop." Roscoe had a minor genius for creating inventively allusive nicknames for new people in FSG. His method was Cockney rhyming, an associative slang in which, for example, the number five is referred to as "Lady" because Lady is short for Lady Godiva, and Godiva rhymes with "fiver," the colloquial term for the old British 5-pound note (as in "Can you lend me a fiver?"). In this spirit he dubbed a newly hired Pakistani programmer "Mander," because his true name was Salah, reminiscent of Salamander. He christened me "E-man," which I liked, because it was almost identical to the shortened version of "Emanuel" that my family and friends in South Africa had always called me since childhood, and, like Roscoe's other christenings, it stuck with me for the rest of my time at Goldman. After the 1994 fixed-income market slump, Roscoe left Goldman to work for Iris, a financial software company in San Francisco run by an old friend of mine, ex-Wells Fargo quant Jeremy Evnine.

Another new hire at Goldman was a fellow South African, Jonathan Berk, who had come to work at Goldman as an analyst with an undergraduate degree. He was wildly fired up about finance and markets and I soon got my first glimpse of capitalist thinking. Shortly after I arrived, the Challenger space shuttle exploded, and Jonathan, young and naive and enthusiastic, rushed off to call his Goldman stockbroker to buy puts on Morton Thiokol, hoping to profit from a drop in the price of the company that designed the leaky seals in the booster. Witnessing his quick response to the shuttle disaster, I thought Jonathan was destined for the business world, but I was wrong. Stimulated by financial theory, he left Goldman a few years later to get a PhD in finance and is now a professor at Berkeley. I met him again 15 years later, in November 2000, at a meeting of the sponsors of the new Berkeley degree in financial engineering, where I represented Goldman. Fervent as ever, he told me that in 1986 he had expected finance to become the theoretical physics of the twenty-first century. We laughed a little at the mismatch between fantasy and reality.

Jonathan traveled from business to academia. Others at Goldman took the reverse route. Another South African colleague in FSG was Ron Dembo, an academic and expert at optimization whom Mutt and Jeff had brought in as a consultant to help structure bond portfolios. Ron flew down from Toronto to New York for three days a week, staying in an apartment provided for him by Goldman, and in turn hired several other academics. For many of us it was our first glimpse of the perquisites of life with an expense account, and we marveled at it. Ron had an entrepreneurial streak and understood the value of systems and software for managing portfolio risk. He left Goldman in 1987, and shortly thereafter founded Algorithmics, a now prominent company that produces risk-management software.

I also began a long association with Bill Toy, who was already working for Fischer Black in the Equities Division when I arrived. Bill and I had both come to Goldman from physics by way of Bell Labs, and we had the same mutual scorn for the Bell environment and its bureaucracy. Fischer, whom I met only briefly in my first few weeks at

Goldman, was in charge of the small Quantitative Strategies group in the Equities Division that built models and trading software for the equities business.

Another immensely talented programmer in FSG was Dave Griswold, who had been hired into Financial Strategies from Grumman Aircraft on Long Island only a few months before me. In his late twenties and armed with a BS in Computer Science from Rensselaer Polytechnic, Dave loved software in general and object-oriented programming, a methodology then beginning to penetrate the commercial world, in particular. Perhaps because there are several famous Griswolds in academic computer science, as well as the character Chevy Chase plays in "National Lampoon's Vacation" series, Dave liked to refer to himself as "Griswlod." It was sophomoric, but it grew on you.

Dave was less a Wall Streeter and more a genuine computer science aficionado at heart. In classic UNIX style, he liked to first build the tools he needed for any new job. He always thought big. Asked to write a new program, he would ambitiously decide that it should be capable of running on any hardware and under any operating system. In order to achieve that, he had to shield his program from the details of a particular machine by creating his own version of all the infrastructure his program needed. Dave therefore created his own portable version of most of the facilities (windows, menus, files, databases, and so on) that DOS or UNIX provided.

I have seen many smart programmers indulge themselves by attempting to create everything *ab initio*; most of them who try fall into bottomless pits from which they never emerge, ceaselessly spiraling inwards in their effort to recreate portable versions of everything you could normally take for granted and get for free. What distinguished Dave from the ordinary stubborn people who wanted to build their own hammers, saws, and levels before starting to build the house was that he knew where to stop; he would finish building just the tools he needed and then use them to create the system itself.

David was a great fan of elegant and consistent computer languages. He loved Lisp and adored Smalltalk, one of the many Xerox PARC inventions that inspired the Macintosh environment. He was a devotee of Objective C, a Smalltalk-flavored C dialect that was an integral part of the operating system for Steve Jobs's Next computer before he returned to Apple. A few years later Dave wrote his own object-oriented language, which he called GoldC, for internal use at Goldman. In the long run, his interests would take him back to the software world.

Only three months after I arrived, Ravi departed to run Prudential-Bache's fixed income strategies group a few blocks away on Water Street. Several of Diller's senior strategists in FSG had already left, and now more of them continued out the door. Dennis Adler left for Dillon Reed and eventually ended up at Salomon Brothers, both firms that no longer exist as independent entities as a result of the enormous consolidation in financial services over the past fifteen years. Diller called me once to invite me to join him at Bear Stearns, but, disturbed though I was by Ravi's abrupt departure, it was much too soon for me to leave a place where I had just arrived. Instead, I put my head down and concentrated on work.

The bond options traders who were using *Bosco* began asking for many enhancements, and so, sometime in mid-1986, they authorized Dave Griswold and me to build them a more advanced trading system. I would provide the analytical and computational subroutines which Dave would embed in his infrastructure. For several months we all fiercely debated which computing platform to use. I was vehemently in favor of UNIX, the richest development environment, and the one I knew best. Bill Toy, who claimed great experience with the UNIX file system from the Labs, thought it was unreliable. Dave, predictably idiosyncratic and uncorporate, wanted to use Symbolics Lisp machines, then the cutting-edge computers for artificial intelligence. He envisaged that their massive amount of RAM would store the entire trading system in memory rather than on disk. (Massive is highly relative. The 64 Mb RAM of yesteryear's shared Symbolics machine is puny compared with the now modest 640 Mb on the personal Apple laptop that I use today.) Eventually we built the system on Sun workstations running UNIX.

Thus passed my first few happy months in the financial industry. At Bell Labs, from the day I had arrived, I had felt like someone past his prime. Now, at Goldman, despite the forty years behind me, I felt renewed. In the evenings I rode the subway home along Broadway to the Upper West Side and pored over textbooks by Cox and Rubinstein or Jarrow and Rudd, excited to be learning stochastic calculus and using my head again. One evening, someone from my old vanpool to the Labs got into the same subway car as me on Fourteenth Street. Seeing me engrossed in symbols, scribbling proofs on my lap on the shaky train, he laughed good-naturedly but incredulously at me for sitting there and doing mathematics on the subway—that was what you were meant to leave behind when you joined the business world!

But I remember thinking quite the opposite: What an enormous relief it was to be in a place where people actually wanted you to spend your time on what you liked! I told my vanpool friend that I could easily imagine doing this sort of work for another ten or fifteen years.

Chapter 10

Easy Travel to Other Planets

■ *The history of options theory* ■ *Meeting and working with*
Fischer Black ■ *The Black-Derman-Toy model* ■

W all Street had never been a place for academics. Yet, from the day I got to Goldman in late 1985, I kept hearing people talk with awe about Fischer Black, codiscoverer of the Black-Scholes equation for options pricing and the head of Goldman's Quantitative Strategies group. I saw him once at a meeting in the first few months after I arrived, but never spoke to him until the traders on the bond options desk arranged for us to meet.

Some traders are scornful of models; others will rely on them blindly. Our bond options traders knew that you need to layer visceral trading smarts over and above a consistent options pricing model. They understood they needed something beyond Ravi's original model, and so they approached Fischer about taking the next step. Since I had earned some credit for having diagnosed and then eliminated one small but glaring inconsistency in Ravi's model soon after I arrived, they therefore suggested that I join Fischer in an effort to build a better model.

Before I went up to his office on the twenty-ninth floor to meet him, to show him what I had done so far, and, implicitly, to see if he would have me work with him, I read a little more on the history of options theory.

Until the early 1970s, no one knew how to estimate the value of options in a convincing way. A call option that paid off when the stock price rose seemed much like a bet on a horse: The more optimistic you were about the stock's future prospects, the more you should be willing to pay for it. Each person set his own fair price.

Then, in 1973, Fischer Black and Myron Scholes published their eponymous Black-Scholes equation for the value of an option. That same year, Robert Merton provided a more rigorous and insightful way of understanding the argument behind their equation. Eventually, his formalism came to supplant theirs, and became the standard. Merton and Scholes won the 1997 Nobel Prize in Economics for their work, but Fischer, who was certainly their equal, died in 1995. Had he been fortunate enough to have lived a couple of years longer, he would surely have been a corecipient of the Prize.

I used to find it almost impossible to understand why the Nobel committee didn't award the Prize for options theory before Fischer died. Everyone in the finance community knew that it was only a matter of time before Black, Scholes, and Merton would receive the award, and it had also been common knowledge for several years that Black was mortally ill with throat cancer. I've heard speculations that the Nobel committee was reluctant to give the award to someone who worked in the business world, especially in the profitable and untheoretical business of investment banking.

Fischer, who had a PhD in Applied Mathematics from Harvard, had been a management consultant at Arthur D. Little and Co. when he developed the Black-Scholes model. One did not think of management consulting as the locus of groundbreaking theorists, but Fischer was always proud of his practical and unorthodox background. Once his contributions were recognized, he became a professor of finance at Chicago and then at MIT, finally leaving academia for Goldman Sachs in 1984. Though Merton and Scholes had each kept at least one foot in the academic world, both of them had worked as consultants or employees of Salomon Brothers at various times, and in 1994, became partners and attractors of capital at Long Term Capital Management, the leveraged hedge fund run by John Meriwether and his ex-Salomon "arb group." I noticed that the 1997 Nobel Prize citation referred only to the university affiliations of Merton and Scholes, and not to their corporate connection—perhaps the Nobel committee really did have an aversion to the business world. Though the Nobel Prize sounds as though it is awarded by the gods, committees are merely groups of people with their own preferences.

Throughout his life, Fischer was genuinely in love with the idea of equilibrium, and he invented the Black-Scholes equation in the late 1960s by applying the condition of equilibrium to markets themselves. Equilibrium is a common and very powerful concept in physics; in equilibrium, the numerical values we observe for quantities of interest in a stable system are the values that cause two opposing forces to cancel exactly. For example, the temperature of a body stops rising at that equilibrium temperature at which the heat flowing into the body is canceled by the heat flowing out. Fischer believed that market prices were determined by similar cancelations.

Fischer first obtained the Black-Scholes equation by demanding that an option on stock and the stock itself be in equilibrium with each other, in the sense that their respective prices should each provide investors with the same expected return per unit of risk they carried. An investor would then be impartial between buying the stock and buying the option. This condition, written down mathematically, was the Black-Scholes equation; it determined the value of the option. It took several years more before Black and Scholes provided the eventual solution to the equation.

Merton, working in parallel, went deeper. He showed that there was a recipe for synthesizing a stock option out of a mixture of shares of stock and cash, a mixture whose proportions must be readjusted continuously by exchanging some shares of stock for cash, or vice versa. An investor who bought the initial mixture and then carried out the readjustment recipe would end up with precisely the same payout as the stock option, and so the option's value should be exactly the cost of purchasing the initial mixture.

The recipe for synthesizing an option was called *dynamic replication*— replication because you were reproducing the option, dynamic because you had to keep changing the mixture in order to do it. Replicating an option was like riding a toboggan with your eyes closed down its serpentine track—you needed a recipe for which way to bank at each point in time. Black-Scholes gave you that recipe. Merton justified it.

That you could dynamically replicate an option was an almost confounding result. Until Black, Scholes, and Merton, came along, no one imagined that you could create an option out of simpler securities. Now an option was seen to be merely a subtle mixture of simpler securities, stock and cash, in constantly changing but known proportions.

Merton relied on a mathematical formalism called *stochastic calculus*, the study of the rate of change of randomly varying quantities such as the price of a stock or the position of a dust particle in a room. At graduate school in the 1960s, 1970s, and throughout my subsequent life as a postdoc, I had never heard of stochastic calculus. Nowadays, its methods are commonplace to all quants and graduate students in finance; every ex-physicist looking for a job on Wall Street begins by studying the subject. Black and Scholes's 1973 paper, in which they presented both their own and Merton's derivation of the equation, was sufficiently arcane that it took several years to get it published. Indeed, it was repeatedly rejected until Merton Miller at the University of Chicago interceded on their behalf.

The two simultaneous but complementary derivations of the theory of options pricing in the early 1970s, Black and Scholes's and Merton's, reminded me of the complementary derivations of renormalizable quantum electrodynamics by Feynman and Schwinger in the late 1940s. Feynman and Schwinger each used drastically different approaches to reach similar results, their respective formalisms so dissimilar that no one understood their equivalence until it was demonstrated by Freeman Dyson. Thereafter, Feynman's more intuitive approach became the standard. Black and Scholes and Merton also utilized different approaches; over the long run Merton's more formal and powerful methods became the standard, and were eventually used by Fischer himself.

From the moment it appeared in print, the Black-Scholes-Merton theory was embraced, not only by academics but by options dealers. Before the advent of the model, a dealer who sold a call option to a client had to take the other side of the trade; the dealer then bore the risk, if the stock price went up, of having to pay the client out of pocket. After the model's dawn, a dealer could use its recipe to roll his or her own option out of stock and cash, and estimate the cost of doing so. The dealer could then sell the homemade option to the client, ideally being left with no risk at all.

Options dealers soon began to use the Black-Scholes model to manufacture options out of raw stock and then sell them. Dealers charged a fee for this manufacture, just like any other value-added reseller.

On Wall Street, quants, traders, and salespeople make daily use of the stock options model and its extensions. During the past thirty years, academics in business schools, mathematicians in math departments, and quants in investment banks and hedge funds have applied similar methods to produce models for options on bonds, options on interest rates, options on credit ratings, options on energy, and even options on volatility itself. Though the simple and profound idea of Black, Scholes, and Merton has remained unchanged, the mathematics has become more elaborate, complex, and daunting.

Black and Scholes's original model assumed almost platonically simple markets. They allowed for the uncertainty of future stock price movements, but ignored other more detailed complexities. However, their model proved to be extensible and robust—one could augment it to take account of the imperfections of actual trading. The model accommodated these and other refinements while leaving the basic strategy substantially unchanged. Options theory is one of the great triumphs of economics, conceptually simple and pragmatically useful despite its complex mathematics. If only the rest of economics had similar efficacy!

I knocked on the door of Fischer's office and entered. Inside, it was quiet and low-lit, a location for work rather than meetings. At Goldman an office was a token of seniority, a very expensive pocket of personal real estate. Many of the fancily furnished offices on the equity floor were largely uninhabited, filled with tombstones of past deals executed by the traders and salespeople who had no time for office work. Fischer's office was much less glamorous; it was dominated by a large Nike poster of a long road disappearing into the distance and, below it, the caption: "The race is not always to the swift, but to those who keep on running."

Brought to Goldman Sachs from MIT by Bob Rubin in 1984, Fischer was one of the first finance academics to head for Wall Street; he became a Goldman partner in 1986. Unlike other professors in the industry who maintained their umbilical links to the safe haven of academia, Fischer embraced the business world wholeheartedly. Now I was about to meet him.

After a brief introduction, I began to show him *Bosco*, the bond options model and its graphical user interface I had built for the options desk. Fischer, like everyone else in the less numerate Equities Division, used a PC running DOS, but I had developed my software on the more advanced VAX we all used in Fixed Income. I logged on to the VAX through a VT-100 terminal emulator on Fischer's PC. Almost as soon as my program started running the VAX itself crashed, and we were left looking at the frozen screen image of my calculator. I couldn't run the program, I couldn't toggle or change the values of any of the fields—we could only observe them carefully on the monitor. I offered to come back later when the VAX was up again, but Fischer was quite unperturbed. He spent the next hour carefully examining the screen I had built, commenting on its layout.

Those were the days of limited computer-screen real estate: I had 24 lines of 80 characters to work with, and all of the approximately twenty-five input and output fields used in *Bosco* had to fit in that space. Fischer meticulously inspected each field, making reasonable but almost picayune comments about some of their labels. Because of the lack of space, I had had to abbreviate most labels, and had half-jokingly contracted the variable named *bond duration* to the inelegant *durn*, which he particularly disliked. Later in the conversation—because I was unschooled in finance and had been in the field only a few months—I periodically referred to "an option on a future contract" and each time Fischer quickly corrected me by brusquely interjecting "*futures* contract."

I was surprised at his willingness to spend so much time on the mere interface to Ravi's model, when he hadn't yet seen the calculator work or listened to my explanation of how I had modified it. When I returned to my fixed-income colleagues later that day, my feelings a little bruised by his criticisms, I scoffed at his attitude. But I soon discovered that Fischer was always a stickler for precision, and clear expression was an invariant devotion of his. Over the years, I became a convert and tried as hard as I could, in anything I subsequently wrote, to be as clear and didactic as possible.

During the weeks after he first examined my frozen *Bosco* computer screen, I learned much more about Fischer's computer prejudices. Some of them were quite reactionary. He disapproved of "mice" and other computer pointing devices. He thought keyboards were the ideal means of data entry; he insisted that anything one could do with a mouse could be done better with macro redefinitions of particular keys on the keyboard. Finally, he disliked graphics, and claimed that unadorned tables of numbers were more evocative and revealing. There was no persuading him on these issues; they were a part of his near-magnificent obsession about presentation style.

There were other quirks, harmless but irritating. He demanded strict standards on the display of numbers, intensely objecting to any printout that included more digits after the decimal point than was warranted by the accuracy of the calculation. Now everyone agrees that it is objectionable to report a measurement of room temperature as 73.1457° F—the implied precision is false—but Fischer logically extended his disapproval to the display of any excess zeros at the end of a decimal number, a feature he dubbed "trailing zeros." If a bond had a yield of 12 percent, he wanted it printed as a confident "12%" rather than as a tentative "12.00%" which would have suggested that it was only accurate to two decimal places. If Fischer did not find the display satisfactory, you could spend too much time talking to him about style and never progress to the content.

Eventually, therefore, everyone who worked with Fischer for even a little while wrote their own version of a subroutine that stripped all the trailing zeros off a number before displaying it. Bill Toy and I used to joke that you could identify Fischer's collaborators by searching their hard disks for a subroutine called *removeTrailingZeros*( ).

Sometimes Fischer took this a little too far. One day a few months later I made use of an options calculator built by someone in his group. It required that you enter the stock's dividend yield, and so I entered the number "0" in the field. For a brief subliminal instant I saw the numeral zero I had entered fluoresce onto the screen, and then vanish, leaving an empty field. Thinking I had made a typing mistake, I entered the zero again. Again, miragelike, the ghostly zero flickered and deliquesced. Then I realized what was happening. The programmer had blindly followed Fischer's dictum to remove all trailing zeros, and since the number "0" was all zeros, it removed the entire number, leaving the impression that nothing had been entered. The program had no respect for the philosophical distinction between nothing and zero.

Just as on the first day I visited him, Fischer was always quiet and calm, always in visible equilibrium. He never seemed to allow his work life to become an exercise in the exhausting multitasking (and the macho pride in coping with it) that quickly became a way of life for people at investment banks. Most often, when you went to visit him, you would find him reading, or on the telephone, or sitting with his back to the door, his PC keyboard on his lap and his chair swiveled 180 degrees to face the PC on the bureau by the window behind his chair, entering notes into Thinktank, a late-1980s organizer program he used constantly.

Fischer filed all his memos and notes in Thinktank; Beverly Bell, his editor at Goldman, said that he accumulated over 20 million bytes of text in it, from addresses and phone numbers to thoughts and ideas. People I knew in his group claimed that he conducted a continuing and eager correspondence with the Thinktank designers in order to suggest additions or modifications he wanted to see.

Fischer was precise and organized, quite punctilious. Every day he ordered the same ascetically healthy meal delivered to his desk. He liked to wear a Casio information-storing watch, which prompted some of his employee-admirers to do likewise. In his office giving audience, if you said something he found useful, he wrote it down with his fine-pointed mechanical pencil on a fresh sheet of his ruled white pad, and then tore it off and inserted it into a new manila folder which he labeled and then placed in one of his file drawers. In an article published after his death, Beverly described the 6,000 files he left behind, now archived at MIT.

Fischer was unashamed of his nerdish enthusiasm for technology, in contrast to most of Wall Street in the 1980s, where important managers prided themselves on their ignorance of computers. Some managers I knew eschewed not only computers, but even desks in their offices, preferring a large conference table to signify their major role as decision makers.

When I began to work with Fischer, I thought he had some strange tastes. You couldn't easily guess his attitude to one question by knowing his opinion about another, though what he said was always thoughtful and sensible. But over subsequent years I learned that he was a rarity, one of those people you only occasionally meet, someone whose character is a coherent whole even though its parts seem uncorrelated. At bottom, he simply liked to think through everything for himself. This didn't make him a great rebel, but rather an outsider whose work had vast impact on the world of insiders. It was impressive to watch.

Back in FSG after meeting Fischer, I continued studying the classic Black-Scholes model for stock options and the way in which Ravi had modified it for use on the bond options desk.

Options have value because future stock prices are uncertain, and the further out into the future you go, the more uncertain they become. A great deal of options theory is concerned with the modeling of future uncertainty. Figure 10.1 illustrates in a simplified way how Black and Scholes pictured the uncertainty of a stock's future price. As time passes, the region in which the future stock price is likely to lie progressively widens. A stock worth $100 today could be worth anything between zero and a very large number thirty years from now. (If you bought internet stocks in the late 1990s, you understand this all too well.)

Bonds are different. While no one knows the future price of a stock, a $100 initial investment in a thirty-year Treasury bond is guaranteed to pay you back exactly $100 when the bond matures. The shaded region in Figure 10.2 illustrates the approximate range of a bond's future price: It widens as we move away from the known bond price of $100 today, and then converges towards the certain value of $100 thirty years from now.

The straightforward but simplistic way to value bond options in 1985 was to use the Black-Scholes model as is, thereby implicitly assuming that bond prices followed the distribution of Figure 10.1 rather than

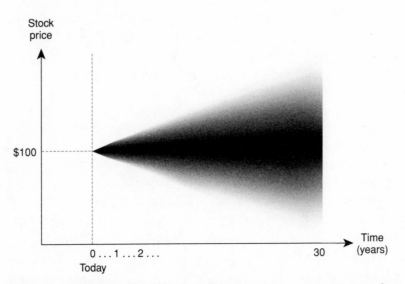

Figure 10.1 The distribution of possible future prices over 30 years for a stock whose price is $100 today. The more time passes, the greater the uncertainty in the future price. The darker the shading, the more likely the price will be in that region.

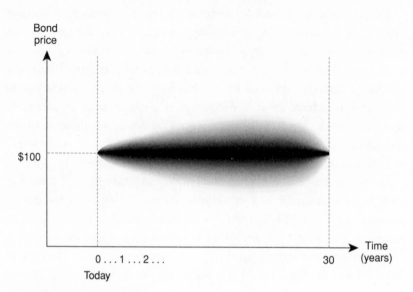

Figure 10.2 The distribution of possible future prices for a bond whose price is $100 today. After thirty years, the bond must again be worth exactly $100. The darker the shading, the more likely the price will be in that region.

Figure 10.2. For short-term options expiring within a year or two, it didn't matter much. You can see that, for the first year, the distribution of bond prices closely resembles the distribution of stock prices. Consequently, the Black-Scholes model is not a bad approximation for short-term (one-year) bond options. But for longer-term options, the bond and stock distributions are vastly different. For long-term bond options, a different model is needed.

Various academics had attempted to alter some of the assumptions about the future evolution of stock prices in the Black-Scholes model so as to make it better mimic the bond price distribution of Figure 10.2. In a similar spirit, but with greater practicality since he was part of a business, Ravi had invented the then-current Goldman bond options model by cleverly modeling the future behavior of bond yields rather than bond prices. A bond's yield is the average annual percentage return you will earn if you buy it at its current price and then hold it to maturity while collecting all the coupons and the final repayment of principal. Ravi simply assumed that a bond's yield rather than its price obeyed the ever-widening Black–Scholes distribution of Figure 10.1. In that case, as time passes and the bond gets very close to its maturity, the future value of its yield, no matter how high or low it ranges, becomes irrelevant to the bond price; too little time is left until maturity for the yield to have an effect. Therefore, although the distribution of bond yields in Ravi's option model grew limitlessly high or low as time passed and resembled Figure 10.1, the bond prices computed from these yields looked much like those of Figure 10.2.

Ravi's model did a reasonable job of capturing the future behavior of a bond's price. It also matched the intuition of the traders, who were already used to thinking about bonds in terms of their yields, and so took naturally to thinking about the range or volatility of yields. The same good idea often occurs to several people simultaneously, and versions of the model soon popped up independently at other Wall Street firms. When I came to work at Salomon Brothers a few years later, I found they had a similar scheme.

But there were deeper, subtler problems with the model that arose from its origin in the Black-Scholes framework. Just as the Black-Scholes model treats each stock as an independent variable, so Ravi's model treated each bond as independent. Doing so led to a host of conceptual inconsistencies. For, while there is nothing obviously wrong in imagining that the future prices of a share of IBM and a share of AT&T can vary independently, it is inconsistent to model the future prices of, say, a five-year bond and a three-year bond as varying independently. If you do, things fall apart.

Bonds are connected to each other. The future behaviors of a five-year bond and a three-year bond are *not* independent, but overlapping: Two years from now, the five-year bond will be a three-year bond, so you cannot model one bond's future without implicitly modeling another. In fact, it is impossible to model one bond without modeling all of them.

A five-year bond and a three-year bond have other commonalities, too. You can think of a five-year Treasury bond that pays interest every six months as a collection of ten zero-coupon bonds with maturities spread six months apart over the next five years. Similarly, a three-year Treasury bond is a collection of six zero-coupon bonds respectively maturing every successive six months over the next three years. Decomposed in this way, the bonds' ingredients are shared: Both contain the first six zero-coupon bonds. Therefore, in modeling the three-year bond, you are also implicitly modeling parts of the five-year bond.

In essence, Ravi's model allowed impermissible violations of the law of one price that lies beneath all rational financial modeling. This law demands that any two securities with the same final payouts must have the same current value. Now, there is a combination of short-term options on long-term bonds that has exactly the same payout as a short-term bond, and therefore, the combination of options should have the same theoretical value as the short-term bond, despite their formally different names. But Ravi modeled long-term bonds independently of short-term ones, and so the model had no way of enforcing this equivalence.

Every hard look at Ravi's model led to the same insight: It is impossible to model bonds piecemeal, one bond at a time. You must build a model of the future evolution of all bonds, that is, of the yield curve itself. This was our aim.

I had left Fischer's office a little chastened by his sharp remarks about the names of the fields on my calculator, but in a few days he let me know that I could join him and Bill Toy in their effort to create a new bond options model. It was a singular opportunity that had a large and beneficial effect on my life.

That spring of 1986 I attended my first options conference, an annual event organized by Howard Baker, Menachem Brenner, and Dan Galai at the Amex. I was one of about a hundred participating quants, traders and academics, all of us actively involved in the field at a time when options meetings were still a rarity, before the conference-for-profit organizations like *Risk* magazine began to dominate the market and eventually put the Amex options conference out of business. I recall several presentations on new models for valuing bond options, one in particular by Rick Bookstaber, then at Morgan Stanley. You could sense a rising urgency, almost a race, to solve the problem. Fischer told Bill and me that Bob Merton was working on the same problem as a consultant for another investment bank.

The Goldman contingent at the conference had more than an academic interest—our traders were making daily markets in long-expiration options on long-dated bonds, precisely the domain where the contradictions in Ravi's model were most severe. The traders were aware of their need for a better model, and as such were at the forefront of the impetus to replace it.

We knew that we had to model the future behavior of all Treasury bonds, that is, the evolution of the entire yield curve. How to set about it was neither obvious nor easy. A stock price is a single number, and when you model its evolution, you project only one number into an uncertain future. In contrast, the yield curve is a continuum, a string or rubber band whose every point, at any instant, represents the yield of a bond with corresponding maturity. As time passes and bond prices change, the yield curve moves, as illustrated in Figure 10.3. To evolve the entire yield curve forward in time is a much more difficult task: Just as you cannot move the different points on a string completely independently of each other, because the string must stay connected, so bonds close to each other must stay connected, too.

How, then, to project bond prices into the future? Fischer, Bill, and I were pragmatists. We were building a model for traders, and we wanted it to be simple, consistent, and reasonably realistic. Simple meant that

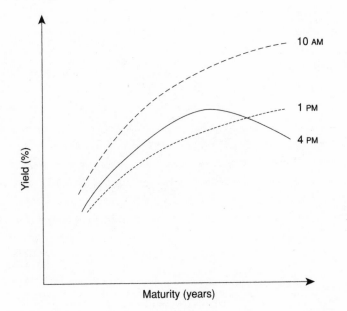

Figure 10.3 Yield curves can vary during the day.

only one random factor drove all changes. Consistent meant that it had to value all bonds in agreement with their current market prices; if it produced the wrong bond prices, it was pointless to use it to value options on those bonds. Finally, realistic meant that the model's future yield curves should move through ranges similar to those experienced by actual yield curves.

When physicists build models, they often first resort to a toy representation of the world in which space and time are discrete and exist only at points on a lattice—it makes picturing the mathematics much easier. We built our model in the same vein. We imagined a world in which the shortest investment you could make lasted exactly one year, and was represented by the one-year Treasury bill interest rate. Longer-term rates would then be a reflection of the market's perception of the probable range of future short-term (that is, one-year) rates.

In this spirit, we built a simple model of future one-year rates that resembled a discrete version of the stock price distributions of Figure 10.1. The initial one-year rate, as shown in Figure 10.4, was known from the current yield curve. As you looked further out into the future, rates could range over progressively wider values.

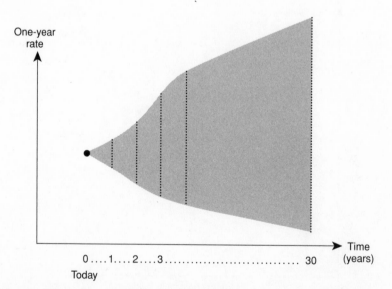

Figure 10.4 The Black-Derman-Toy model focuses on the distribution of future short-term rates. Here, each dot corresponds to a particular value of the future one-year rate. The more time passes, the greater the uncertainty of future rates.

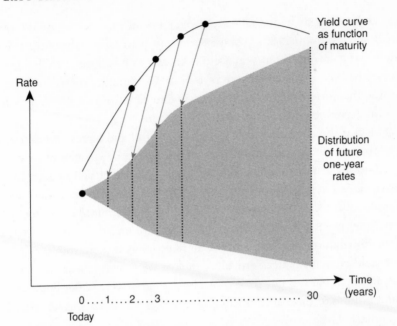

Figure 10.5 How the distribution of future one-year rates is deduced from the current yield curve in the Black-Derman-Toy model. The two-year yield to maturity fixes the distribution of one-year rates after one year, the three-year yield to maturity fixes the distribution of one-year rates after two years, and so on.

In order to complete our model, we now had to determine the range of future one-year rates at every year in the future. In our model, the key principle was to think of longer-term bonds as being generated by successive investments in short-term bonds. From this point of view, two years of interest is obtained by two successive one-year investments, the first at a known rate, the second at an uncertain one. The market's price for a two-year bond today depends on its view of the distribution of future one-year rates. You can calculate the logical value of the current two-year bond yield, from the current one-year yield and *the distribution of one-year rates one year hence*. Similarly, you can calculate the volatility or uncertainty of the current two-year yield from the volatility of the distribution of one-year rates one year hence. Alternatively, working backwards, since the current two-year yield and its volatility is known from the market, you can deduce *the distribution of one-year rates one-year hence*, as shown in Figure 10.5.

In the same way, the value of the current three-year yield can be found from the current one-year rate, the known distribution of one-year rates one year hence (already deduced from the current two-year yield) and *the distribution of one-year rates two years hence*. But, since the value of the current three-year yield is known, you can use it to deduce *the distribution of one-year rates two years hence*. Continuing in this way, you can use the current yield curve at any instant to pin down the range of all future one-year rates, as illustrated in Figure 10.5.

This was the essence of our model. When Bill and I programmed it, it seemed to work—we could extract the market's expectation of the distributions of future one-year rates from the current yield curve and its volatility. There was nothing holy about the one-year time steps we started with. Once the model worked, we used monthly, weekly, or sometimes even daily steps on a lattice, determining the market's view of the distribution of future short-term rates at any instant from the current yield curve. A typical lattice (or tree, as we called it, because of the way an initial interest rate forked out into progressively wider branches) had hundreds or thousands of equally spaced short periods, as illustrated in Figure 10.6.

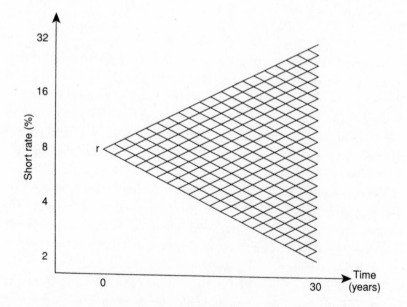

Figure 10.6 A schematic illustration of a multiperiod short-rate tree in the Black-Derman-Toy model with equal periods extending for many years.

We had aimed to make our model simple and consistent, and it was—we could match all current bond prices with one tree. We could then use the same calibrated tree to value *any* security whose payouts in the future had a known dependence on interest rates by averaging those payouts over the distribution. In particular, we could value the payout of an option of any expiration on a bond of any maturity.

It was particularly attractive that our new model satisfied the law of one price. Our tree functioned as a computational engine that produced the current value of a security by averaging its future payouts; you put future payouts onto the end of the tree, cranked the handle that averaged and then discounted them over the interest rate distribution, and ended up with the current price. The engine didn't care what name you gave to the security that produced the payout—bond, option, call it what you like. As long as the future payouts were identical, the engine produced the same price.

By late 1986, less than a year after I came to Goldman, we had most of the model implemented and running at reasonable speed. Now we began trying it out on actual options traded by the desk, cataloging the ways in which its prices differed from those of Ravi's model. Our traders' intuition had been honed on the old model, and they were sensibly conservative about switching—it is never wise to start using something new until you understand how well it glues on to what you used before. You need a feel for a model before you can begin to rely on it. Therefore, some of the sales assistants in Financial Strategies began to test it, and slowly convinced themselves that it satisfied the law of one price, something that was theoretically obvious to us but not yet practically clear to them.

I was tremendously excited by what we had done. Still at heart a physicist, and still philosophically naive about financial modeling, I half-thought of what we had built as a grand unified theory of interest rates, and imagined we could use it to value every interest rate-sensitive security in the universe.

Fischer, however, disliked this view of our model. More practical and much more experienced, he knew that there were financial forces that lay outside our model; it seemed perfectly possible to him that the model might be good (if it was good at all) for one sector—simple

How we grope our way to an understanding.

options on Treasury bonds, for example—but not for callable bonds, caps, or a host of other optionlike fixed-income instruments. He called what we had created an "as if" model, by which he meant that we were assuming that the world of bond market investors behaved *as if* only short rates mattered.

Despite my desire to have done something grand, I, too, began to recognize our model for what it was: a simple phenomenological model in the sense that physicists use the adjective, a useful but limited toy that we should take tentatively but seriously, trying to see how far we could push it. We had assumed that markets care only about a single factor, the short-term interest rate, and that all longer-term rates simply reflect the market's opinion of future short-term rates and their volatilities. Was that strictly true? Of course not! The world is indescribably more complex. But what we had was a good starting point from which to capture some of the rational linkages between long- and short-term rates. Our model may not have been *the* real world, but it was a *possible* real world, one of many, and that made its prices interesting.

Fischer wanted the paper we were writing to be clear, accurate and yet not overly mathematical. Over the next year I wrote multiple drafts which he read and then returned with comments, and with the help of his editor Beverly, the paper grew progressively shorter. In my previous life as a physicist I had been a somewhat careless writer with little patience for revision. That year of draft writing taught me the importance and pleasure of formulating concepts qualitatively but precisely, and from then on I was willing to struggle over small things to communicate them clearly.

scientist can communicate

Our paper, *A One-Factor Model of Interest Rates and Its Application to Treasury Bond Options*, eventually appeared in the *Financial Analysts Journal* in 1990, almost four years after we had developed it. To my pleasure and surprise, it was widely adopted and rapidly became known by the acronym for our names, BDT. It was a pity we hadn't published earlier, but Fischer was a perfectionist, reluctant to release it until he was truly satisfied.

We weren't the only builders of consistent models of the yield curve. At Salomon Brothers, my friend Mark Koenigsberg and his boss, Bob Kopprasch, who later came to head up Financial Strategies at Goldman, had also built a fairly simple model of interest rates, though it wasn't quite as general as ours. Oldrich Vasiçek, always a pioneer, had published the first Black-Scholes-style model of interest rates a good ten years earlier, in 1977; Cox, Ingersoll, and Ross had published a more complex but related model in 1985. There were others, too. So why was our model so widely embraced?

— not irreha... abstraction

I can think of three reasons. First, we were practitioners and therefore knew what a trading desk needed. While Vasiçek and the Cox-Ingersoll-Ross team had been focused on the general problem of modeling yield curves, we aimed squarely at bond options just when that market was expanding.

Second, our model was easily accessible to practitioners. It was written in a down-to-earth style using the language of binomial trees, a poor man's description of volatility that everyone on Wall Street could grasp. What we described was so close to an algorithm that anyone who took the effort could implement our model as a computer program. Most other contemporary models demanded a stronger grasp of stochastic calculus to understand them and a separate effort at numerical analysis to turn them into a useful computer program; in our model, the medium was the message: The description and the implementation were almost one.

Finally, unlike most prior models that produced analytical formulas that didn't match the shape of actual yield curves, ours could be calibrated to almost any curve, and therefore was ready for the trading world. Indeed, the description of the calibration was a critical part of our paper.

In subsequent years, hosts of new yield-curve models appeared, each known by their authors' acronym, and ingenious academics and quants keep finding new and perhaps more realistic ones. You can now pick from BK (Black and Karasinski), HW (Hull and White), and HJM (Heath, Jarrow, and Morton) or its extension BGM (Brace, Gatarek, and Musiela). The process continues, though which model to employ is still a matter of taste and compromise. Selecting a model becomes a question of finding one that is rich enough to represent most of the risks your product faces, efficient enough to run on a computer in a tolerable amount of time, and simple enough so that programming it is not too complex and burdensome a task.

BDT was simple and consistent, but, like any model, it was not entirely realistic, and its limitations became increasingly apparent over the years. At bottom, it had only a single factor of uncertainty, the future distribution of short-term rates, and so all rates, both short and long, tended to move together, preserving the curve's initial shape a little too well. Therefore, though the model was good for valuing options on bonds, it was not well suited to valuing options on more arcane properties of the yield curve, such as its slope or curvature.

Still, the model's simplicity made it an easy entry point into the art of yield-curve modeling for both practitioners and academics, and it left its mark. It continues to be used even after superior but more complex models have arrived on the scene.

Building the model had been tremendously absorbing, just like the old days in physics. For most of each day I had banged my head single-mindedly against the same problem, thinking about the trees, writing the computer program that embodied it, searching for ways to speed it up, speaking with Fischer and Bill, examining the computer's results, making further modifications. Sometimes I had difficulty sleeping, waking up spontaneously in the middle of the night, unable to return to bed until I had tried out a new scheme.

Unlike me, Fischer was patient. He took an efficient-market attitude towards building models: Each day you looked at what you knew and decided what was the best way to proceed next. On at least two occasions he thought we could do better if we stopped everything and started again from scratch. It was a trait I admired, but I didn't have the stomach for it. Bill and I were new to the field and eager to have our first contribution complete and disseminated.

The first time Fischer wanted to begin all over again was when we learned how to introduce the mean reversion of interest rates into our model, an insight that, not untypically, came from an accidental observation. Until then we had always run the model with equal time periods in the tree. In order to speed up the program, I experimented with varying the period length in the tree, letting it start out small in the present and then grow large in the future. In this way I aimed to make our valuation engine take a detailed look at distributions in the present but only a coarse look at their behavior in the far distant and uncertain future.

When I tried to calibrate these unequally spaced trees to the current yield curve, I ran into trouble. It often became mysteriously impossible to find any distribution of future short-term rates that were consistent with the yield curve. The mystery disappeared when we drew the trees and examined their topology. Figure 10.7a shows a tree with equal-length periods. We could now see that the increasing period lengths of Figure 10.7b caused the tree to grow visibly wider over time, reflecting a tendency for interest rates to move *away* from their mean, a runaway behavior that doesn't mesh too well with reality. This was what caused the difficulties with calibration. Similarly, if we decreased the future period lengths as shown in Figure10.7c, we observed that short-term rates reverted to the mean and the tree tended to grow ever narrower with time. This narrowing tree incorporated a restoring force that stabilized interest rates, akin to what happens in real markets when governments and central banks intervene to stabilize economies.

When Fischer realized that a tree with decreasing periods could describe mean reversion, he wanted us to drop our equal-period version and begin all over again. Bill Toy and I were more anxious to complete what we had started, and eventually we prevailed. The trees with variable periods eventually became part of the Black-Karasinski model.

Fischer was the first to notice the link between period length and mean reversion by examining the topology of the trees, and it made me aware of his intuitive powers. Looking at the tree, he could see the dynamics that its shape implied. It was only much later, after completing our paper, that we worked out the description of our model in the elegant language of stochastic calculus, the way it is now described in textbooks.

On a second occasion, sometime during early 1987, Fischer became entranced by the idea of adding a second stochastic factor to our model. The idea was sensible; our original model had simplistically assumed the entire yield curve was driven by short-term rates, and we were tempted to make the model truer to life by allowing longer-term rates to vary independently of the short-term rate. Adding a second factor in our framework meant working with two-dimensional trees. We played around with calibrating such trees to the yield curve. But trees with two or more dimensions are not only harder to visualize or draw, as you can see from Figure 10.8, but also appreciably more difficult to handle in a computer program, and I was again relieved when

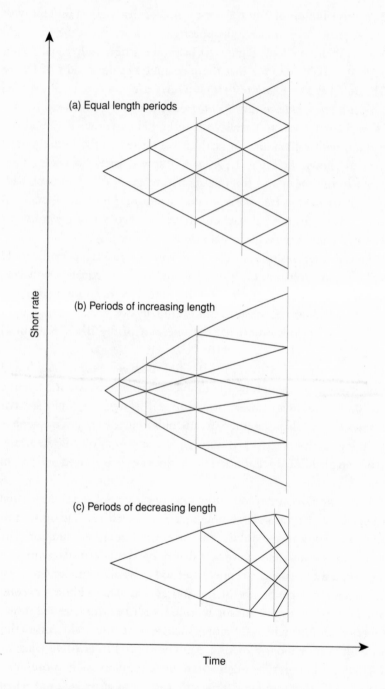

Figure 10.7   BDT short-rate trees with constant volatility but varying periods.

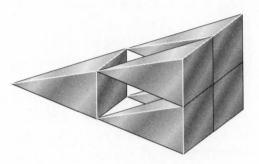

Figure 10.8   A two-dimensional tree of future interest rates.

we postponed this elaboration in favor of completing the delivery of our simpler model to the trading desk.

Several years later, Fischer, Iraj Kani, and I began investigating a two-dimensional version of the BDT model, but we never completed the work.

It takes only a good idea and a few people to develop a model, but it takes many more people to turn the model into a usable tool. For that you need a graphical user interface, a database that contains the details of traded products you own, and current market data for calibration.

But even collecting data isn't as simple as it seems—models are everywhere. What one thinks of as "market data" are often prices filtered through another model or calculation. Yields are extracted from collections of bond prices. Volatility is calculated from historical returns. Each year, as markets mature, products become more liquid and traders calibrate their quotes to greater numbers of related securities, sometimes so many that their prices must be obtained via electronic price feeds. All of this involves software. Sooner or later everyone who creates a useful model gets exposed to the truth that building a trading and risk management system around the model is a huge and often overwhelming software project that requires many more programmers than quants. Models, critical though they are, are only a small part of the story.

Back in 1986 when we developed our yield curve model, traders were quite willing to enter a yield curve into the system manually, and

I was perfectly capable of building most of the system and user interface around the model myself. I delivered it to the traders on the bond options desk and they began testing it immediately.

As they began to use our model I ran into my first taste of battle with "middlemen," the people appointed to intermediate between the producers and users of models. Middlemen—usually one per desk—sat with the traders and got to know their business well.

Middlemen serve a useful task. It's not easy for a quant to understand the finance, build the model, do the math, write the program, and still have the time to work closely with the trading desk. Traders, always rushed, need a middleman to coordinate their requirements, to make them agree on their most urgent needs. Since traders and quants speak slightly different languages, it's good to have someone who can understand both sides' dialects and serve as the designated mediator.

Unfortunately, the middlemen on the corporate and Treasury desks at that time preferred that the model creators remain invisible; one of them who used our model to generate prices for traders wouldn't even admit to doing so. Since you are paid in proportion to the perception of your benefit to the business, this was not good.

There wasn't much I could do about being front-run, but I decided to at least confirm my suspicions. A few days later I went back to the source code of my program and temporarily added a few lines that ensured that, when you tried to use it, you got a pop-up window saying "Model Under Repair." Within a few hours I started to get calls from the middlemen asking what had happened to the model they had not admitted that they were using.

Ever since, I have been wary of people who stand between model creators and end users. Quants everywhere have firsthand experience of being bypassed by more technically challenged people who extract information from you and then pass it on to other people at meetings you're not invited to. For a long time afterwards, whenever I wrote programs for traders, I used to include a swatch of code that kept a log of who used my program, and when. I encouraged people in my group to do the same. That way I had documented proof of our utility, even though I couldn't put a dollar value on it. In 1994, when the investment banking industry was forced to lay off people and Goldman went through difficult times, I sent a copy of the log to my bosses, showing how many tens of thousands of times some of our Quantitative Strategies group's programs had been used. No one in our group was laid off that year, and that bit of information may have helped a little.

I met with Fischer regularly over the next eight years, though we never again worked as closely as we did when we developed BDT. He was the most remarkable person I met at Goldman.

His most noticeable quality was his stubborn and meticulous devotion to clarity and simplicity. In writing and speaking, he put weight on both content and style. When we wrote the first draft of our paper on a one-factor model of interest rates, Fischer wanted no equations in it, and I had to struggle long and hard to satisfy his standards: He wanted accuracy and honesty without the technical details, which meant that you had to understand the model viscerally, and then explain that understanding. I think it was the clarity of the mechanics of our model that made it so popular and widely used.

Because he liked clarity, and perhaps because his training was not in economics, Fischer avoided excessive formalization. His papers were the antithesis of the unnecessarily rigorous lemma-filled research papers of financial economics journals. He tried to write as he spoke, in a terse but good-natured conversational style, using clear but casual, unadorned English. There was a touch of jerkiness to his prose because it lacked the technically superfluous conjunctions—and, but, thus, and therefore—that people commonly use to link the flow of sentences in scientific articles.

Fischer expected clarity and directness from others, too. Though he was generous with his time and didn't care about rank, you had to prepare for an audience with him. If it was evident that you hadn't thought carefully about your question, you quickly discovered that he wasn't going to do the thinking for you. And, if you didn't grasp his answer and repeated your question, he would simply repeat his answer.

A very direct man, he was uncomfortable with small talk. When he had nothing to say, he said nothing; this could be disconcerting on the telephone, where he often simply kept silent for a minute or two without terminating the conversation. Sometimes, this led you to babble in an attempt to fill the silence, until Fischer simply said an abrupt goodbye and hung up.

He once told me that one of the things that limited his influence was the fact that he always told people the truth, even if they didn't want to hear it, a characteristic I can vouch for myself. When he grew skeptical of some of the information technology managers in his division at Goldman in the early 1990s, he purposefully met with them all and then made a frank list of who was good and who was bad, and handed it over to his bosses. He laughed sheepishly but half-proudly when he conceded that he had been naive to think that he would gain anything from this.

Among Goldman partners he struck me as always a bit of an outsider. In the era before the firm went public, a "class" of partners was appointed once every two years, and each of them then advanced by being allowed to buy progressively larger shares of the company. Fischer once said to me that he was proud of possessing fewer shares than anyone else in his class of 1986.

This directness and informality characterized his research, too. His approach seemed to me to consist of unafraid hard thinking, intuition, and no great reliance on advanced mathematics. This was inspiring to lesser mortals. He attacked problems directly, with whatever skills he had at his command, and often they worked. He gave you the sense (perhaps misguided) that you could discover deep truths with whatever skills you had, too, if you were willing to think hard. He was guided by his great economic intuition; though his mathematical skills were unexceptional, his instinct was strong, and he was tenacious in trying to attain insight before resorting to mathematics.

In modeling he had a taste for the concrete: He liked to describe the financial world with variables that represented observable phenomena rather than hidden statistical or econometric factors. He thought practical usefulness and accuracy were more important than elegance, despite the unquestionable elegance that lends so much appeal to the Black–Scholes–Merton framework he founded. He had a strong pragmatic streak; he was at least as much a practitioner as an academic, willing to devote time and attention to software, trading systems, and user interfaces. He thought that these were just as important as the models themselves.

Fischer preferred reality to elegance in modeling. In one of his last published papers, *Equilibrium Exchanges*, he succinctly stated his attitude in the last part of his introduction. "In the end," he wrote, "this entire article amounts to a series of conjectures about the nature of equilibrium, if one exists. I have been unable to provide an exhaustive and precise analysis of the implications of my assumptions, but I would rather guess about what follows from more-relevant assumptions than derive precise conclusions from less-relevant assumptions."

Clearly, though style was important to him, content was paramount. Between 1990 and 1995, when he worked first in Goldman Sachs Asset Management and then in Fixed Income Research, I invited him to come and listen to the occasional seminar speaker we had visit the Quantitative Strategies group I ran. I noticed that he didn't attend if the seminars were on new or improved numerical solutions to problems that were already soluble; it's not that he was uninterested in numerical solutions, but rather that he was more interested in financial economics. Similarly, he didn't get carried away by the need to find analytical solutions to equations; he was just as happy to use numerical methods when fast computers were available.

Fischer also had a good grasp of the overwhelming importance of computing in making effective use of models. People have often asked why we publicized our research on the BDT model in 1990, given that we worked at a profit-making investment bank. In fact, when we published it, traders at Goldman had already been using it for several years. But more importantly, Fischer distinguished between releasing models (which he thought legitimate) and releasing a computer implementation or trading system that incorporates the model, which he thought should be sold.

The truth is that models are rarely an unambiguous source of profits. What counts as much or more is the trading system and the discipline it imposes, the operational errors it disallows and the intuition that traders gain from being able to experiment with a model.

Fischer had his own way of thinking about markets. He was deeply inspired by the so-called "general equilibrium" approach of the capital asset pricing model, the idea that prices and markets equilibrate when the expected return per unit of risk is the same for all securities. This belief was the source of much of his intuition, and was the method he first used to derive the Black-Scholes differential equation. In late July of 1995, shortly before his death, in response to a question I sent him about these matters, he emailed me: "I view all our work on fixed-income models as resulting from the application of the capital asset pricing model to fixed-income markets."

I had a touching glimpse of his love for this approach a few years before he died when, together with a few of my colleagues, I tried to assess the effect of transactions costs and hedging frequency on our trading desk's options prices. We built a Monte Carlo simulation program that dynamically replicated each option as the stock price changed, adding the assumed transactions costs as each rebalancing of the hedging portfolio took place. In the long run we intended to use the program to see how much this caused options prices to deviate from the Platonic Black-Scholes value; in this way we could estimate the actual cost of our hedging strategy rather than accept the value of the idealized value embodied in the Black-Scholes model.

Whenever you write a program to do something new, you should first make sure that it does the old things correctly. In testing the program written by one of my colleagues, we first ran it assuming that there were no transactions costs and that you could hedge continuously, in order to ensure that we obtained the exact Black-Scholes replication price. Of course, you cannot really hedge continuously in a computer simulation, so we rehedged very often, several times a day. To our amazement, we discovered that even for 10,000 rehedgings on a one-year option—that is, for more than thirty rebalancings in a day—we still couldn't obtain the exact Black-Scholes value. There was always a residual discrepancy. This seemed wrong, so I wrote my own version of the program and found the same small but significant discrepancy. This was very puzzling; it suggested that the Black-Scholes formula was less applicable to the conditions of actual markets than we had expected.

I was perturbed enough to want to speak to Fischer about this, and went over to his office in another building on Goldman's growing campus. When I explain what I had found, he briefly became quite excited at the apparent inability of Merton's replication method to produce the exact Black-Scholes value, and said something like, "You know, I always thought there was something wrong with the replication method."

Sad to say, I discovered a little later that both my simulation program and my colleague's contained small but different errors, which, once corrected, confirmed that the replication method rapidly converged to the exact Black-Scholes value! In his heart, though, Fischer mistrusted the Merton derivation and preferred his original proof.

Fischer's independent thinking led him to unorthodox but well-thought-out ideas, many of which sounded obvious once he articulated them. He voiced some of them in speeches, and others in a collection of brief, pointed notes that he circulated informally at Goldman in the early 1990s.

In one short essay he struck at the foundation of financial economics, writing that "certain economic quantities are so hard to estimate that I call them 'unobservables.'" One unobservable, he pointed out, is *expected return*, the amount by which people expect to profit when buying a security. So much of finance, from Markowitz on, deals with this quantity unquestioningly. Yet, wrote Fischer, "Our estimates of expected return are so poor they are almost laughable."

In another essay entitled *Managing Traders*, he argued that a trader should be judged on the rationale behind his or her methods and rewarded only if it is sound, irrespective of whether or not he or she profited in the most recent period. "It's crucial to judge the stories they trade on," he wrote about traders. "Stories can be wrong, but I'm uncomfortable trading without one. . . Looking only or primarily at their profit and loss statements is a recipe for disaster." He wanted to reward intelligence and long-term thinking rather than the short-term vagaries of markets.

In his speech on being named the Financial Engineer of the Year by the International Association of Financial Engineers (IAFE) in 1994, Fischer said that he had always preferred applied research to academic. University professors, he claimed, should be paid and hired for their teaching, not their research; he believed that their desire to teach well would then lead them to do good research.

When he became terminally ill, he neither hid it nor announced it, but informed the necessary people, and spoke about it in a detached, objective way that I found admirable. I never heard him complain.

He had a massive operation, and was full of genuine praise for the surgeon, who he said was "a genius"; it made me briefly envious of people who help others rather than work on theories. After the operation, he had a temporary recovery, and worked again, assiduously. For a while we sometimes spoke on the telephone about building models of options valuation that included jumps in the underlying index.

He was always frank if you asked about his health, but never volunteered any information if you didn't. Later, when one could sense from occasional remarks and rumors that his condition had worsened, I summoned the courage to ask how he was doing. He said simply that things looked "pretty iffy right now."

When he finally stopped coming to work, he communicated with anyone who wrote to him via email. I liked to keep in contact, and would send him comments or short bits of news from work. If my emails were insubstantial, consisting of small talk or complaints, then, true to his style, he seldom replied. But if you wrote to him about some genuine issue in finance, you received a prompt answer. I asked him once if these email questions were bothering him, and he immediately replied to say no, and then stressed in a postscript that he liked to receive these questions.

At his memorial service in Cambridge, I heard a moving speech by Jack Treynor, former editor of the *Financial Analysts Journal* and, in many respects, Fischer's mentor, who concluded by saying that as regards death, "Fischer wasn't afraid at all." This is the way I saw it, too. He rarely seemed to delude himself about the way the world really worked.

what a man.

Whenever I think of Fischer I think of him as a consummately unsentimental realist. Once, when I was about to travel to Vienna to speak at a conference at which Robert Merton would be present, I called Fischer (already ill but more than a year before his death) and left him a voicemail asking the appropriate way to refer to "the model"— should I call it "Black-Scholes" or "Black-Scholes-Merton?" Fischer replied with a message saying it was OK to call it the Black-Scholes-Merton model, because it was Merton who had come up with the replication argument for valuing an option. Then he added, quite imperturbably, that "that's the part that many people think is the most important."

On a professional and personal level, Fischer always seemed more free of artifice than anyone I knew, though this sometimes made him difficult to deal with. He didn't soft-pedal in giving you his opinion of work you had done or actions you had taken, but just told you what he thought. He had a strong sense of what was important, and he always took the long view, in corporate politics as well as in research. For that reason, he was the perfect person to call when you needed a clear view about an issue. In the midst of corporate politics, he told you to concentrate on quality even if people around you sometimes didn't appreciate it. He kept your eye on the goal, which was to help the business in the best way you could, to try to keep breaking new ground. He didn't sympathize with holding on to turf; instead, he always encouraged the search for new opportunities.

Fischer's last paper, written but not fully completed while he was dying, was submitted to the *Financial Analysts Journal*. He called the paper *Interest Rates as Options*, and cleverly pointed out that short-term interest rates themselves resemble call options, a consequence on which he then elaborated.

In a footnote to the article, the managing editor of the journal explained the circumstances behind the paper's publication:

> Fischer Black submitted this paper on May 1, 1995. His submission letter stated: "I would like to publish this, though I may not be around to make any changes the referee may suggest. If I'm not, and if it seems roughly acceptable, could you publish it as is with a note explaining the circumstances?" Fischer received a revise and resubmit letter on May 22 with a detailed referee's report. He worked on the paper during the summer and started to think about how to address the comments of the referee. He died on August 31 without completing the revision.

Chapter 11

Force of Circumstance

■ Manners and mores on Wall Street ■ The further
adventures of some acquaintances
■ Volatility is infectious ■

N o one stays happy on Wall Street for long. The people who work there don't usually think of it as an avocation, like physics or medicine. Instead, most investment bankers want to get rich as fast as they can and then retire. And so, as Heraclitus wrote, all things happen because of strife and necessity.

At Goldman, in the pre–IPO days, the route to getting really rich was to become a partner and acquire a stake in the profits of the firm. Those who succeeded in gaining a partnership tended to last another decade or so and then retire, some voluntarily, some forcibly. Many partners were gone by their late thirties.

To join the partnership, or even to be considered for it, you had to have made a clear contribution to the profits of the firm. As a result, the vast majority of partners came out of sales, trading, and investment banking, where the money you made for the firm could be unambiguously counted. Almost no partners came from information technology or research, whose contributions, while substantial, did not carry a clear dollar value. Even Fischer, though he appeared to be an exception to this rule, had reportedly made millions of dollars for the firm by taking careful account of a mathematical subtlety in the definition of certain futures contracts of which most traders were unaware.

In troubled FSG, everyone seemed to know that whoever ran us properly might get the ultimate Goldman reward, a partnership and all that it guaranteed. The self-assured young kid in the cube next to me was certain that Mutt or Jeff would make it. "There are about 7,000 people at Goldman," he intoned. "And there are 70 partners. That's one partner per 100 people. There are over 100 people in FSG, and they're in charge. Therefore, one of them will be a partner."

It didn't work out that way. Instead there followed a succession of new FSG rulers and corulers who entered and exited like lovers in a French farce. It would take more than a few tries to fix it, but Goldman eventually got it right.

First came Bob Kopprasch from the Salomon Brothers Bond Portfolio Analysis (BPA) group, where he had run the options research team in which my friend Mark Koenigsberg now worked. Kopprasch's team had written reports containing some of the best research on fixed-income derivatives in the 1980s, high quality, well-written pieces that straddled and almost dissolved the border between academia and practice. It was their publications you turned to if you wanted to understand how to value swaps and swaptions before the necessary methodology appeared in textbooks. John Meriwether's arb group at Salomon cherry-picked some of their best people from Kopprasch's team, men like Victor Haghani and Greg Hawkins, who later moved with Meriwether to Long Term Capital Management (LTCM). When I ran Goldman's Quantitative Strategies a few years later, I always regarded the work done by Kopprasch's group as a model for what I tried to achieve. Nowadays, quantitative groups on the Street devote much less effort to these kinds of publications.

For a while, Kopprasch tried to manage us in an uneasy triumvirate with Mutt and Jeff. It must have been difficult. Soon Mutt made a graceful exit to the less quantitative world of asset management. Then Jeff left for a large Savings & Loan that, like many others, had benefited from the FSLIC guarantee on their deposits to become a speculative investor in securitized pools of home-owner mortgages. Then, only a few months into his reign, Kopprasch seemed to tire of the politics and went upstairs to work with the futures salespeople. Eventually he left Goldman to join an investment firm started by Lew Ranieri, former head of mortgages at Salomon Brothers and one of the creators of the market for mortgage-backed securities.

Then things turned around. In 1987 Bob Rubin appointed Ed Markiewicz to manage FSG. Ed was a down-to-earth, longtime Goldman accountant, about forty years old, who was said to be Bob's *consigliere*, his troubleshooter in difficult situations. Ed knew little about models, software, or options trading, but he could distinguish flim from flam, a skill in short supply. He spent his first few months as boss of FSG questioning everyone. "What do you think of so-and-so?" he would say to you behind closed doors. Slowly he figured out who had useful skills and who was merely along for the ride. A semblance of order returned; the overpaid consultants left; the professional administrators were trimmed. Presuming that I was one of the good guys, Ed moved me from a cube into an office and put me in charge of creating a fixed-income software group. Our mission was to replace our antiquated FORTRAN financial library with something we eventually called GS-ONE, an object-oriented unified framework for constructing Goldman Sachs fixed-income trading systems.

By early 1988 Ed had restored order. It was reassuring to see that excess had its limits, and impressive that he accomplished the turn-around so efficiently, because in truth he understood so little about what people in FSG really did. But he did understand instinctively when people were feeding him a line. Temporarily triumphant, he seemed to us to have a good chance of becoming the partner who would now reign over FSG. Over the next year he seemed to bloom; he became more confident, working out at the Health and Racquet Club some lunch times and spending time on the trading floor with Jacob Goldfield, whose influence kept growing.

New partners were picked every second November at Goldman, and people who were in the running had some idea of their odds. After the final deliberations, on the morning when their names were about to be made public, the head of the firm called up each new partner to congratulate him. Candidates in the running hovered around their desk from early that morning, waiting for the call or its absence. I was no longer working at Goldman the day they announced the partners of 1988, but friends told me that when the call didn't come, Ed left the office for the remainder of the day. A few months later he left FSG, and went on to troubleshoot other problem areas of the firm.

David Garbasz, who took me under his wing when I first came to Goldman, had his share of subsequent strife, too.

Trained as a scientist but now a Goldman trader, he was always willing to debate options markets and their theory. It was stimulating to walk upstairs to the bond options desk and hang out with the aggressively humorous traders around him. One day a group of us were chatting on the trading floor, kidding around about the rash of teenage suicides who had apparently hung themselves in toilets or attics. According to the newspapers, these boys were the victims of autoerotic asphyxia, a search for the extreme pleasure that purportedly accompanies a reduction in oxygen supply to the brain at the time of orgasm. When someone in the group questioned the authenticity of the phenomenon, David pointed casually over towards one of the tallest new recruits on the desk and said "Of course it's true. Why do you think he's so tall?"

Like many people on the Street, David wanted faster advancement and more control. Once every few weeks, he would reportedly talk to Rubin. Less than a year after I came to Goldman, he resigned and went to work as a senior options trader at O'Connor, the renowned and very savvy options trading firm in Chicago.

David was ambitious and volatile, though not, by Wall Street standards, extraordinarily so. A year or so after joining O'Connor, he departed together with two software engineers he had met there to start a company to produce fixed-income risk management software. They based themselves in Chicago and called their firm RMS, an evocative name that I greatly admired.[1]

David's plan to build a commercial fixed-income risk management system was an inspired one, several years ahead of its time. Although many trading firms and investment banks, including Goldman, wrote their own risk-management software, at that time no one had yet marketed that type of product commercially. Stan Diller at Bear Stearns

---

[1]RMS is a common mnemonic for both Risk Management System and Root Mean Square. Volatility—a crucial measure of risk that is defined as the square root of the mean of the squares of the stock's daily returns, or "root mean square" in common statistical parlance. Root mean square is also suggestive of Brownian motion, the process by which a randomly moving stock price diffuses from its initial value in such a way that the average price change is proportional to the square root of the elapsed time.

was pushing in that direction; as head of FAST, their fixed-income research group, he was building a system called AutoBond, which was intended to first be used by the trading desks and then, once polished and debugged, to be sold to clients. He was pursuing every quant's dream: to convert his work for the desk into something that would generate measurable dollars and cents for the firm, thereby eliminating the gap between the *luftmensch* PhDs and the revenue-generating "real" businesspeople.

David and his partners hired programmers in Chicago, where rents and salaries were low compared to New York. There they embarked on the creation of an elegant bond-and-options-risk system, object-oriented and written in C++ to run on Sun UNIX workstations. Most investment banks' financial software had always been behind the times, but RMS was strikingly modern: It had an up-to-date graphical user interface with drag-and-drop features, graphs, and icons. Several years would pass before other small companies, among them Renaissance, C-ATS, Infinity, and Algorithmics, began to build similarly stylish systems. Consolidation has been swift in this business, too, and only Algorithmics now survives as an independent company.

Then things accelerated. David returned to New York and took a position as a trader at E. F. Hutton, where, I heard, he had negotiated a golden parachute in the event of a change of ownership. I think he intended to use RMS as the provider of his trading software at Hutton. It was the perfect confluence; he would be paid for trading, and RMS would have immediate users to test and improve their software.

Within a year, E. F. Hutton, damaged by a check-kiting scandal, was acquired by Shearson (another famous company whose name finally disappeared after mergers with Lehman Brothers and American Express). As a result of the restructuring, David pulled the ripcord. With the cash he received, he continued to fund RMS's development in Chicago throughout 1988. He told me they were close to making a sizable sale of their system to Shearson's trading desk.

David was excited about all these possibilities, and was spending lots of time in New York drumming up clients. I invited him over for a Rosh Hashanah dinner. He was tightly wound; he kept everyone entertained, working the table after dinner like a comedian in a club, sliding from chair to chair to engage different people, telling everyone about how well things were going.

Each year the Securities Industry Association has its annual meeting in New York with many exhibits devoted to financial software and hardware. RMS took a booth there in 1988 and displayed their risk system. It was beautiful: You could alter a yield curve by dragging at it with a computer mouse, and then see the subsequent effect of the change in interest rates on your bond or options portfolio.

Then came Euripidean disasters. Sometime in late 1989 we heard that O'Connor & Co. had obtained a preliminary injunction to stop David from selling the RMS system. We heard that O'Connor claimed that RMS had used O'Connor's trade secrets. David told me that he was fighting them in court. He said that they imagined that the well-known duration hedging techniques he provided in RMS were proprietary to them, whereas they were widely used on the Street—industry practice, in fact.

One summer weekend that year he and Ted Dengler, an ex-oceanographer friend of David's who had also become an options trader at Goldman, visited us in a house that we rented for the season on Fire Island. As we threw frisbees on a deserted stretch of beach, talking while keeping a watchful eye on my daughter Sonya, I remember David telling me that he had gone to see the movie *Tucker: The Man and His Dream*, directed by Francis Ford Coppola. It was the true story of how an inventor in the late 1940s tried to take on Detroit by building a much better car, and how Detroit then both copied and crushed him.

The expensive legal battle and the injunction put an end to RMS. In 1995, after giving a talk at a conference, I was approached by someone I knew who had worked at O'Connor during the RMS episode. When I asked if he had known David, he told me that O'Connor had been intent on shutting down David's enterprise. With their deep pockets, he said "they had guys spending all their time running *diff* on RMS's files and the O'Connor code." (*Diff* is one of the great suite of UNIX tools that make a programmer's life easier. It compares two different files of text and finds any common strings of words in them, a simpler version of current bio-informatics programs that search for common strings of DNA in the mouse and human genome.) I have no idea whether there were in fact commonalities, but even independent people coding the same well-known algorithm might end up writing vaguely similar chunks of code.

O'Connor eventually disappeared, too, absorbed into Swiss Bank, which itself subsequently merged with UBS. Starting in 1990 David disappeared into some alternate nonfinancial New York; none of his old friends saw him anymore. Someone reported that he'd become a gourmet cook. I called him once and left a message, but was unable to track him down. I never resented it; I understood from my own experience the embarrassment of leaving a field. Ted told me that he ran into David in Central Park one afternoon in the mid-1990s, and exchanged a few words with him.

One Sunday morning in the early summer of 1998 I went for a run on Riverside Drive. The road was filled to overflowing with the annual AIDS march. Returning to my apartment, I walked past the crowds watching marchers on the corner of Eighty-Third Street. Suddenly I heard a vaguely familiar voice behind me, and turned to look. On the corner were a man and a woman with whom I briefly exchanged glances, and their child of four or five. A moment later I realized it was David, and I watched as he turned around and headed back down Eighty-Third Street towards Broadway with what I presumed were his wife and child.

Then, in October 2000 I was named the Sungard IAFE Financial Engineer of the Year, and gave a speech at the annual dinner in which I thanked several people, including David. The speech later appeared on the IAFE website, and a friend of David's, "googling" him in early 2002, found my reference. Suddenly, after more than twelve years of silence, David called. Now a successful entrepreneur and investor, he was passionately interested in mathematics education, and was working to persuade Israel, his native country, to adopt a more rigorous school mathematics curriculum. He wanted me to get involved. We met once or twice subsequently, and he was the David of old, confident and energetic. He and his wife and two children lived in New York and spent weekends on their farm in upstate New York. He seemed to have everyone's idea of a good life.

Peter Freund, though he was head of the burgeoning bond options business, also did not stay very long at Goldman. About eighteen months after I arrived, he left for Bankers Trust to start up their credit derivatives business, and is now commonly regarded as one of the founders of that industry.

Dave Griswold, who had used my models to build the new options trading system for Peter's group at Goldman, followed him to Bankers as a software consultant. There he created yet another object-oriented language he called *Seymour*, a pun on C++. Later, Dave started several small companies in succession, most of them focused around his love of computer languages in general and Smalltalk in particular. The last of these companies, Animorphic, used its Smalltalk expertise to produce a very fast Java interpreter, and was acquired by Sun Microsystems in 1997, presumably leaving Dave independent enough to continue to follow his true interests.

Like so many of the firms on the Street in the mid-1980s, when I began, Bankers Trust no longer exists as an independent entity. It became unviable in the mid-1990s after its involvement in the derivatives scandals of Orange County and Procter and Gamble, and was acquired by Deutsche Bank.

Jacob Goldfield, the *wunderkind* on the bond options desk when I arrived, was the only one of Peter's traders at that time who went on become a Goldman partner, and he did so quite rapidly.

Jacob had a precocious trading-genius aura that was augmented by his conspicuous idiosyncrasies. While almost everyone new to Wall Street in those days wore suits and carried briefcases, he arrived each day lugging his belongings in a Jansport backpack. His face stubbled and impassively pale, he traversed the trading floor and rode the elevators up and down 85 Broad Street in stockinged feet, a silent character in a Munch painting. I still run into people nowadays who visited Goldman in the late 1980s and, though they don't recall his name, ask me about the trader who wore no shoes.

Jacob was very good at saying very little, an excellent quality in a trader. He had an intimidating email style, radically terse—no "Dear" or "Hi" at the beginning, no "Thanks" at the end, no punctuation, grammar or capital letters, no unnecessary segues or conventional lead-ins or fadeouts—just one cryptic sentence or query encapsulated entirely in the subject heading of the email, with no subsequent body. It was instant messaging ahead of its time, I suppose. *"What do u think about xxxx?"* the subject of an email might say. I would reply in a carefully thought out paragraph and then receive a three-letter message with *"Thx"* in the subject. I always ended up feeling like an uninhibited babbler.

One day in 1986 or 1987, Jacob called down from the trading floor to my office in FSG to ask me to check out a young man who had been introduced to Goldman through a friend of Bob Rubin's wife. I went up to Rubin's office on Goldman's executive floor. The interviewee was a young Israeli, aged 19 or 20, who told me that he had completed high school at fourteen and proceeded straight to medical school. Several years later, he said, he had decided to abandon medicine and study physics at the Sorbonne. Now he had come to New York. Bob Rubin had asked Jacob to speak to the young man, and Jacob passed him on to me.

When I asked him why he was interested in working at Goldman, he replied that people had told him that because he was so smart, he should "go into options." This didn't impress me; I have always been skeptical about intellect in search of problems. We spoke for a half hour or so, and several things about his story seemed curiously illogical. Medicine seemed an unlikely choice for someone accomplished enough to finish high school at fourteen; I found it hard to imagine a fifteen-year-old with the aplomb to dissect cadavers and perform gynecological exams. And why go all the way from Israel to the Sorbonne to study physics?

I began to quiz him about physics and found that his knowledge was semipopular. When I asked him what he had read, he mentioned Capra's *The Tao of Physics*, an entertaining and fashionable mystico-physical book about quantum mechanics and Buddhism. Though he knew a little about the definition of an option, he knew nothing about the theory of how to value them. I pointed out these inconsistencies to Jacob, and said I wouldn't hire him.

A few months later, sitting at my desk, I picked up the ringing phone to hear Jacob, again calling from Bob Rubin's office. In his usual give-no-information style, he queried me: "Tell me, do you remember that young Israeli guy you interviewed? What did we conclude at the time?" The reverberating tone indicated that my voice was coming out at the other end on speakerphone.

I answered carefully.

"I thought there was something fishy about him," I said. "He seemed to know too little about the things he was supposed to be good at. For someone who was supposed to have studied physics, he didn't have much depth. Why do you ask?"

"He was arrested a few days ago in Ace Greenberg's office at Bear Stearns—entering under false pretenses," replied Jacob, only slightly more loquacious than usual. I think he wanted Bob Rubin to hear what a good call he and I had previously made.

After Peter Freund left Goldman, Jacob soon became head of the bond options desk, and then, a few years later, one of the youngest Goldman partners ever, eventually running the entire swaps desk. He left the firm in 2000 to pursue his own investments, and recently became Chief Investment Officer for Soros Fund Management.

Observing all this mobility had its effect on me, too. By 1988, after only two and a half years in FSG, I had grown weary of the constant instability. I had worked for four heads of FSG in less than two years, and a fifth one, Markiewicz's replacement, was clearly looming.

I had also began to feel that my lack of a formal economics background would count against me. After completing my work on BDT and GS-ONE I began to think about new projects. When I told Ed Markiewicz that I would like to work on a better model for valuing the delivery option embedded in Treasury bond futures contracts, he said I should check with the "brains trust" on whether that was reasonable.

The brains trust was Jacob's apt name for Bob Litterman, José Scheinkman, and Larry Weiss, three very smart PhDs in economics who were also in FSG. Jacob, now making lots of money for the firm, had begun to refer to them by that name, and Ed, who admired Jacob, used it, too. Though Bob, Larry, and José deserved their reputation, I was uncomfortable with further intellectual constraints.

Finally, there was the question of pay, always forefront in everyone's mind. In those days at Goldman, the value of your annual bonus was communicated to you just before Thanksgiving, and then paid in mid-December. The archaic payroll system was unable to cut a check for more than $100,000 dollars. If, on that December day when Goldman delivered the actual bonus payment to you, your year-end bonus was, say, $1,000,000, then you received ten checks, each one sealed in its own envelope, the whole bundle neatly stacked and secured by a rubber band. Bonuses were all paid on the same day, and someone senior went around the floor handing out the check bundles to each employee. Thus, although bonus amounts were private and company heads encouraged you to keep them that way, you could guess the order of magnitude of someone's bonus by the thickness of their deck of checks. Even a minibundle of two checks was instantaneously distinguishable from one. Some traders received a fat stack and some of them flaunted it. One well-paid young trader had a habit of taking his bundle and silently riffling through it, meticulously counting the envelopes one at a time in full view of his colleagues. Nowadays, the payroll system has no check-size limit, or, more honestly, no limit my bonus was ever able to cross.

Goldman was wisely conservative and pay grew slowly. As long as you kept working at the same firm, your future bonus was determined by your past. The raise you got in a good year, or the cut in a bad one, was quoted as a percentage of what you made the previous year, which had the effect of damping a raise and cushioning a decline in your compensation. It wasn't easy to move to a new level. Some people who worked for me have detested this smoothing, arguing heatedly you should be paid "what you're worth" each year. Personally, I didn't dislike it that much. In research, who knows exactly how to put a number on your contribution?

More than pay, I cared about doing something interesting; had someone offered to make me the Goldman Sachs partner in charge of Information Technology for the back office, I would have refused. Nevertheless, in early 1988, even I started to become dissatisfied about my compensation prospects in FSG.

I took to on-and-off commiseration with Bill Toy, also an ex-physicist and my collaborator on BDT. Bill, who had arrived on Wall Street a year or so before me, was already in the far reaches of "disgruntledom." Somehow, he had internalized the trading-and-sales view of quants as unworldly *luftmenschen*, and had by now acquired a disdain for the stigma of having a PhD that bordered on self-hatred. Though he wanted to be one of "them"—the front-office real "businesspeople"—to them, however, he was still just a quant.

Once a week we had lunch with Ramine Rouhani, who had been working with Fischer on the theory of portfolio insurance, the trading strategy that later played a part in the 1987 stock market crash. We would eat cheap lunches at the long-since-shut Italian Alps on William

Street, where I slowly became slightly depressed and even more cor-
rupted by listening to the two of them feverishly and incessantly talking about their dissatisfaction with their role. Ramine and Bill were
intent on becoming a part of "the business," and were always planning
routes of escape to parts of Goldman that were closer to "the business."

"I've got to get out of here," Bill would say repeatedly, shaking his
head slowly from side to side and wiping his brow with the back of
his right hand. Over the years, Bill and I would continue to commiser-
ate, and on occasional bad days I, too, would repeat the mantra "I've got
to get out of here." Whenever I did, Bill would say to me scornfully,
"You'll never have the guts to leave!"

Ramine left Goldman within a year and now runs fixed income trading at the New York branch of the French bank CDC IXIS. Bill sol-
diered on at Goldman; he became a true expert at the legal, regulatory,
and financial-engineering aspects of structured equity derivative products, and coedited a book on the subject. Finally, no doubt after many
additional lunches similar to the ones we shared back then, he joined
Ramine at CDC in 1999.

Part of me, of course, liked being a dissident. Recently I experienced a burst of recognition while reading the autobiography of
Erwin Chargaff, the Vienna-born discoverer of the eponymous base-
pairing Chargaff rules that led to Watson and Crick's discovery of the
double helical structure of DNA. Chargaff, who disliked the imagina-
tive, shot-in-the-dark, theoretical-physics-like style that characterized
Watson and Crick's approach to model building, grew bitter at being
asked why he had not made the discovery implied by his rules. In his
autobiography he wrote: "Most people are wise and applaud the
inevitable; but I, inexplicably, love to be on the losing side."

By this route I came to the point where, in 1988, I began to interview for positions at other investment banks. It wasn't hard to get out
of Goldman's office unobserved during the day. I had been advised that
if you left your jacket at your desk no one would even realize you were
gone, and it was true. Soon a headhunter introduced me to the fixed
income group at J. P. Morgan (now J. P. Morgan Chase) just a block or
two away, and I periodically walked over there for a series of protracted
interviews with banking people who were waiting for the end of the

Glass-Steagall era so they could enter the investment banking business whole-heartedly. It was somewhat disheartening: Most of my interviewers were more interested in asking me what it was like to work at Goldman than they were in assessing my credentials, and nothing came of it in the end.

Another headhunter sent me to Shearson, where I was offered a position in charge of a small group supporting bond futures trading under Stan Jonas. At that time Goldman still had a simple hierarchy of titles consisting of Analyst, Associate, Vice President, and Partner. I found it almost impossible to comprehend the seniority that went with the VP title offered me by Shearson; their bureaucracy seemed to be deeper and closer to that of Bell Labs. A friend there explained to me that there were divisional VPs and firmwide VPs, and that it was better to be a firmwide VP than a divisional one.[2] I liked Stan a great deal and was impressed with his grasp of theory and practice, but I was still not quite ready to leave Goldman.

Then, early in 1988, David Garbasz, by now in charge of RMS, introduced me to Tom Klaffky, the head of the BPA group at Salomon Brothers. Although Salomon had a fearsome reputation as a place with a coarse and brutal culture, they were without a doubt the best fixed-income trading firm in the world, and BPA was the premier quant group on the Street. I was definitely interested in working there.

At David's suggestion, I sent Klaffky my résumé. Then, a few days later, I walked the 100 yards from 85 Broad Street to One New York Plaza to meet him. His claim to fame at Salomon was his participation in the creation of zero-coupon Treasury Strips out of Treasury bonds. Now in charge of BPA under Marty Liebowitz, Tom's empire consisted of several subgroups. Among these was Bob Kopprasch's former options research group, now run by Janet Showers, and Mike Waldmann's mortgage research group.

I proceeded to meet with Tom on several occasions in the middle of 1988, and each time he displayed a burst of fitful interest in having me join Salomon, but then nothing much would happen. Whenever things slowed down, David Garbasz would encourage me to push forward, and

---

[2] A few years later a lady who cut my hair asked for my title at work. When I said I was a Vice President at Goldman Sachs, she congratulated me on having only one person above me. She didn't understand that I was one of probably 3,000 VPs.

I would write Tom another letter outlining my thoughts about how I could contribute to Salomon Brothers. Then I would surreptitiously walk across the street to drop my letter off at One New York Plaza.

The physical delivery was tricky. My friend Mark Koenigsberg worked for Janet Showers, and I was always wary of bumping into him in the lobby of One New York. I didn't want him to know I was interviewing there. One lunchtime, walking over to deliver a note to Klaffky on the Forty-Third floor of One New York, I met Mark coming out of the ground-floor elevator I was about to enter. Flustered, I told him I was there to get a haircut at the barber in the basement, and he promptly escorted me down there to show me where it was. I had to improvise quite fast to avoid getting an unwanted trim.

Against my nature, I was slowly becoming a little more daring in dealing with this unfamiliar, nonacademic and money-centered world. I told Tom (in writing, not in conversation—that would have required a greater quantity of *chutzpah* than I possessed) what level of pay it would take to make me move firms. That I was able to do so impresses me, for inside I still heard my mother's unarticulated but clearly communicated sentiment that one worked for love and interest, and that it was crass to talk about pay.

When Klaffky asked me how much money I was making at Goldman, I exaggerated a little. As a result, I approximately doubled my annual pay when I moved to Salomon a few months later. In those days, I'm afraid, it was common to lie about your salary and bonus. In some sense, we regarded a question about past pay as an invasion of privacy that didn't deserve an honest answer. Many of the people I knew in fact interpreted it as equivalent to a question about how much money you'd *like* to earn at your next job. Nowadays, firms hire companies to conduct background checks on new employees before they begin work, and you cannot hire anyone whose résumé differs in the smallest way from the ascertainable facts.

Klaffky seemed uncertain where to place me inside Salomon, and eventually arranged for me to have lunch with John Meriwether's team, the famed arb group that later became the core of Long Term Capital Management. It must have been my collaboration with Fischer that made them agree to see me, and I worried that I knew a lot less than they thought. Garbasz, like many traders a fluent bluffer, tried briefly to coach me about pari-mutuel betting, a topic he claimed was of interest to members of the arb group. I shudder a little when I think of the day I finally went over to have lunch with them in one of the catered dining rooms high up in One New York Plaza.

I don't remember exactly who was at the lunch. I recall about eight men, some subset of Larry Hilibrand, John Meriwether, Victor Haghani, Bill Krasker, Greg Hawkins, and a few of their more junior team members. I was a comparative novice; *in toto*, I had had just over two years of experience on the Street. The work I had done with Fischer and Bill Toy was inventive and useful, and was later to become a market standard. Nevertheless, most of my knowledge was theoretical. In contrast, the members of Meriwether's group were more savvy than anyone I had ever seen. They understood both theory and practice.

My lunchtime interviewers were unfailingly polite. I recall their asking me some general questions about my work with Fischer; sensibly, they tried to determine to what extent I had truly been his intellectual collaborator. It was hard to answer; no one I've known in finance has displayed Fischer's determination to approach any problem without preconceptions and to think it through for himself. They posed me a technical question about the relative value of an Asian option and a European option, and I gave what I later learned was the wrong answer. They nodded at my reply but didn't correct me. A few days later Klaffky told me that they didn't want to hire me for their group, but thought that I would be a reasonable hire for someone else.

One morning in 1999, more than a decade later, I participated in a conference call with some of the same people. I was at Goldman Sachs and they were at the now collapsed LTCM, being overseen by the consortium of investment banks who bailed them out. Together with my colleagues Kresimir Demeterfi, Mike Kamal, and Joe Zou in the Quantitative Strategies group at Goldman, I had written an expository paper on volatility swaps, a new over-the-counter instrument that allowed retail clients to trade volatility itself as an asset. LTCM was interested in buying volatility swaps in order to offset the volatility risk in some of the still open positions that had contributed to its demise.

That morning its overseer from Goldman had a few of the LTCM partners telephone us to discuss the subtleties of swap valuation. The questions they asked us in that brief conversation showed an immediate understanding of theoretical subtleties that was far more insightful and sophisticated than any questions we had been asked by the Goldman traders we knew. It was a shock to realize that people whose great experience and knowledge straddled both the quantitative and the trading worlds had, despite their sophistication, brought themselves into such a catastrophic state.

With no position available for me in the arb group, Klaffky turned to his own area, BPA, and introduced me to his head of mortgage research, Mike Waldman, who needed someone to lead a new Adjustable Rate Mortgage (ARM) group he was forming. Within a few weeks I had an offer to work for Mike.

I had one brief moment of foreboding when I met with Klaffky to discuss my offer and he asked if he could answer any questions for me.

"I've heard that people at Salomon are much tougher and more hard-nosed than people at Goldman," I said. "Is that true?"

"That's not quite right," he said to me. "I think Salomon's a bit like a shark, in a way. You know, sharks have to keep swimming, keep moving all the time, or else they die. That's more or less what Salomon's like."

I thought it merely odd that he would try to allay my fears by comparing his firm to a shark. I ignored the analogy as well as the advice of many acquaintances, headhunters, and former Salomon employees, who warned me that Mike could be a difficult boss. When I was being courted he was congenial. Always cautious, I agonized through the summer of 1988 and then decided to take the job.

Early in the fall I told Ed Markiewicz I was going to leave Goldman for Salomon. He spoke with Fischer and Jacob, and, when I told him how much money I was being guaranteed, did not come back with a counter-offer. Though I was happy about my soon-to-increase pay, I was just a little disappointed that they didn't try to lure me back.

On my last day at Goldman, when I had completed my exit interview and given up my ID card so that my next exit from the front door of 85 Broad would be my last, I received a call from Scott Pinkus, Goldman's head of Mortgage Research. Scott tried to persuade me stay on at the firm and work on applying the BDT model to asset-liability management. But he played up the software side of the work, and I felt that he, too, viewed me more as a physicist-turned-programmer than a financial modeler. In any event, it was too late for me to reverse my course. I took a short vacation in the Caribbean, and a few weeks later started work at Salomon Brothers.

Chapter 12

A Severed Head

*■ A troubled year at Salomon Brothers ■ Modeling
mortgages ■ Salomon's skill at quantitative
marketing ■ Mercifully laid off ■*

Throughout the next year I was falling in the dark. Each day I could sense the ground rushing up to meet me, like a bad plane-crash dream that ends in a startled awakening. That year at Salomon, from October 1988 to Thanksgiving 1989, was the worst I ever experienced, and much of what happened to me was as much my fault as theirs. Most of the time I simply felt incompetent. I kept thinking that perhaps I would eventually adjust. I didn't, though I learned a lot.

Mike Waldman, my new boss in Mortgage Research, had quit graduate school to move to Wall Street in the 1970s, very early in the quant game. I soon found out that though he had a quick sharp businesslike mind, he had a brusque manner and some strange habits to go with it. Early every Monday, right after I dropped Sonya at her nursery school, I would rush to our early morning mortgage group meeting where Mike led a discussion of the status of all our modeling projects. We all brought our own breakfast, and as the meeting started, Mike would devote several minutes to scratching out a circular moatlike groove in each half of his sliced bagel, throwing away the doughy detritus and leaving behind a scooped-out half bagel crust into which you could then put butter or jam. It was very disconcerting. I was enviously impressed one morning when someone else in the group got the nerve to ask him "Does it taste better that way?"

I was Mike's lieutenant in charge of research on adjustable rate mortgages (ARMs, for short), something I knew little about when I arrived. I had never had any formal education in mortgage markets; flung into the middle of this, and supposedly supervising people who knew more about it than I did, I began to read the Salomon Brothers research papers on the topic.

The American mortgage market, I learned, was gigantic, comparable to that of Treasury bonds. At the individual level, savings banks all over the country lend money to homeowners who need to finance their housing purchase. In exchange, homeowners contract to repay the loan over 15 or 30 years in equal monthly installments of interest and principal. ARMS are mortgages with an *adjustable* rate of interest that, every six months, for example, floats up or down in approximate synchrony with short-term Treasury interest rates according to some specified formula. Correspondingly, every six months, the homeowner's monthly mortgage payment changes, too.

ARMs have all sorts of additional wrinkles. They start out the first year with a "teaser," an unusually low and tempting interest rate. Then, over time, as the rate adjusts, there is a cap on how high it can float and a floor on how low it can sink. Finally, although a mortgage may have a nominal life of 15 or 30 years, a homeowner can choose to terminate the loan early by prepaying the unpaid balance—a smart thing to do if interest rates have fallen so low that a totally new mortgage with a lower interest rate is preferable.

Banks who lend to homeowners own the mortgage, the claim to the homeowner's future monthly repayments. Periodically, the banks turn around and sell the mortgages they have acquired to GNMA, FNMA, and FHLMC, government agencies that act as financial intermediaries by pooling together vast quantities of similar but not identical mortgages into more standardized securities. They then resell these pools to large investors—mutual funds, pension funds, insurance companies, hedge funds, and the like—in search of interest-bearing investments. This process of asset acquisition, pooling, standardization, and subsequent sale provides a liquidity that frees the savings banks to make more loans. As a result, the percentage of residents who own their own homes is greater in the United States than anywhere else in the world.

Mortgages are messy, though it takes only a little careful high-school math to work out the monthly mortgage payment that will draw the loan down to zero over 15 years. But that's just the start. Everything about an adjustable rate mortgage pool—the interest payments, the principal repayments, and so on—varies with the future level of interest rates, so an ARM is really a complex option whose payments are contingent on interest rates.

To estimate what a mortgage pool is worth, you have to rely on a model of future interest rates, something like the BDT model I had worked on, in fact. You then simulate the pool's future cash flows, averaging over thousands of interest-rate scenarios generated by the model. You want to represent the future evolution of long- and short-term interest rates as realistically as possible, and then, for each future scenario, compute the adjustment in the floating ARM interest rate that a homeowner will pay each month. You also want to try to estimate from past experience what percentage of homeowners will prepay their mortgage as a consequence of the change in rates on each scenario, since this prepayment alters the cash flows, too. The output of this Monte Carlo simulation model is the current value of the mortgage pool.

Mortgage valuation models involve a witch's brew of assumptions about yield curve movements and how homeowners respond to them, none of them well-tested. Even the ZIP code of the homeowners who owned the houses that were financed by the mortgages in a pool is important—some localities, based on their socioeconomic classification, had a greater tendency to prepay than others—and I had heard of investors who actually went to check out the neighborhoods for themselves. Compared to the rigor and predictability of physics or even the simple elegance of the Black-Scholes formalism, mortgage valuation is ugly. I once remarked on this to Steve Ross whose investment company, Roll & Ross Asset Management, specialized in mortgages. "Whenever I see something complex and confusing in the investment area," he retorted, "I see the scope for getting a little extra benefit out of being smart."

It's a good answer, and probably true, but I still find mortgages unattractive. Black-Scholes is clean and simple, like the theory of the hydrogen atom. Modeling mortgages is involved and approximate, more like trying to explain the structure of the energy levels in the uranium isotope U^{238}. I prefer clean problems. Still, mortgages were what I had signed on to deal with.

Salomon was a tough place. The first thing I noticed when I started work was that everyone came late for meetings. The most senior people arrived last, each of them popping their heads into the door to see if everyone else was there and then quickly leaving again if they weren't. The junior people took advantage of this chronic lateness to be late themselves. Everyone was so determined to not have his or her own time wasted that they collectively wasted everyone else's. This would not have happened at Goldman.

The level of fear that permeated Salomon was more evident, too. Friends of mine who wanted to leave the firm were semiparanoid that their bosses would discover that they were interviewing elsewhere and then fire them before they left. I never heard anyone at Goldman speak this way; despite the natural tension between employer and employee, most Goldman workers never imagined that exercising their right to look at other jobs would naturally lead to being fired.

There were other signs of Salomon's take-no-prisoners culture. In the 1980s, the BPA group had written a series of renowned reports for clients on valuing swaps and other recently invented derivatives contracts. Each report's distinctive light brown cover bore the names of its authors printed in a darker brown. Then, over the years, as one or more of the original authors left the firm for other banks or trading houses, BPA would reprint the report, having removed the departed authors' names. Eventually there were old but popular reports still being distributed that apparently had no author at all. This Orwellian rewriting of history struck me as particularly petty and ineffective, an affront to the notion of research.

At Goldman the enemies were competing firms; at Salomon the enemies were competing colleagues. Shortly before they were acquired by Citigroup, I met with an old friend still working there and asked him what had caused a well-known acquaintance of ours to have been laid off by the firm. "Oh him," my friend said, "It turned out he couldn't even code a Black-Scholes model!" Now, the Black-Scholes model is so fundamental and ubiquitous that I had little doubt that this was false. But, more interestingly, I asked, how did anyone actually know that our friend couldn't code the model? Who had put him to the test?

Everyone in the Salomon quant group, I was told, had to recreate their own computer code for even the simplest things that other people could already do, because no one who had created something independently was willing to share it. This was in diametric contrast to the situation at Goldman, where, because this kind of backstabbing was frowned upon, software was shared. At Goldman it would have taken longer to find out that someone couldn't do something as straightforward as code a simple model.

The most impenetrable barrier was the wall between Meriwether's group and everyone else. Occasionally I would catch distant glimpses of the arb group. Meriwether, Haghani, Hawkins, Krasker and their colleagues sat together in the center of the trading floor, a world apart from everyone else, a little Persian carpet marking the center of their privileged domain, an exalted clique of happy people who awed everyone and knew it. They had their own inviolably secret models, their own inaccessible data, their own computer systems and system administrators, all exclusively theirs. They also had access, if they wanted it, to the best models and minds in BPA, via a one-way street that ran only in their direction. They were an elite force, a Republican guard who could do whatever they wanted, and everyone half-envied, half-resented them for it. They had it all—knowledge, independence, prestige, and lots of money.

I attributed many of these cultural divergences between Salomon and Goldman to the structural differences between a public company and a private partnership. Goldman, then still private, functioned more smoothly because it was run by partners seeded uniformly throughout the firm. They were the daily overseers who didn't possess a liquid stock to sell, and so their long-term profit depended on the firm remaining intact. As a result, any excessive egotism was eventually squelched, sooner rather than later, because someone in control, despite his or her desire to win that particular battle, realized that it was harmful to the firm. Goldman people always told you that Goldman people were nicer, worked better together, were less political. Though this was not entirely true, the constant talking about it helped make it a self-fulfilling prophecy. No matter how self-interested the partners were, their long-term interests were tied up in the entire company, not just in their little piece of it.

In the words of a famous Goldman ex-partner, Gus Levy, Goldman was long-term greedy rather than short-term greedy. At Salomon, I thought, it was every man for himself and God against them all.

The key responsibility of my research group was to support the ARMs dealers, who, unlike the arb group, were more interested in earning a spread by servicing clients than in carrying out genuine proprietary trading. We helped them by writing short quantitative marketing reports that provided generally truthful ammunition for use by the salespeople. When the desk acquired some new pool of mortgages, we ran our models on them and tried to explain where their value lay.

There was a range of different models and corresponding metrics that you could use to gauge the value of a pool. The simplest measure was the total profit that the pool would yield to a purchaser over its lifetime, assuming interest rates in the future remained unchanged. The most complex, which used interest-rate simulation models of the BDT type I had helped develop at Goldman, was Salomon's option-adjusted spread model that reported the spread over Treasury bonds the pool would generate, on average, over all future interest-rate scenarios.

We ran daily reports on the desk's inventory using both these models. Different clients preferred different metrics, depending on their sophistication and on the accounting rules and regulations to which they were subject. We also did some longer-term, client-focused research, developing improved statistical models for homeowner prepayments or programs for valuing the more exotic ARM-based structures that were growing in popularity.

The traders on the desk used the option-adjusted spread model to decide how much to bid for newly available ARM pools. The calculation was arduous. Each pool consisted of a variety of mortgages with a range of coupons and a spectrum of servicing fees, and the option-adjusted spread was calculated by averaging over thousands of future scenarios, each one involving a month-by-month simulation of interest rates over hundreds of months. Because the number and size of the monthly payments received from the pool varied in a complex path-dependent way with changes in interest rates, in 1989, on even the fastest computers, it took vast amounts time to perform the calculations that led to the model's recommended bid.

What made all of this complex work so unpleasant was the extreme urgency of the demands from the desk coupled with the archaic nature of the computer models we used. Often, we had less than thirty minutes to prepare a bid for a pool. The outdated and unfriendly FORTRAN program used to calculate the option-adjusted spread had been written many years earlier. In order to value the pool, the program needed the parameters that described its constituents: how many subgroups of mortgages it contained, each subgroup's coupon and maturity, the caps and floors on the interest rate, and so on. You had to type these numbers into a file in a prespecified order with exactly the right number of blank spaces between each number. Then the program ran on a powerful supercomputer bought solely for this purpose.

On a typical day, the starting gun fired when the desk received a page-long fax from a savings-and-loan with the pool's parameters. We then had a half-hour to type the parameters into the input file and submit it to the supercomputer, which in ideal circumstances took about ten minutes to complete its calculations. So, every ten minutes impatient traders would call from the desk for the answer.

Unfortunately, the program was totally unforgiving about input: If there were just one blank character too many or too few, the program silently hiccupped, and then went into an infinite loop, pointlessly churning away on misread data without ever producing an answer. As a result, for the first ten or fifteen minutes you would sit there nervously waiting for the program to terminate and an answer to appear on the screen, all the while wondering whether the supercomputer was simply running a little slowly that day, or whether you had mistyped the number of blanks and were now in purgatory. If fifteen minutes elapsed without an answer, you could assume you had made a mistake; you then killed the program and started over. It was agonizing.

This schedule of pool valuations dominated our life. Someone always had to be on duty, preferably someone who could type very fast. It was maddening to stand by and watch the one slow typist in our group chicken-peck her way across the keyboard when there was a rush to bid. If you left your desk for a while, you had to tell the secretary where you could be reached. No one thought of taking more than a one-week vacation. When I did take two weeks in the summer of 1989, I could sense Mike's displeasure at my lack of professionalism.

Once a week there was an early-morning meeting of S, T, and R, as the hollowly upbeat sales manager liked to refer to sales, trading, and research, linking their names together in an effort to give equal status to research. Occasionally I had to deliver a brief two-minute presentation to the salespeople on the attractive characteristics of some new ARMs pool we had acquired. The first time I did this I was still shaky and insecure about the peculiarities of mortgages, and a consultant was brought in to prep me on how to talk from a script without seeming to look at it. His trick was to use very large type, so you could invisibly scan ahead and memorize one phrase at a time with a quick glance down, all the while maintaining apparent eye contact with your audience. The rehearsals and videotaping were demeaning, but it was an illustration of their totally professional approach.

What impressed me most about Salomon was precisely the professional way they used quantitative research to generate business. I thought of financial research as a scientific endeavor, and I loved it with an amateur's passion. At Salomon, they were businessmen: They used financial modeling as a marketing tool, and they tackled it like merchandisers. They were experts at using models as yardsticks to measure and then rank different securities by value, and they were proficient at then using those rankings to push securities to clients.

I wasn't good at marketing and I disliked it, but I learned a lot that year. I also grew to see the logic of using models as sales tools. The truth is that there are so many different securities in the world, so many varieties of stocks, bonds, options, and even bonds with embedded optionality, that it's very difficult for anyone to know which security in a class provides the best value. A model can provide you with a conceptual basis for thinking about value; it can project a scattered universe of bond prices onto a one-dimensional line that orders them by value.

I came to see that creating a successful financial model is not just a battle for finding the truth, but also a battle for the hearts and minds of the people who use it. The right model and the right concept, when they make thinking about value easier, can stick and take over the world. A firm whose clients start to rely on the results that its model generates can dominate the market. This is what happened with Salomon's concept of option-adjusted spread—a short while after they invented it, every other firm on the Street was writing their own version of the model to do the same analysis, because clients demanded it.

Salomon people, who had been in the quantitative business much longer than Goldman, thought about research in this way instinctively. As soon as I arrived, I noticed that their salespeople and quants were prodigiously agile at using quick, back-of-the-envelope methods to compare bonds in terms of yield to maturity or option-adjusted spread. All new hires, not only traders and salespeople but even quants, went through a several-month-long training program. I say "even quants" with real admiration, because at Goldman, in those days, it was considered a luxurious waste of resources to send quants to a training program. Salomon's fixed-income program was exceptional. It was taught by traders, salespeople, and quants who together covered market conventions as well as quantitative concepts and the use of quantitative tools. There were regular exams, and the trainees became expert at bond math. Everyone had studied Homer and Leibowitz's classic *Inside the Yield Curve*; they emerged from the program with a visceral feel for yields, forward rates, and durations.

To my admiration, it was clear that someone at Salomon had once understood the advantages of a firmwide, uniform interface to all its models. The sales tools and models that everyone in the firm used in 1989 ran on an outmoded and clunky Quotron terminal, an infrastructure that had been built in the 1970s under the farsighted leadership of Michael Bloomberg. Awkward though it was, everyone at Salomon had learned how to use the Quotron proficiently to access internal and external information, in much the way that people used Web browsers a decade or more later. In 1989 Bloomberg was no longer at Salomon but already the head of his burgeoning information and modeling-tool empire, and his Bloomberg terminal for clients was by that time far in advance of the Quotron. A few years later I was pleased to see that the BDT model, too, was available through his terminals.

Throughout 1989 my problems worsened. In truth, I was still a bit of an amateur who didn't know as much about the world of sales as most of the comparably senior people around me. My friends Mark Koenigsberg and Armand Tatevossian still tease me about a stupid answer

I gave to a question about the term structure of volatility that Mike squeezed out of me at a BPA meeting. I can only plead guilty. It didn't help that Mark would joke publicly about how much money he imagined I had been guaranteed to join BPA.

Month after month I clenched my teeth and tried to stick it out. Sometimes I imagined that with enough time I would eventually manage to become one of them. Most of the time, however, I longed to leave, but since my employment contract guaranteed my bonus for 1988 and my total compensation for all of 1989, I was reluctant to give that up, and so I struggled on.

Working for Mike was no pleasure, though, even for someone with fewer faults than I had. He seemed to have to control everything. Sometime in early 1990 Phelim Boyle, a well-known pioneer of quantitative finance and a professor at the University of Waterloo in Canada, invited me to speak at an academic conference on the BDT model, which had just been published. Mike refused to allow me to attend and to talk about my previously published work, even on my own time. When I asked why, he smiled and said that we shouldn't help the competition. Like many bosses on Wall Street, he thought he owned the people who worked for him. I suppose I believed that, too. I turned down the invitation.

I wasn't the only unhappy person in the mortgage group. In the end, I noticed that those who had previously enjoyed some semblance of an independent life, in business or academia, could not long tolerate Mike's need to stifle them. Most of the senior people who joined during that year were gone a year later. Some, like me, had to leave because they were too different from Mike; others I knew, like Ravi Mattu who had moved to Salomon from Citibank, had to leave because they too closely resembled Mike in their skill sets and felt suffocated. Only fresh young recruits who had been imperceptibly eased into servitude before they knew any other kind of life could tolerate the incessant control. Finally, a few years later, I heard that Mike himself had to leave.

My personal end came fast. In late 1989, in a bad market, Salomon began to lay off staff. Layoffs are always more convenient for a firm than firings; it is easier to let someone go because of adverse economic conditions than because of some inadequacy that might be challenged in court. Firms do not publicize the names of the people laid off, but this is how it works: First, you hear the general rumor that layoffs are about to occur. Then you begin to hear mention of one or two people who have suddenly disappeared from work. Finally, you notice that some of the people you normally interact with are beginning to avoid you. Later, you realize that they knew in advance. The sad truth is that when you know that friends or colleagues are about to be laid off and you can do nothing about it, you avoid them, too.

One day, walking together down the stairwell between floors, Mike encouraged me to explain really thoroughly to the young man working for me exactly how far I had progressed with my regression model of ARMs prepayment rates. "Got to keep bringing the younger generation up to speed!" he smirked unconvincingly, as he tried to make sure nothing would be lost when I was gone. I understood subliminally that I was going to be let go, but I couldn't quite absorb it. I continued to think of sticking it out until I found a better job, but I didn't really look for one.

Then, one afternoon, early in the Thanksgiving week of 1989, I received a call at my desk from Mike, who asked me to descend a few floors to see him in an office downstairs. I felt my heart sink into my stomach. I quickly called Eva, telling her I thought that "it" was about to happen. She told me in the nicest way not to worry about it. Then I left my office and went downstairs.

When I knocked on the door of the unfamiliar office to which I had been summoned, Mike opened it. Inside were Tom Klaffky, who had hired me, Marty Leibowitz who ran all of BPA, and someone from Human Resources or the legal department to ensure that everything was done properly. I sat down and, in words I no longer recall, they told me that I was being laid off, but that I would continue to be paid (at a lower rate, *sans* bonus) for a few more months. They told me to debrief the people working for me about the state of my projects and then to leave the building.

When you're told to leave, you feel as though you've done something shameful and you simply slink out. I spent a short time with the young man who worked for me, who had obviously been told what was coming, and then, without a farewell to anyone, set off to meet my wife and daughter Sonya at a pediatrician's appointment, glad to have a distraction. Finally, it was just about over.

We celebrated Thanksgiving with friends in upstate New York a few days later; then, on the last Sunday of the holiday weekend, I drove downtown to my office at Salomon at 7 A.M., when it was certain that no one would be there to see me, to pack my books into boxes for shipping. A few days later I received confused calls from Mark and Armand, who had no idea why I was no longer at work.

Ultimately, it wasn't that bad. I like to imagine there was a kind of karma working its way with me: If I hadn't left FSG for Salomon, if I hadn't suffered the humiliations of the inadequacy I felt at Salomon that year, I would never eventually have come back to a position at Goldman that suited my skills and personality so much better.

I never saw Mike Waldman again, though for about a year I often had fantasies of what I would say if we met on the street. But, about six years later I was invited to give a speech about Fischer Black on the occasion of his posthumous induction into the Fixed Income Analysts Society Hall of Fame. At the award luncheon I found myself seated at the table of honor adjacent to Marty Leibowitz, by then the Chief Investment Officer at the TIAA-CREF, Teachers Insurance and Annuity Association-College Retirement Equities Fund. As Waldman's boss's boss at Salomon, he had delivered my sentence on that November day in 1989. This time he was cordial and complimentary, and neither of us mentioned the circumstances in which we had last spoken to each other.

Chapter 13

Civilization and Its Discontents

■ Goldman as home ■ Heading the Quantitative Strategies Group ■ Equity derivatives ■ The Nikkei puts and exotic options ■ Nothing beats working closely with traders ■ Financial engineering becomes a real field ■

O ut on the street in December 1989, I grew slightly panicked. I visited headhunters, went on job interviews and called most of the people I knew. Several possibilities emerged, none compelling. I had no desire to fall into the wrong position; I had seen too many people move from one one-year job to another, making money but spoiling their reputation.

Through all these mental peregrinations I thought of Fischer as my lender of last resort. Holding no grudge against me for having left Goldman, he brought me in to interview with the Quantitative Strategies (QS) group he led in the Equities Division. There I reacquainted myself with Jeff Wecker, who was in charge of the trading systems being built in the group, and Bill Toy. I also met Bob Granovsky, a yellow-bearded, perpetually perplexed-looking equity options trader whom everyone called "Granny"; he had been there trading options for as long as anyone could remember. Then Fischer offered me a job.

I had been the head of a group in FSG and at Salomon, but QS was a small, flat organization with no managerial slot for me. Nevertheless, I thought the position would suit my abilities—at bottom, I liked doing research. I did worry a little about pay—Bill Toy, now departing the quant world to realize his dream of moving to the business side, warned me that compensation in equities was lower than it was in fixed income. I queried Fischer who brushed this aside. Without further anxiety, in mid-December I accepted my destiny and agreed to return to Goldman and begin working for Fischer on January 22, 1990.

It didn't go as planned. A few days before I was to start, Fischer unexpectedly called me at home to say that he was leaving the Equities Division for Goldman Sachs Asset Management (GSAM), and that he had recommended that Jeff Wecker and I jointly comanage QS. Shortly thereafter, the heads of the Equities Division sent out a Memo To All that announced Fischer's move and our ascension to his former role. Nowhere did the memo mention that I was not currently an employee of Goldman Sachs. In subsequent years I learned that there's nothing the firm likes more than the appearance of a smooth transition.

For Fischer, GSAM may not have been the best place, and I suspect they twisted his arm to move him there. Coinventor of the world's most famous and useful financial model, he was more of a thinker than the manager or salesman that GSAM needed. Though his attitude to change was invariably positive and though he had only praise for the firm, I felt that they had not completely figured out how to use him to their greatest advantage.

For me, though, this was a lucky stroke and the beginning of several years of the most absorbing work I had ever had, a time of almost drunk delight, tempered though it was by battle with my peers (and bosses) far on the ringing plains of lower Manhattan. I was immensely happy to return to Goldman Sachs, and lucky, too. By Wall Street standards it was a civilized place. During bad times in bad organizations, I had sometimes childishly wished for retribution, willing to be hurt myself as long as it hurt my employers, too. I never felt that way about Goldman. It was the only place I never secretly hoped would crash and burn.

Jeff thought it wonderful that he and I had an opportunity to step into Fischer's shoes, and predicted that we would be Goldman Sachs partners in a few years. Older, less upbeat and more battered by history, I was dubious about our prospects. Still, I set about acclimating to my new home after so many years as a fixed-income person.

In 1990, Equities was the most old-fashioned division at Goldman. Its workers radiated a genteel white-collar, white-shoe pedigree, and they looked down on the rough-and-tumble *nouveau riche* world of the Fixed Income bond traders, who in their turn thought themselves a little classier than J. Aron, the commodities and currencies business Goldman had acquired in the 1970s. That year I met a woman from Aron who didn't have the obvious Harvard/Wharton aristocratic pedigree typical of so many Goldman employees, and she unashamedly told me that she would never have been at Goldman had she not been a part of J. Aron when they were acquired. Aron had a scrappy make-do culture, and by 2004 their people were running most of the trading divisions in the firm, including equities.

The QS group Jeff and I inherited was a hodgepodge mix of about four employees and five long-term consultants who together occupied a messy warren of shared offices and cubicles in a corner of Equities on the twenty-ninth floor of 85 Broad Street. I liked the augury of my new phone number, 902-0129, whose last four digits I superstitiously interpreted to indicate that I was Number One on Twenty-Nine.

We were ideally located about forty feet away from the derivatives trading desk, distant enough so you could concentrate quietly when necessary, but sufficiently close to feel part of the same team. You could stroll over and talk to traders about the market at the end of the day without seeming too pointed. This proximity to the trading desk lasted only six months; after that, as both QS and the derivatives business expanded, we moved a few floors away and lost our sense of community. From then on it became much harder to acquire the skill of communicating with traders, one of the more difficult tasks facing a new quant.

Our offices were crowded and littered; piles of documents blocked the corridors between the cubicles, and the disorganization made a bad impression on clients who occasionally visited the sales and trading floor. Periodically one of the heads of Equities would walk by and threaten reprisals if order were not restored. The worst culprit was Bill Toy, whose desk and office floor was stacked one to two feet high with every squirreled-away piece of paper he had ever read or written on— he was unable to part with anything. When Bill used to complain about wanting to make more money, Jeff would tell him that the easiest way to get a $50,000 raise was to clean up his desk, and I think it was true.

The only traditional financial modeler in Fischer's ex-group was Piotr Karasinski, then still busy writing the paper on the Black-Karasinski yield-curve model. Most of the other members were talented hardware and software consultants who had been hired and managed by Jeff to focus on electronic stock-trading software. Long before most people, Fischer had foreseen the application of information technology to trading; in 1971 he had written an influential paper entitled *Toward a Fully Automated Exchange*. Now, together with Jeff, he was nudging the firm in that direction. It was prescient work, but a little early; if he had lived another ten years to witness the growth of computerized exchanges he would have had a riper laboratory in which to test his ideas.

The hardware focus of the QS consultants permeated our surroundings. Shelves piled high with old computer parts ran along the walls of the long, narrow, dark office I inhabited, reminding me of the garbage dump of broken robot parts that C-3PO used to repair himself in the movie *Star Wars*. I remember the look of suppressed puzzlement on John Hull's face when he visited me there that year and found that people he thought of as quants were spending so much time and energy on technology. In truth, though, that was what the business needed. I had seen over and over again during the past few years that a model only gains its power when embedded in a useable trading system.

The QS consultants were paid by the hour and many of them worked the shifted day of computer geeks, starting late in the morning and programming away spacily with CD players on their desk and headphones on their ears. This was an unfamiliar and unprofessional look in 1990, especially on a floor that clients visited, and we tried to bring a more superficially businesslike look to the group. It wasn't easy. One consultant who left his CD player inside his unlocked desk drawer overnight found it gone one morning. He spent the first half of that day speaking to Security in an attempt to find it, and the second half arguing that we should reimburse him for the stolen player. It was with great difficulty that I refrained from pointing out that he had spent the last eight hours looking for the CD player, and that his hourly rate for that time had already exceeded the cost of it.

The Equities floor I now worked on had a character very different from the Fixed Income atmosphere I knew so well. In 1990, Equities had not yet lost its aura of a small, exclusive, old-world club. Partners had their daily lunch brought to them on a large silver tray delivered by a gracious, white-coated food server, each plate covered by its own elegant warming dome. There were luxuries for less important people, too. Employees on the trading floor received free food during the day; when you arrived in the morning, a gentleman dropped by to pick up your food order on which you could select anything you liked from a collection of local restaurant menus. The point was to keep you at your desk while the markets were open and clients were calling.

Almost everyone ordered monumentally large helpings of lunch, drinks, and snacks. It was simply hard to resist. Sitting surrounded by individual plastic containers of fresh carrots, celery sticks, strawberries, quartered kiwis and sliced peaches, nibbling the day away, you saw that someone else had ordered a container of cherries and thought "What a good idea. I'll do that tomorrow." At 11:30 A.M. the hot food started to arrive—swordfish, steak, potatoes, rice, asparagus, whatever you wanted. To help wash it down, our food server Neil delivered six-packs of Evian or Perrier, the smallest round lot. Some people actually left for home in the late afternoon with doggy bags of food and mineral water.

I disliked the free-food perk. By noon, I had grown bloated from consuming a day's worth of food in only a few hours, and I was genuinely relieved at the loss of that privilege when QS was moved off the trading floor in mid-1990. It was easier to simply pay for what you really wanted. Later, after the fixed-income market's losses of late 1994, everyone on the trading floor had their food privileges revoked, and from then on traders, salespeople and their assistants had to go to the cafeteria or a local takeout place and buy their own food. There was an elegant VP lounge at the top of 85 Broad Street, where vice presidents could reserve sit-down formal lunches at tables bedecked with white tablecloths, waited on, for some mysterious reason, by uniformed, German-accented, middle-aged women who reminded one vaguely of Rosa Klebb. The restaurant was shut down in 1994, too, and it was high time; it harkened back to an age when being a vice president was something rare and significant. Ten years later during the dot-com boom of 2000, when casual clothing ruled, free snacks made a temporary comeback and every day each floor received Snapples, bottled water, and very fancy, presliced, Harry-and-David-style fruit. This, too, disappeared when the technology IPO market collapsed. You could see Wall Street's behavior—its manic depressive, feast-or-famine style of hiring and firing, expanding and contracting, large raises followed by large cuts—all mirrored in the waxing and waning of the food supply.

My boss was Dexter Earle, a partner at Goldman and a salesperson. This was the time in my life when I began quite unselfconsciously to refer to the person I worked for as "my boss." My wife didn't like to hear me use the phrase; she was still in academic life and thought it a dysphemism, but I had learned over the years to regard it as merely realistic. Dexter's expertise was in portfolio rebalancing, so he didn't know that much about options and volatility, but he was willing to joke about his ignorance, smiling charmingly as though it didn't matter when, at group dinners, people occasionally roasted him by handing out blank books entitled *Dexter Earle on Derivatives*. With the confidence of graciousness, polish, silk ties, and matching suspenders, he outlasted by many years the more knowledgable but abrasive comanagers the firm brought in to assist him in running the equity derivatives business. Dexter was terrific with clients—we all used to laugh at the story of how, when Dexter was asked by a client about Goldman's approach to AI (artificial intelligence software), he parried by replying that "we are going to take a global approach and go slow." But what impressed me most was his ability to tell when someone was misleading him about topics he didn't understand. When we listened to the occasional confident-sounding information technology fact-spinners whom I knew to be half-charlatan, the heads of trading usually bought their stories of expertise, but Dexter, a salesman himself, could identify the hollowness beneath the surface.

Dexter's secretary was a pleasantly stern woman with a penchant for odd, homeopathic remedies. The first time I went to speak to her, she made me stand impatiently at her desk for five or ten minutes while she unhurriedly filled out various administrative forms. As I waited, an old Mother Goose couplet I used to read to my children suddenly flashed through my consciousness: *I am his Majesty's dog at Kew/ Pray tell me sir, whose dog are you?* Years earlier, reading it aloud without thinking, I had thought it only a forced rhyme about a talking dog. Now, I suddenly understood it. Though I was "upstairs" and more critical to the business than she was, she was "downstairs" in a finer establishment. As years went by I learned that quants, like the little boy in A. A. Milne's poem, are always halfway down the stairs.

The new new thing in the derivatives world in 1990 was exotic options. My absorption in this world was triggered by the excitement at Goldman over what we all referred to as the "Kingdom of Denmark puts."

On the last trading day of 1989, the Nikkei 225 index of Japanese stocks reached its zenith of 38,915.90. Throughout its ascent during what is in retrospect called the Japanese equity bubble, many Japanese companies had come to the capital markets to borrow from investors. Sometimes, in order to pay even lower interest rates, the companies had promised to eventually pay back more than they had initially borrowed, provided the Nikkei were to drop by the time the loan came due, an event to which they ascribed little probability. The greater the drop, the more yen the companies promised to repay. In options parlance, the companies had given their bondholders put options on the Nikkei, thus providing them with an insurance policy against a Nikkei decline. Some bondholders kept the bonds but sold the attached puts for cash to interested parties.

As the Nikkei ascended to ever higher levels during the late 1980s, Granny had adroitly and systematically bought large numbers of these puts that now collectively constituted a gigantic insurance policy against a decline in the Nikkei. He had bought them inexpensively, probably because the companies that issued them did not believe a sustained decline in the Nikkei was possible back in those days of soaring Tokyo property values and rising Japanese equity markets.

When I arrived in QS at the start of that year, everyone in derivatives was talking about the Kingdom of Denmark Nikkei put warrants. I heard that it was puzzled-looking Granny who had come up with the idea that Goldman issue a listed put on the Nikkei. Since we owned the inexpensive insurance against a Nikkei decline that Granny had bought, we could now sell similar protection to the public. So, in January 1990 Goldman created the Kingdom of Denmark Nikkei put warrants, struck at a Nikkei level of ¥37,516.77 with an expiration date in early 1993. They were listed on the American Stock Exchange, and the Kingdom-of-Denmark prefix referred to the issuer of the warrants,

the sovereign Kingdom of Denmark to whom we paid a fee to guarantee that they would stand behind the put warrants in the event that
Goldman's credit failed.

Our issuance was exquisitely timed; the Nikkei was just past its peak,
and many buyers were willing to bet on its further decline. Granny had
bought cheap Nikkei volatility from Japanese yen-based counterparties
who didn't believe that the Nikkei would drop, and was now able to sell
it to American dollar-based investors who were betting it would. Most
profitable options strategies I have seen have had the same formula: Buy
some simple, less attractive product wholesale, use financial engineering
to transform it into something more appealing, and then sell it retail. It's
a transformation that requires an understanding of clients' needs as well
as technical skills.

To accomplish this, Granny added a custom-tailored, exotic subtlety
to the structure of the Kingdom of Denmark Nikkei put warrants that
I haven't yet mentioned. The Nikkei is an index of 225 Japanese stocks
whose prices are quoted in yen. An American dollar–based investor in
the Nikkei index effectively owns Japanese stocks denominated in yen,
and then faces two risks: that the Nikkei drops and that the yen weak-
ens against the dollar. American investors were happy to buy insurance
against a drop in the Nikkei, of course, but they didn't want their insurance payment to decline if the yen were to simultaneously weaken as
the Nikkei fell, a not unlikely occurrence. Therefore, the Kingdom of
Denmark Nikkei put warrants also carried built-in protection against a
drop in the yen by guaranteeing that, irrespective of what happened to
the actual yen-dollar exchange rate, the payoff of the warrant would be
converted to dollars at an exchange rate guaranteed in advance.

For example, if the Nikkei were to drop from 37,500 to 25,000, a
drop of 12,500 index points or 33 percent, the holder of a put warrant
with a face value of $1,000 and a guaranteed conversion rate of $1 per
yen would receive $333, even if the yen (to take an extreme scenario)
were to become worthless in dollar terms. If the conversion rate had not
been guaranteed, the holder of a warrant whose payoff was converted to
dollars at the prevailing exchange rate would have received no dollars at
all. This was a very attractive feature for American investors, who naturally measure their profits or losses in dollars—it allowed them to profit
from an overdue decline in the Japanese stock market without worrying about its effect on the yen.

The market came to refer to this feature as a "quanto" option, though I always preferred calling it a "guaranteed exchange rate" (GER) option, which seemed more apt. This was the first nonstandard or so-called exotic option I remember encountering, and like most successful structured products, its payoff reflected investors' needs.

This is where the role of financial engineering enters the picture. Even though Granny had bought yen-based puts cheaply and sold the Kingdom of Denmark puts more expensively to avid investors and speculators, there was a dangerous mismatch between their payoffs that could have eliminated our profit. The options we bought would pay us in yen if the Nikkei declined, but the Kingdom of Denmark puts we sold would oblige us to pay our counterparties in dollars. A move in the dollar-yen exchange rate could therefore diminish or even wipe out our profit. To prevent this from occurring, we would have to continually hedge the effect of any move in the dollar-yen exchange rate on the value of both the options we had bought and those we had sold.

Just as a clothing designer must factor the cost of labor, cloth, and trimmings into a garment's price, so we had to reflect the cost of hedging in the price we charged for our GER option. The hedging strategy involved daily trading in the Nikkei and the yen, a strategy whose estimated cost we had to include in the price we charged for the Kingdom of Denmark puts.

Black and Scholes had shown in 1973 that the fair value of a standard stock option was the price of hedging it over its lifetime. They derived a partial differential equation for the option's value and had shown how to solve it. Ever since, academics and practitioners had kept busy by extending that insight to all sorts of other options. Now, in late 1989, Piotr Karasinski had found an analogous partial differential equation for the fair value of the Kingdom of Denmark GER put. Much to the surprise and near disbelief of everyone on the desk, he had shown that its value depends on the correlation between moves in the dollar-yen exchange rate and moves in the Nikkei index. It was counterintuitive, almost paradoxical that the degree of correlation between the Nikkei level and the yen should influence the value of a GER Nikkei put whose payoff was designed to be independent of the value of the yen.

When I returned to Goldman in that first month of 1990, everyone was focused on the Nikkei puts, in particular on how to value and hedge them. I soon met Dan O'Rourke, an options trader newly hired

by Granny a few months earlier, and now responsible for the daily hedging of the Nikkei book. Dan and I saw the world similarly. First, we both
understood that models alone were inadequate, no matter how good
they were. What traders need is standardized systems that contain the
models, systems that force them to use the models in disciplined ways.
Our traders were managing their books on an inadequate and unreliable Lotus spreadsheet that any trader could modify at his whim. It was
not the right way to run a business. We felt it was critical to build a risk
management system tailored to Nikkei options, analogous to the sort of
trading system I had helped build in FSG for the bond options desk,
similar to the sort of system Garbasz had tried to create in Chicago. You
needed a dedicated computer program to keep track of the hedging of
the hundreds of options, futures, and currency positions that constituted
our desk's Nikkei volatility book. Second, and more importantly in the
short run, Dan and Bill Toy convinced me of the importance of demon-
strating to the traders that Piotr's counterintuitive formula for the value
of a GER put was correct.

I began by trying to penetrate to the essence of Piotr's formula for the
value of a GER option. If you wanted to explain an options formula to
a trader, you couldn't resort to stochastic calculus and partial differential
equations. Even now, when traders are more likely to have a mathematical background, you still need to have an intuitive way of showing them
that a formula makes sense. I'm never satisfied with myself until I understand equations in a low-tech, visceral way. Therefore I decided to forget about deriving the partial differential equation for the Kingdom
of Denmark GER option, and instead tried to obtain a more easily understandable explanation of its fair value. Feynman's rules for quantum
electrodynamics are a poor man's tool for calculating the probability of
complex scattering events correctly. In a lesser but similar way,
I wanted to find a set of consistent rules that would let you convince a
poor trader that an option formula was right without resorting to the
advanced mathematics behind dynamic options replication.

I thought about what the Black-Scholes formula really tells you.
In principle, you can derive the formula from the Merton strategy of
dynamic replication; from this point of view, the formula dictates in ex-
quisite detail exactly how to synthesize a stock option out of a chang-

ing mixture of stock and riskless bonds. But looked at more naively, the formula gives you the fair price of the option in terms of the current price of the stock and the current price of a riskless bond. Its key insight is that the option is a mixture. Like the ancient Greeks' mythological centaur, part horse and part man, a call option is a hybrid, too—part stock and part bond. From this point of view, I came to regard the Black-Scholes formula as a simple and sensible way of interpolating from the known market prices of a stock and a bond to the fair value of the hybrid. Several economists, Paul Samuelson among them, had come almost imperceptibly close to obtaining the Black-Scholes formula before Black and Scholes by means of this kind of reasoning.

When you want to estimate the price of fruit salad, you average the prices of the fruit the mixture contains. In a similar vein, I thought of the option formula as a prescription for estimating the price of a hybrid by averaging the known market prices of its ingredients. So I experimented with making myself a set of rules that a poor man could use for valuing options as mixtures; I tried to see if I could use them to get the right formula for the GER option. I eventually came up with the following rationale.

First, as in any mathematical problem, you have to choose your units, the *currency* in which to quote all security values. You can choose any currency you like—yen, dollars, or even shares of IBM stock as the unit measure of value; it's like deciding on inches or centimeters in reporting heights. The cost of creating an option or an apartment building should not depend on which currency you choose to perform your estimates.

In practice, a little thought often suggests a natural choice of currency that can immensely simplify the problem. To take an example outside the options world, stock market analysts often cite a stock's P/E ratio—its price divided by its annual earnings—as a measure of a stock's value. This is equivalent to using the stock's annual earnings in dollars, rather than the dollar itself, as the unit in which to report a company's stock prices. The stock price, quoted this way, automatically tells you how many years of presumed earnings you are paying for when you buy the stock at its current price.

Many of the advances in options theory in the 1990s involved nothing more than Black, Scholes, and Merton's original insight augmented by the clever choice of a more subtle unit of value than the dollar, a trick first exploited by Bill Margrabe soon after Black and Scholes invented their model. Options theorists of a mathematical bent call this trick "the choice of numeraire."

Since risk is what you are dealing with, you must then specify the *risky ingredients* of the option, those elements whose future values are unknown. Here, you aim to think of the complex option as a mix of the simplest underlying securities whose risks you understand. Options modelers call these the risk factors. For a standard stock option, for example, the stock price is the major risk factor. For the Kingdom of Denmark Nikkei put, the most important risk factors were the level of the Nikkei and the value of the dollar-yen exchange rate.

Next, you must describe *the range of future scenarios* that the values of the risky securities can take. The range is usually described by several model parameters that will have to be specified when the model is calibrated. Once you know the range of future scenarios for the risky ingredients, you can then estimate the value of any other risky security (an option, for example) as the average of its future payoffs over each of the scenarios, discounted to the present time. In the Black-Scholes model, for instance, one assumes that future stock returns lie on the common bell-shaped distribution familiar to all users of elementary statistics. This distribution is specified when you know the parameters that determine its center and width, or, put more mathematically, its mean and its standard deviation.

You must then *calibrate* the model, which means you must make its scenario parameters consistent with the current prices of the simpler, risky, underlying securities in the natural currency you've chosen. In the Black-Scholes model, calibration means ensuring that when you use the model to calculate the value of the stock itself, you reproduce the current stock price, and when you use the model to calculate the value of a riskless bond, you reproduce its price. This constraint is almost enough to pin down the Black-Scholes formula. Calibration is absolutely critical. Anytime you use your model to calculate the value of a simple risky security whose risk you understand and whose market price you know, your model must match that price—if it doesn't, you're starting off from the wrong place.

Once the model is calibrated, you can use it to calculate the value of the option as a discounted average of its future payouts over the distribution of scenarios. I like to call this interpolation, because the model is used to calculate the "middle" value of a mixture from the known prices of its ingredients at either end.

There is nothing especially original about my prescription, but it does demystify the method of options valuation while still preserving much of the economic logic. I found it a helpful way to explain models to traders, and a useful intuitive way of thinking myself. You can get the answer to many complex derivatives problems with less mathematics than you think.

I now proceeded to apply this logic, one step at a time, to the Kingdom of Denmark GER Nikkei put. Since it paid out in American dollars, I chose dollars as the natural currency. The relevant risk factors were the level of the Nikkei (in yen) and the value of the yen (in dollars). Piotr had assumed the common bell-shaped scenarios of future returns for both the Nikkei and the yen—good enough at that time when no one yet worried about the fat tails in the distributions and their effect on options prices.

To calibrate the model, I chose the values of the respective centers of the bell-shaped distributions of the Nikkei in yen and the yen in dollars so that both the prices for the Nikkei and the yen, quoted in dollars, matched their current market values. Now the model was fully specified and ready for interpolation.

Next I calculated the fair value of the put option by averaging its payout over all future Nikkei and yen scenarios, first converting that payout to dollars at the guaranteed exchange rate. To my great gratification, I immediately obtained Piotr's formula more directly. The value of the option did indeed depend on the correlation between the Nikkei in yen and the yen in dollars. My method was much easier to explain to traders; always on the search for pricing discrepancies, they instinctively grasped that a model had to be calibrated to agree with the market's dollar prices for the Nikkei and yen, securities they could buy or sell at any instant.

In physics I always used to do calculations at least two different ways and see if they agreed. I decided to do that here, too. If my rules were right and if I was careful to use them correctly, I should have obtained the same final answer for the value of the GER put even if I chose an unnatural currency. To confirm this, I perversely decided to choose the yen rather than the dollar as my currency, a more contrived choice of numeraire for evaluating a GER put that pays out in dollars. Now I calibrated the distributions to the market prices of both the Nikkei in yen and the dollar in yen. I worked out the fair value of the Nikkei put warrant in yen, even though it paid out in dollars. When I converted the warrant's final yen value to dollars at the current exchange rate, the answer was identical. Everything was consistent no matter which currency you used to solve the problem.

There was an element of paradox to the appearance of the Nikkei-yen correlation in the final formula, but over time we got to understand better why this correlation was so important. The Kingdom of Denmark Nikkei put's payout in dollars was independent of the dollar–yen exchange rate; it varied only with the level of the Nikkei. But, in order to hedge the put, you had to hedge its exposure to the Nikkei, which required taking a position in Nikkei futures whose value depended on the level of the Nikkei in yen. Owning these Nikkei futures induced a secondary exposure to the yen, which now had to be hedged, too. It was this secondary (yen) hedging of the primary (Nikkei) hedge that induced a dependence on the correlation. Once I included the cost of carrying out both hedging transactions over the lifetime of the option, I obtained the correct value for the GER put.

I was very pleased with my poor man's rederivation of Piotr's elegant result, and ran from trader to quant, excitedly explaining my understanding to anyone who would listen. Over the next few months Piotr, Jeff, and I wrote a paper, *Understanding Guaranteed Exchange-Rate Options*, intended to be the first of a new series of Quantitative Strategies Research Reports. Though it contained some mathematics, it was written in a relatively casual style, intended to educate clients and salespeople about these products. For a brief period I felt that we knew something interesting that few other people understood, and I looked forward to sending our report to academic friends and clients. I was happy to be in the publication business again.

It wasn't that easy, however. When you send clients a research report from an investment bank you have to be careful that nothing you write can be construed as a recommendation that might cause legal problems. Statements about hedging require disclaimers on the limited efficacy of theoretical models in the face of actual markets. Furthermore, you obviously don't want to reveal anything that could damage your business franchise. Therefore, after preparing our report, we took it to the new head of the trading desk for approval.

Several days later he asked us not to distribute the report outside the firm. Though I was frustrated at not being able to communicate what we knew to people in our field, I could see that he honestly felt that option pricing formulas were akin to trade secrets that neither competitors or clients should know about.

I thought he was wrong. The true commercial value lay in Granny's great idea—selling Nikkei insurance that was insensitive to a drop in the value of the yen to American investors who thought that the Nikkei was overpriced. But this idea was already in the public domain, since we had listed the warrants on the American Stock Exchange; sure enough, it was almost immediately copied by other banks.

Within a few months, finance academics at several universities published papers on the valuation of GER options. One or two of them got it wrong the first time, because it was subtle, but several got it right. Had we published our paper, Goldman would have given up little; they might even have gained some minor kudos as a haven for analytically talented people. A few copies of our internal report did leak out over the next year, probably distributed by salesperson eager to set up a dialogue with clients. Ten years later it was finally reprinted, belatedly but verbatim, in a book on currency derivatives.

Later that summer I gave a talk on GER options at a course organized by John Hull at the University of Toronto. While listening to the other speakers, I began to realize how lucky I was to be working in equity derivatives at Goldman. GER options were merely the forerunner of many new and intriguing problems that the blossoming equity options markets were beginning to throw our way, problems of which academics were unaware.

The problems of intellectual and business interest often came to us as questions, ill-posed by traders, who knew they had a difficulty but could not always articulate it. The first battle was understanding what the problem was. The traders didn't always have the patience to listen to our solutions. Sometimes, as we discovered from the salespeople, it was the firm's clients, especially in mathophiliac France and Japan, who had a greater taste for learning about financial models and exotic products. I began to realize that there was a market for honest, simple, direct and nonpatronizing writing about complex topics.

During the next ten years in Quantitative Strategies we wrote many reports on the subtleties and complexities of equity volatility. We tried to straddle the line between academia and Wall Street, attempting to explain the theory of trading and valuation in a picturesque and pedagogic style using only a modicum of academic rigor, the latter often relegated to an appendix. We aimed to make our papers accessible to an audience of intelligent traders, salespeople and clients, all with a presumed short attention span.

In my mind's eye I retained a 1980s view of quant groups, an outlook I had absorbed by osmosis from Stan Diller and Fischer. I felt that we were advantaged by working at the intersection point between theory and the real world. I saw that it was good to have one foot in both the academic and practitioner universes; I found that publication of our models could simultaneously move financial economics forward while bringing prestige to Goldman Sachs, thereby helping to attract people of high quality to the firm. Finally, I learned that persuading the world to measure value with your model is an effective and honest endeavor.

People outside Goldman thought that we spent all of our time doing abstract research and writing it up for publication. It wasn't so. Our main activity was always building models and trading systems for use by the derivatives desks, trying to solve their practical problems with our theories. In the time we had left we wrote our reports, often for love rather than money. We were immensely lucky to be the theorists living in the experimenters' laboratory, with the opportunity to be the first to hear about new irregularities and the difficulties they posed for trading desks.

The success of Granny's structured deal made everyone hungry for more. It was clear that further deals would require more quants and better risk management systems, and the QS group began to grow.

Though no one used that term in those days, it was Piotr's "financial engineering" that showed us how to eliminate the mismatch between the risk of the warrants we owned and the GER puts we sold. Executing the hedge in practice was more complicated. The trading desk was long a diverse assortment of yen-valued Nikkei puts. They were correspondingly short a large homogeneous batch of the dollar-valued Kingdom of

Denmark Nikkei puts that Goldman had issued. To hedge the mismatch, they had to continually trade varying quantities of Nikkei futures and yen currency, as well as some individual Japanese stocks. This entire "Nikkei book" had to be hedged at least once each day, and sometimes more often.

When I arrived in January 1990, all this complexity was being handled on a vintage DOS-based PC running a Lotus spreadsheet into which various Black-Scholes options formulas had been embedded. It was neither flexible nor robust enough for interactive risk management.

I was lucky to have come to QS from the fixed-income world, which has always been a few sophisticated steps ahead of equities in these matters. The rapid rise of interest rates in the late 1970s, after years of stable returns with low volatility, had forced fixed-income clients and the trading desks that serviced them to become the early pioneers of portfolio hedging systems. As a result, I knew a great deal about designing and building risk systems, and saw that this was where I could contribute.

In a month or two, Piotr and I, together with Rao Achyuthuni, one of the QS consultants, quickly designed and built a rudimentary Nikkei risk management system that we called *Samurai*. It was simple, but it did the job: We entered our trading positions in tabular fashion into a flat computer file, one security to a row. Within each row the first column indicated the number of securities we owned, the second specified the security type (stock, option, index, futures contract, currency, and so on), while the remaining columns spelled out the details (strike, expiration, and so on) necessary for valuation. Each day we edited the file to reflect new trades or expirations. Samurai read the positions in the file and then reported the model value and hedge ratio for the entire portfolio at current market levels. It also reported the impact on the portfolio of more extreme scenarios in which the Nikkei level, the yen, interest rates, and volatilities moved up or down by as much as 20 percent. This latter feature was perhaps the most useful; we could use it to discover the potential "hot zones" in the book that might take us down, and we could estimate what types of new trades could ameliorate these potential disasters.

Samurai made a giant splash; simple as it was, nobody in the division had ever seen a built-from-scratch, risk-management system for derivatives portfolios before. The desk embraced it and invited Jeff, Piotr, and me to demonstrate it to Roy Zuckerberg and David Silfen, the daunt-ingly patrician heads of the Equities Division.

What we had built suited the desk so well because we had collabo-rated so closely with Dan. Traders have their own vernacular and, though he spoke it himself, Dan was one of the few traders I met who was will-ing and able to bridge the language gap. He would spend hours with us on the chalkboard each day, trying to help specify and test the system; he would patiently debate with me what should be displayed on the screen and in what format. Dan was also a bit of a closet quant, who one day proudly took out of his desk drawer the senior thesis on option pricing he had written years earlier. Most of the programs we wrote in QS over the next several years worked so well in part because Dan took on the role of the trading desk's agent.

Unlike many traders, Dan also knew that success comes from incre-mental improvements. We weren't building the space shuttle, whose specifications had to be written down in minute detail and handed over to the engineers. When we began to build risk systems for the develop-ing business of equity derivatives, we had entered uncharted terrain, and there was no commonly acknowledged best path through it. Every time we spoke with the traders, we faced such a flood of demands and choices that it was difficult to decide what to do first. Dan, more than anyone else I worked with from trading, understood what physicists call pertur-bation theory, the approach by which you get the most critical feature completed first, and then at each next step you tackle the next most important feature. In contrast, many other traders and desks were like the "old sailor my grandfather knew" in A. A. Milne's poem "who had so many things he wanted to do that whenever he thought it was time to begin, he couldn't because of the state he was in." Dan perceived his job to be the definition and creation of a uniform and well-designed trading infrastructure for the entire desk, wherever they worked, so that traders could move from one country to another and find a consistent environment. Most traders just want to trade; Dan was willing to think about the tools you need to trade safely. When the firm moved Dan to London a few years later, no one adopted his role, and from then on giv-ing the desk what they needed became much harder. For more than ten years afterward, the methodology we created in Samurai remained the core of our risk system, despite manyfold increases in the size of our desk and our book.

By the early 1990s, the Soviet Union had collapsed, the end of history was ostensibly upon us, and global capitalism was rampant. In equity derivatives, the era of exotic options had begun. Exotics seemed the preferred way for investors in one country to gain just the exposure they wanted to the markets in another. Suppose you were an American investor who wanted to gain if the French stock market rose. In the old days you had to buy and hold a diverse collection of French stocks and face the detailed bother of tracking their prices in francs, collecting their dividends, converting them to dollars, paying income and capital gains tax; after all that, however, you were still exposed to the risk that the French franc might deteriorate against the dollar. Now you could instead come to our equity derivatives desk and buy a call option on the CAC-30 French equity index, GER'd into dollars; you got the simplicity of looking at the daily closing level of the CAC-30 in the newspaper or on a screen and knowing what your P&L was, as traders like to refer to their profits and losses. You could leave the messy stuff to us.

Exotic options like these and others were taking off, and Goldman was determined to build a Structured Equity Products business. The success of Samurai made QS the natural support framework, and during the next five years we grew to about 30 people, with approximately three software developers in our group for every pure quant. Each day we thought about new options we could design and value, all of them providing exposure to more granular contingencies than the coarse, standard options on which we had sharpened our teeth. There were barrier options, options on the maximum of a stock price, options on the average of a stock price, lookback options, outperformance options, rate-contingent options, options on options themselves. When, during the late 1970s and early 1980s, these structures had first been invented and their value found by means of ingenious mathematical manipulations, they were merely a curiosity, a pushing of the theoretical limits. Now, ten years later, investment banks saw them as tailored instruments in the business of giving customers exactly the risk profile they desired—for a premium of course.

Behind all of these exotic structures, if they were successful in the marketplace, were two obvious principles. First, since an option is a type of bet on a future scenario that may never occur, investors want to pay as little as possible for it. Second, in order to minimize an option's cost, you must define as precisely as possible the exact scenario you are betting on. The more precise you can be about the scenario from which you want to benefit or protect yourself, the less you pay.

We had options for every attitude. The classic was a standard call option. A call on the Standard & Poor's (S&P) 500 index, for example, was a straightforward bet that the index would rise by the expiration date; when you bought it you paid for all scenarios in which the index would ultimately rise, including those in which the index first dropped and then recovered.

There were more exotic flavors. A *knock-in barrier* call option was a bet that the index would first drop below some barrier level and then regain its ground. If you thought that this dip followed by a rise were likely, you could pay only for that scenario, and it would cost you less than a standard call. There were many similar variations on this theme.

If you didn't want to worry about small fluctuations in the S&P 500 as long as its trend was upwards, you could buy an *average* (or *Asian*) call option on the index, whose payout depended only on the average level of the index over the life of the option. Since the time average of an index is a more stable quantity than the index itself, this option, too, was generally cheaper than a standard call.

Alternatively, if you thought that the stock market would rise only if the Federal Reserve kept interest rates low, you could buy a rate-contingent call option on the S&P 500 that would extinguish (or *knock-out*, in options parlance) if interest rates were to rise. Again, since this call would pay out only if interest rates were to stay low *and* the index were to rise, a less likely occurrence than the index rising under all circumstances, you paid less for it.

A typical buyer of our options was a European commercial bank that, as interest rates kept falling, wanted to attract depositors by giving them a chance of earning a higher return. The bank would promise its depositors an enhanced rate of interest proportional to the rise (if it occurred) in the one-year average of the CAC-30 over the next year. To provide that payout, the bank bought options on the average of the CAC-30 index from our desk. Instead of providing its depositors with a simple fixed-income investment, it was giving them a hybrid product they couldn't get elsewhere, a bond combined with an equity "kicker."

Conversely, many of the sellers of equity options were European pension and mutual funds or insurance companies who, unhappy with the decline in bond yields, sold options on equity indexes to enhance their return. They gambled that the indexes wouldn't rise and that the options they sold would finish out of the money.

The development of new options structures resembled an arms race. Any firm that created something popular with clients had a few months to press their advantage before another firm copied them. It took that long to reverse-engineer a product, add a few wrinkles, develop a risk management strategy, put in place the legal and technical infrastructure, and then market it.

Early in the 1990s, most options were written on simple global equity indexes, like the S&P 500 in the United States or the FTSE 100 in Great Britain; the exotic nature of the option lay not in the nature of the underlyer, but rather in the definition of the way in which the payout of the option depended upon the level of the underlyer. During the technology and biotech bubbles of the late 1990s, investors became more interested in options on complex underlyers, baskets of technology or pharmaceutical stocks, for example. As firms tried to outdo each other, options payouts became more refined and harder to apprehend. By the end of the decade, the most popular options were being created at French banks by elite École Normale Supérieure–trained mathematicians with a characteristically French taste for formal mathematics. The exotics they marketed were options on baskets of stocks whose actual composition kept changing over time. In one, for example, the number of constituent stocks in the basket each year decreased as the best-performing stock of the previous year was eliminated. As in any business, the salespeople liked tailoring and complexity because not only could you charge more for it, but it was also more difficult for a client to assess the value of its individual features. Complexity was also harder for competitors to copy.

Variations flourished. Riding the crest of this wave of innovation, and simultaneously propelling it, was Peter Field's inspired venture, *Risk* magazine, to which we turned each month for its mix of industry news, gossip, and quantitative articles. It was the first glossy in the options world, replete with advertising and cover art, a magazine aimed at quantitative practitioners rather than academics or money managers. It spurned the suffocatingly rigid format of academic periodicals like the *Journal of Finance*, and both academics and practitioners loved it. Fischer, too, commented admiringly on it. For several years in the early 1990s each issue contained topical articles on the newest exotic structures and how to value them. Soon *Risk* was organizing expensive courses on exotic options, a clever arbitrage by which they charged quants from one set of investment banks to listen to the lectures of quants from another set, while *Risk* pocketed the fee.

Other journals sprang up, too. The International Association of Financial Engineers, a new professional organization of quants, began to specify an educational syllabus suitable for the training of a quant. New textbooks and Master's of Financial Engineering programs sprouted and flourished at the increasing numbers of universities that, sensing a need, began to cater to those willing to pay to learn quantitative finance. In 1985 when I entered Wall Street it was amateur heaven, a fluidly makeshift field filled with retreads from other disciplines who could learn quickly, solve equations, and write their own programs. You had to learn options theory on your own and there were only a few textbooks to help you—those written by Jarrow and Rudd and Cox and Rubinstein were the only ones I could obtain. The only derivatives meeting I went to each year was the annual spring meeting of the Amex. By the late 1990s, there were scores of master's programs, hundreds of conferences, and thousands of books. Physicists and mathematicians, either unable to find academic positions or, grown weary of academic politics and pay, increasingly sought out Wall Street jobs.

The quantitative life of practitioners, formerly the happily casual domain of self-taught amateurs, was becoming a discipline, a business, and a profession. It was simultaneously becoming a little less fun, too.

Chapter 14

Laughter in the Dark

■ The puzzle of the volatility smile ■ Beyond Black-Scholes:
the race to develop local-volatility models of
options ■ The right model is hard to find ■

I first heard about the smile in December 1990 from Dave Rogers, our head options trader in Tokyo. I had begun traveling to Japan regularly to bring our traders the latest releases of our risk management tools and to learn what new models and software they needed. Unlike the New York Stock Exchange, the Tokyo market closed at midday; traders grew less frenetic and went out for lunch, salespeople departed to meet clients, and there was time for leisurely conversations. While we chatted, Dave showed me the computer screen he used to watch the prices of options on the Nikkei 225 index. He pointed out a peculiar asymmetry in the Nikkei options prices: The prices of out-of-the-money puts were unexpectedly larger than those of other options.

Everyone referred to this asymmetry as "the smile," or "the skew." At first it looked only mildly interesting, a peculiar anomaly we could tolerate. Then, when I thought about it a little more, I realized that the existence of the smile was completely at odds with Black and Scholes's twenty-year-old foundation of options theory. And, if the Black-Scholes formula was wrong, then so was the predicted sensitivity of an option's price to movements in its underlying index, its so-called "delta." In this case, all traders using the Black-Scholes model's delta were hedging their option books incorrectly. But the very essence of Black-Scholes was its prescription for replicating and hedging. The smile, therefore, poked a small hole deep into the dike of theory that sheltered options trading. If Black-Scholes were wrong, what *was* the right delta to use for hedging an option?

During the 1990s, the smile, initially a peculiarity of equity options, infected other markets, taking a slightly different form in each one. Understanding it became a dominating obsession for me and many of my quant contemporaries. It was an anomaly that sat right at the inter-section of options trading and options theory, and I spent much of my intellectual energy trying to model it.

Our work started in the typical heady rush of energy and ambition that made me feel as though I were in physics again, racing to be the first to find the "right" model for something important and interesting. I fantasized about building a model that, embraced by everyone, would replace Black-Scholes. It wasn't as simple as I thought. During the next ten years I learned that "rightness" in financial modeling is a much fuzzier concept than I had imagined.

One of the things you learn repeatedly in a career in financial mod-eling is the importance of units. You always want the prices of securities to be quoted in a way that make it easy to compare their relative values.

When you need to compare the values of bonds, for example, their prices are insufficient, because each bond can have a different maturity and coupon. Instead, you quote their yields. A bond yield provides an estimate of the return the bond will generate for you irrespective of its coupon and maturity. You may not know whether a discount bond at 98 is better than a premium one at 105, but you do know that, all other things being equal, a yield of 5.3 percent is less attractive than 5.6 per-cent. This conversion of prices to yields is itself a model, albeit a simple one. It is a convenient way to communicate prices, as well as a good first step towards estimating value.

In the options world as well, price alone is an insufficient measure of value; it's impossible to tell whether ¥300 for an at-the-money put is more attractive than ¥40 for a deep out-of-the-money put. A better measure of value is the option's implied volatility. The Black-Scholes model views a stock option as a kind of bet on the future volatility of a stock's returns. The more volatile the stock, the more likely the bet will pay off, and therefore the more you should pay for it. You can use the model to convert an option price into the future volatility the stock must have in order for the option price to be fair. This measure is called the option's implied volatility. It is, so to speak, an option's view of the stock's future volatility.

The Black–Scholes model was the market standard. When I sat next to Dave in Tokyo that day, his computer screen showed the prices quoted in Black–Scholes implied volatilities. Even today, when no one believes that the Black–Scholes model is absolutely the best way to estimate option value, and even though more sophisticated traders sometimes use more complex models, the Black–Scholes model's implied volatilities are still the market convention for quoting prices.

Options are generally less liquid than stocks, and implied volatility market data is consequently coarse and approximate. Nevertheless, Dave pointed out to me what I was already dimly aware of: There was a severe skew in the implied volatilities, so that three-month options of low strike had much greater implied volatilities than three-month options of higher strikes. You can see a sketch of this asymmetry in Figure 14.1. This lopsided shape, though it's commonly called "the smile," is more of a smirk.

With implied volatility as your measure of value, low-strike puts are the most expensive Nikkei options. Anyone who was around on

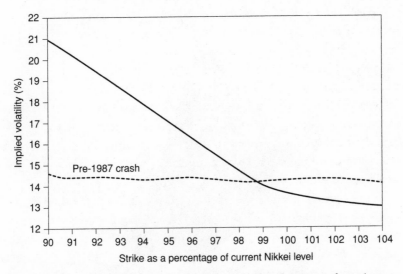

Figure 14.1 A typical implied volatility smile for three-month options on the Nikkei index in late 1994. The dashed line shows the lack of skew that was common prior to the 1987 crash.

October 19, 1987 could easily guess why. Ever since that day when equity markets around the world plunged, investors remained constantly aware of the possibility of an instantaneous large jump down in the market, and were willing to pay up for protection. Out-of-the-money puts were the best and cheapest insurance. Like stableboys who shut the barn door after the horse has bolted, investors who lived through the 1987 crash were now willing to pay up for future insurance against the risks they had previously suffered. By 1990 there were similar smiles or skews in all equity markets. Before 1987, in contrast, more light-heartedly naive options markets were happy to charge about the same implied volatility for all strikes, as illustrated by the dashed line in Figure 14.1.

It was not only three-month implied volatilities that were skewed. A similar effect was visible for options of any expiration, so that implied volatility varied not only with strike but also with expiration. We began to plot this double variation of implied volatility in both the time and strike dimension as a two-dimensional implied volatility surface. A picture of the surface for options on the Standard & Poor's (S&P) 500 index is illustrated in Figure 14.2. Like the yield curve, it changes continually from minute to minute and day to day.

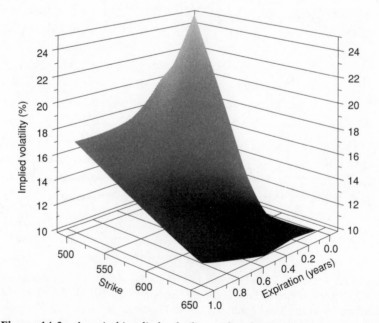

Figure 14.2   A typical implied volatility surface for the S&P 500 in mid-1995.

This tentlike surface was a challenge to theorists everywhere. The Black-Scholes model couldn't account for it. Black-Scholes attributed a single volatility at all future times to an index or a stock, and therefore always produced the dull, flat, featureless surface of Figure 14.3a. The best you could do, if you modified the Black-Scholes model to allow future index volatility to be different from today's, was to obtain a surface that slanted in the time direction, as depicted in Figure 14.3b. But the variation in two perpendicular directions, time and strike, was a puzzle. What was wrong with the classic Black-Scholes model? And what new kind of model could possibly explain that surface?

We knew that the Black-Scholes model oversimplifies the behavior of stock prices. It assumes that a stock price *diffuses* away into the future from its current value in a slow, random, continuous fashion, much like a cloud of smoke from the smoldering tip of a cigarette spreads through a room. Dense near the tip of the cigarette and sparse farther out, the intensity of the smoke cloud at a point represents the probability that a particle of smoke will diffuse to that location. In the Black-Scholes model, a similar cloud depicts the probability that the stock price will reach some particular future value at some future time. Figure 14.4 illustrates that cloud of probabilities for a stock in the Black-Scholes model. The more dispersed the cloud, the more uncertain the future stock price. A single parameter, the stock's volatility traditionally denoted by the Greek letter sigma, σ, determines the rate of diffusion and the width of the cloud. The greater the stock's volatility, the wider the cloud.

Though simplification is the essence of modeling, the Black-Scholes picture of smoke-cloud diffusion is too restrictive. First, stock prices don't necessarily diffuse with a constant volatility; at some times a stock diffuses more rapidly than at others. Second, and more gravely, sometimes stocks *don't diffuse at all*. Diffusion, as shown in Figure 14.4, is a slow, continuous process; in diffusion, a stock price that moves from $100 to $99 passes through every possible price between them. This is not what happened during the 1987 crash, however; on that day the Dow-Jones index jumped its way downward through 500 points like an excited kid on a pogo stick.

Returning to New York from Tokyo, I began working with my QS colleagues Iraj Kani and Alex Bergier. I wanted to extend the Black-Scholes model just enough so that it could incorporate the smile. "Just

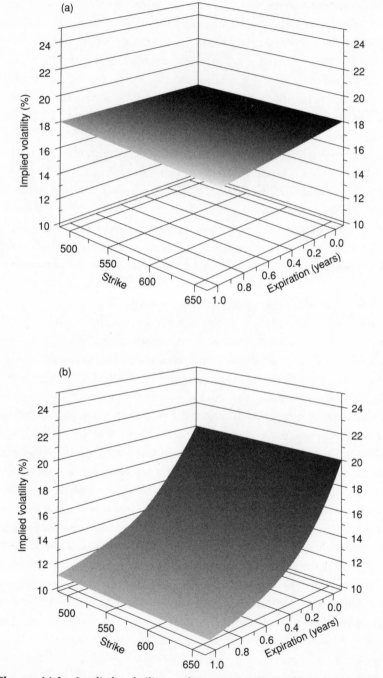

Figure 14.3 Implied volatility surfaces. (a) In the standard Black–Scholes model. (b) In an enhanced Black–Scholes model where volatility varies with time to expiration.

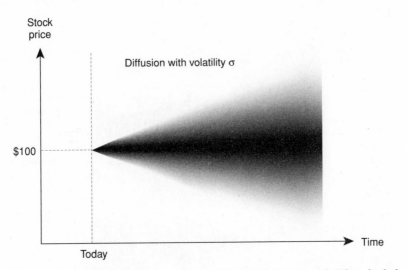

Figure 14.4 Simple diffusion in the Black-Scholes model. The shaded regions illustrate the range of possible future prices for a stock whose price is $100 today. The more time passes, the greater the uncertainty in the future price. The darker the shading, the more likely the price will be in that region.

enough" was always the aim. A model is only a model; you want to capture the essence of the phenomenon, not the thing itself. It is far too easy, in the name of realism, to add complexity to the simple evolution of stock prices assumed by Black and Scholes, but complexity without calibration is pointless.

The overwhelming fear of equity investors was another 1987-style crash, so we added this possibility to Black-Scholes. This was not something new; Merton had done it in his so-called jump-diffusion model in the mid-1970s, and to begin with, we did it even more crudely than he had. To the constant diffusion of stock prices we added just one new feature, the small probability p that the stock price might take one sizeable jump J downward. The probability cloud for this process is depicted in Figure 14.5. It shows the two scenarios the stock can now take: a jump J downward and subsequent diffusion with a volatility σ_H, which is likely to be high because of the after-excitement of the crash; or, more likely, continued diffusion with the normal, lower volatility σ_L.

Typically, we assumed the probability p to be of order one percent, implying that the market assigned about a one-in-a-hundred chance of a crash during the option's lifetime. We chose the σ_H to be about 40 percent greater than σ_L, based on a combination of intuition and expe-

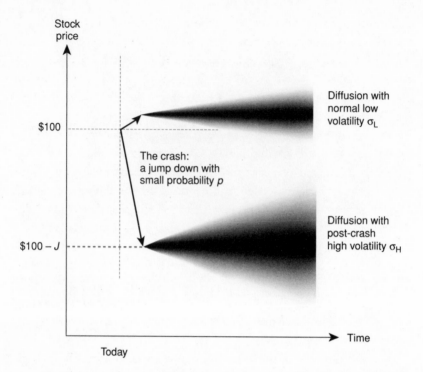

Figure 14.5 The range of possible future prices for a stock that can jump once and then diffuse. The darker the shading, the more likely the price will be in that region.

rience about the after-effects of stock crashes. Our model now had only two unknown parameters, the jump size J of the crash scenario and the volatility σ_L associated with normal behavior. This was just one parameter richer than Black-Scholes, which contained only a single volatility. We calibrated these parameters by matching the model's option prices to the two implied volatilities that defined the shape of the three-month smile, those of an at-the-money option and a put option struck 5 percent out of the money. With a normal volatility σ_L in the vicinity of ten percent and a downward jump J of about 25 percent of the current stock price, we found we could produce smiles like those in Figure 14.1.

Our model looked at the world like this: During the option's lifetime the Nikkei had a roughly one-in-a-hundred chance of dropping about 25 percent. This is why you paid so much more for an out-of-the-money put. We then used the model to estimate the option's delta, the hedge ratio necessary to cancel its index risk. We also used it to value the more illiquid or exotic options that were becoming increasingly fashionable—barrier options, for example—whose prices were highly sensitive to the probability and size of the jump. We wanted our traders to search the market for options whose prices differed significantly from those produced by our model. They could then buy the apparently cheap ones and sell the rich ones in the hope that these outliers would eventually revert to our model's prices and generate a profit.

Though the jump model captured one essential sentiment responsible for the smile, it was ultimately too crude. Its view of a future in which the Nikkei awoke each morning and decided either to make one large instantaneous excited jump downward or else diffuse calmly was still too simplistic. Looking back, perhaps we should have added a distribution of possible jump sizes and jump times. But jumps occur rarely, and since there was little data on their distribution, we would have had to make many unverified assumptions, something that felt unaesthetic. Rightly or wrongly, we preferred a more constrained model whose parameters were totally fixed by calibration to observed options prices. Ten years later, though, more detailed jump-diffusion models of the smile became popular again.

Our initial model of the smile did find users in Goldman's risk arbitrage group, where savvy traders combined worldly knowledge with quantitative methods to take educated bets. Some arbitrageurs focused on acquisitions in which the acquiring company tenders for the stock of a target company at a public offer price that substantially exceeds its current level. If and when regulators approve the acquisition, the target's price will jump to the offer price. Until then, its price reflects an estimate of the probability of completion of the deal. For these situations, our jump model was a theoretically accurate picture, and the risk arbitrageurs made occasional use of it to see whether their estimate of the likelihood of the acquisition's approval matched the jump probability implied by the current price of the target.

Meanwhile, from mid-1991 through early 1993, Iraj and I and the rest of QS turned temporarily to the more pressing problem of enhancing our risk systems to handle the increasing number of exotic options we traded.

Unfortunately, the more we worked on exotics, the more we ran into the problems of the smile: Whenever we used the Black-Scholes framework to value the exotic options in the desk's book, we were using a model that produced the wrong value for much simpler standard options, a model inconsistent with the smile. This wasn't good—you can't trust a model for complex phenomena if it gets the simple stuff wrong. You wouldn't trust a NASA computer program that predicted the trajectory of an interplanetary probe from Earth to Mars if it couldn't first correctly predict the orbits of Earth and Mars around the sun.

The right place to start was with a model that could match the market prices of all standard options, the entire implied volatility surface. Only then, when it was correctly calibrated, could you sensibly use it to calculate the value of an exotic. How could we find a model that matched any surface?

I thought back to our development of BDT. In the mid-1980s, the fixed-income options world had undergone a similar crisis: Practitioners used a yield diffusion model like Ravi's to value an option on any single bond, but felt uncomfortable because it couldn't simultaneously match the prices of all Treasury bonds on the yield curve. BDT was one of the possible solutions to this dilemma.

We had a tremendous advantage in having come to the equity derivatives world with a background in fixed income. Iraj and I perceived the following analogy between bonds and their yields and options and their volatilities:

- Bond prices are quoted using current long-term yields, which reflect the market's expectation of future short-term rates.
- Options prices are quoted using current long-term implied volatilities, which reflect the market's expectation of future short-term volatilities.

Our ambition was to build a post–Black-Scholes model that allowed us to back out the market's expectation of future short-term volatilities from the current volatility surface. We weren't sure how to do it, but we knew that the world needed a better model and would reward its discoverers. Throughout 1993 we felt as though we were in a race with unnamed competitors to find it.

Iraj and I were great admirers of the binomial options model, a simple, picturesque, and yet accurate way of performing options-theoretic calculations on a gridlike tree of future stock prices. On a binomial tree, prices move like knights on a chessboard, one discrete step forward in time and up or down a notch in price. Binomial trees are easy to draw and, in a jerky way, mimic the behavior of real prices or indexes. As the grid of the chess board becomes progressively finer, prices move more and more continuously—they start to diffuse, in fact—and the binomial model becomes equivalent to the Black-Scholes model. Binomial trees were the Feynman diagrams of options theory, easy to picture and use, wonderful for simulating simple trading strategies or developing valuation models. Even the innumerate traders with whom we often dealt could understand them. Initially invented by William Sharpe soon after Black and Scholes wrote their paper, bimonial trees were then cleverly elaborated upon by John Cox, Mark Rubinstein and Steve Ross. As options theorists grew increasingly professional and better educated, binomial models fell into a low-tech disrepute, but we still found them immensely useful.

Therefore, we tried to use a binomial tree of index options prices like the one shown in Figure 14.6 as a guide to extracting the market's view of future short-term volatilities. The left edge of the tree denotes the current index level. Each step up or down from there illustrates a potential future index move. Traditional binomial trees make the key assumption that all moves on the tree are of equal percentage magnitude; at any future time, at any future level, the index, whether it moves up or down, grows or shrinks by an identical percentage. In technical terms, the index has a constant volatility of returns, globally the same across the entire tree, identical at each future instant of time and index level. This constancy of the index's volatility in the Black-Scholes model leads to

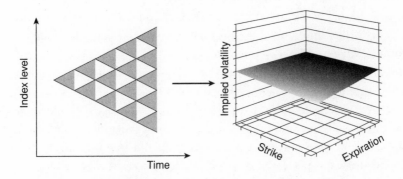

Figure 14.6 At left, a binomial tree of future index moves. Each future percentage move is identical and represents a constant index volatility. At right, the shape of the corresponding implied volatility surface.

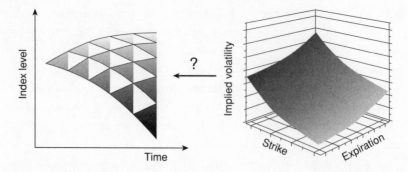

Figure 14.7   At left, an implied binomial tree of future index moves. Each future percentage move has a local volatility that rises as the index level drops. Can one deduce the shape of the implied binomial tree from the implied volatility surface at right?

the associated flat implied volatility surface that is inconsistent with actual options markets.

Iraj and I developed an alternate view of the future tree of index lev-els. We pictured the usual constant-volatility binomial tree redrawn on a flexible sheet of rubber, which we could then stretch and distort so as to resemble the tree of Figure 14.7. On this deformed tree, the size of the moves in the index at each node of the tree could differ, repre-senting a varying volatility whose value differed from node to node. In theorists' jargon, the index would have a varying *local volatility*; by "local volatility" we meant the short-term volatility of the index at a particu-lar future level and time. The constant or global volatility of Figure 14.6 was inconsistent with the market's tentlike implied volatility surface of Figure 14.2. There must be, we figured, an *implied binomial tree* whose local volatility could be chosen to match the market's implied volatility surface. We expected it to look like the tree in Figure 14.7, in which the local volatility of the index rises as the index falls and vice versa, in order to reflect the surface's variation with strike.

It was easy to imagine such a tree. It was even easy to build such a tree by literally making up a rule for how local volatility varied within the tree and then constructing it. Given such a tree, you could use it to calculate the prices of many different options and then plot their implied volatility surface. We could see that it was possible to pick a local volatility whose variation produced a realistic-looking volatility surface. But the ultimate problem we faced was the inverse of what we were doing. We needed to start with the implied volatility surface the market presented and deduce from it the unique local volatilities that reflected it. The implied volatility surface was the primary object, and the whole procedure we envisaged would only constitute a true theory if you could extract from it a unique implied binomial tree.

Throughout 1993, as the QS group continued to build the more elaborate risk-management systems that occupied most of our time, we continued to ruminate over the smile. In spare moments we tinkered with implied trees, still uncertain as to whether there was a truly unique relationship between the volatility surface in Figure 14.7 and the tree we hoped it implied. We knew we could go from the tree to the surface, but what was the incontrovertible way to go from the surface to the tree? We discussed it with Dave Rogers and his traders, who, because of our sheet-of-rubber analogy, always called it the *flexible tree*. We built versions of it and used them to price and hedge varieties of options, but, too busy with supporting the software needs of the desk, we avoided an all-out attempt on the question of uniqueness.

The relationship between surface and tree reminded me of the lecture by Mark Kaç I had heard as a graduate student at Columbia thirty years earlier, when he solved the question of hearing the shape of a drum. Physicists call this an inverse-scattering problem because, whereas most models in physics proceed from the physical law to the results, inverse problems work backwards. Newton's theory of gravitation, for example, commences with the law of gravitational attraction between the sun and the planets, and deduces the planetary orbits. Inverse scattering problems go in reverse—given the observations, they ask, what law would produce them? Imagine, for example, that astronomers observed some strange perturbation in the orbit of the earth. What change in the law of gravitational attraction would account for it?

Our search for a method to extract a unique implied tree from the volatility surface was an inverse scattering problem. This approach is more typical of financial modeling than it is of physics. In physics, the beauty and elegance of a theory's laws, and the intuition that led to them, is often compelling, and provides a natural starting point from which to proceed to phenomena. In finance, more of a social than a natural science, there are few beautiful theories and virtually no compelling ones, and so we have no choice but to take the phenomenological approach. There, much more often, one begins with the market's data and calibrates the model's laws to fit it. This calibration is a kind of inverse-scattering approach, too, and it was what we were trying to do in our attempt to construct implied trees.

Sometime in late 1993 I went to visit our trading desk in London, where I also gave a talk at a *Risk* magazine conference on exotic options. Between conference sessions, I met Graham Cooper, the new editor of *Risk*, and also ran into John Hull. During our conversations I told them what Iraj and I had been exploring. Graham and John told me that they had heard that Bruno Dupire at Paribas Capital Markets in London and Mark Rubinstein, the Berkeley finance professor who was one of the codevelopers of the original constant-volatility binomial tree model, had been tackling the same problem. Worried about giving away proprietary information to our competition, I called Dave Rogers in New York and quickly got his approval to allude in public to what Iraj and I had done. I hurried back to my hotel room and quickly appended a few transparencies to my presentation to describe our implied tree approach. After my talk, Graham invited me to submit an article on our work to *Risk*, while John, hearing me describe our trees sometimes as "flexible" and sometimes as "implied," nudged me towards the use of "implied."

With competition at our heels, Iraj and I anxiously rededicated ourselves to proving the uniqueness of our tree. Most of our day was typically spent enhancing the desk's trading models, responding to requests for pricing new structures, and building trading software. Whenever we had spare time away from desk support, we tried again to define a scheme for uniquely extracting the local volatility at each future node of the implied binomial tree.

We began with the market's implied volatility surface on a given day, as illustrated in Figure 14.2. We then constructed a binomial tree like the one in Figure 14.8. Each shaded triangle in this tree, at each index level and future time, evolves with a different local volatility whose magnitude is represented by the degree of shading. Higher index levels correspond to lower (paler) volatilities; lower index levels correspond to higher (darker) volatilities. How pale or how dark must you choose them to match the initial implied volatility surface of Figure 14.2? That was the question.

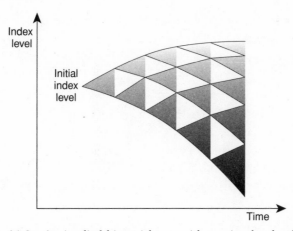

Figure 14.8   An implied binomial tree with varying local volatilities represented by the shaded triangles in the tree.

The *local* volatility in Figure 14.8 is a local quality of the tree, the microscopically viewed volatility within each single small internal triangle. In contrast, the implied volatility in Figure 14.2 is a *global* quality, a wide-angle overview of all the internal triangles seen from 30,000 feet. We viewed the implied volatility of an option as the average[1] of all the local volatilities that the index will experience during the life of that option.

Consider the option whose expiration and strike correspond to the time and index level at the location of the small flashlight in the next-to-last row of the tree in Figure 14.9. The value of its implied volatility depends upon the values of the local volatilities in the shaded right-striped triangles; those are the local volatility regions that the index can traverse in moving towards the strike during the life of the option. It's useful to think of the option expiring at the flashlight as an X-ray source that illuminates all the local volatilities in the internal right-striped triangles in the tree.

Similarly, the option whose strike lies at the location of the lantern in the tree of Figure 14.10 illuminates the local volatilities in the shaded left-striped triangles.

The option with a strike at the flashlight illuminates one part of the tree, while the option whose strike lies at the lantern illuminates another

---

[1]A mathematically complex average, to be honest, but an average nonetheless.

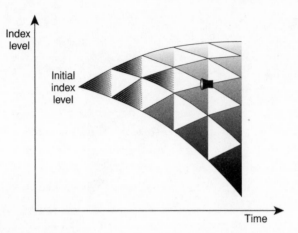

Figure 14.9 The implied volatility of the option whose expiration and strike lie at the circle illuminates the local volatilities in the right-striped region of the tree.

part. But no single option, neither the one struck at the lantern nor the one struck at the flashlight, sheds light on just one triangle in the tree, the single node whose volatility was the obscure object of our desire.

We kept struggling. We wanted a set of options that illuminated the volatilities at just one internal node. But each scheme we tried failed— there seemed to be no recipe for the local volatility at a single node.

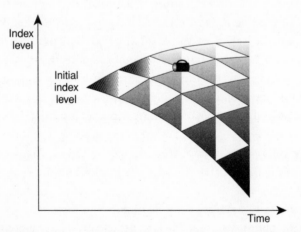

Figure 14.10 The implied volatility of the option whose expiration and strike lie at the location of the lantern illuminates the local volatilities in the left-striped region of the tree.

Then, one day, as we played around with a five-row toy version of our tree on a spreadsheet, we found something miraculous happened, something so strange that for a few minutes we thought it was due to a programming error in the spreadsheet. We noticed, almost by accident, that if we used *three* distinct option strikes to illuminate the interior of the tree, two of them with adjacent earlier strikes and one with a strike one period later—if, so to speak, we directed X-rays into the tree from three different angles—the illumination canceled everywhere except at the single node where they intersected. This is illustrated in Figure 14.11. It was astonishing: We had found an algorithm that determined the local volatility at a single node in terms of the market implied volatilities of the options with strikes at the three surrounding nodes.

Now we knew how to find every local volatility, step by step. We could select any node on the implied tree, read off the implied volatilities of the three options adjacent to it from the market's implied volatility surface, and then extract the local volatility at that node via our algorithm. In this way, one node at a time, we could find all the local volatilities. With those local volatilities and the implied binomial tree on which they sat, we could value and hedge any option on the index in a manner consistent with the smile. We were immensely elated, believing we had made the next big breakthrough in options pricing, an extension of the Black-Scholes model to make it consistent with reality.

We weren't the only excited ones. Mark Rubinstein and Bruno Dupire had also spent the past year developing similar extensions of Black-Scholes. A few weeks later Mark delivered his presidential address at the January 1994 meeting of the American Finance Association on *Implied Binomial Trees*. Speaking to him over subsequent years, I learned that he too imagined he had achieved a great breakthrough.

At about the same time, John Hull mailed me a copy of a talk Bruno had given on his version of implied trees at a meeting of the International Association of Financial Engineers (IAFE) in New York a few weeks earlier. In it, Bruno also claimed to have found a unique way to extract local volatilities from implied ones.

Each of us—Iraj and I together, Mark and Bruno separately—had tackled the inverse scattering problem in characteristically different styles. Iraj and I were used to dealing with the denizens of the invest-

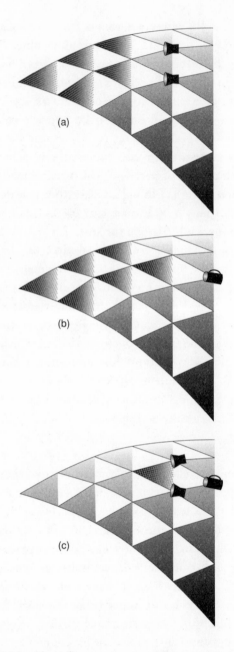

Figure 14.11   How three options can illuminate one node. (a) Two options with adjacent strikes illuminate the triangles to their left. (b) A single option expiring one period later illuminates all the previous triangles plus one more. (c) Subtracting the earlier expirations from the later leaves just one internal triangle illuminated.

ment banking world, the less numerate traders, salespeople and clients, and so we wrote our paper as simply and clearly as possible. We wanted anyone reading it to know exactly how to build their own implied tree. We explained, step by step, exactly how to build the tree and calibrate it to a given volatility surface, and we illustrated it with a fully worked-out numerical example involving a five-period tree that anyone could check.

Mark's presidential address was more discursive and academic, and covered the history of the problem. His initial solution to the inverse scattering problem focused on matching the market's implied volatilities at a single expiration, thereby ignoring some of the additional information embedded in the implied volatility surface.

Bruno's IAFE talk was the most tantalizing. As a Frenchman, he had a taste for formal mathematics, and his very brief report proposed an elegant formula for the local volatilities in terms of the slope and curvature of the implied volatility surface at the same strike and expiration. His paper wasn't easy to understand and people I spoke to were not sure it was correct. Sometimes I thought he was being intentionally obscure, staking out his claim without revealing exactly how he had derived it.

We studied Bruno's report and soon realized that his concise formula was exactly equivalent to what Iraj and I had developed on a discrete tree. Where he had used calculus, we had used algebra. Though it wasn't anywhere near as important or grand, we were playing Feynman to his Schwinger or Black and Scholes to his Merton. In an appendix to our paper we rederived Bruno's results and included a more transparent proof and a reference to his work.

In late December 1993 both Bruno and Iraj and I submitted our respective papers to Graham Cooper at *Risk*. Bruno's appeared in the January 1994 issue of *Risk*, together with an editorial explaining that ours would follow in February. The January issue also contained a page-long news report by Graham Cooper about the work that Mark, Bruno, and Iraj and I had done, referring to it as the new "supermodel," and rather accurately describing the relative merits of our individual approaches. We were all suitably flattered.

For the next several years we toured the seminar and conference circuit. I spoke at dozens of university finance departments and business schools, at the Vienna options exchange, and at countless industry conferences. Salespeople in Japan, France, Switzerland, Spain and Italy, countries where the more sophisticated traders loved learning about quantitative theories, took me to see client after client. We gave day-long seminars to large groups in Zurich and London, Bilbao and Paris, Milan and Munich. It was exhilarating.

Iraj and I, together with Mike Kamal and Joe Zou, two more ex-physicists who joined our group in 1994, continued to enhance the model and to use it to value exotic options. We also worked with two software engineers in QS, Deniz Ergener and Alan Buckwalter, to embed the model in the desk's trading software. Most of all, we struggled to abstract the model's mathematical features into a visceral understanding that would make it accessible to traders. Since all their intuition was based on the Black-Scholes model, we developed a series of simple approximate corrections, rules of thumb that traders could use to nudge the Black-Scholes model in the direction of implied trees.

It turned out to be much harder to explain the model to our traders than to our clients. The traders were busy, their lives dominated by watching screens, servicing salespeople, and entering the terms of their transactions into computer systems. Each day they had to book hundreds or thousands of new trades, often staying late into the night to make sure all the details were correctly reconciled between the front-office risk management system on their desks and the back-office main-frame that held the firm's books and records. They were more interested in automating the bookkeeping aspects of their life than in improving their pricing.

The traders were in charge, and used whatever model they wanted without reason or justification. If you wanted them to hedge differently, the burden of proof was on you. They weren't stupid, just sensibly philis-tine, averse to using new models they didn't understand. Unfortunately, they were also averse to spending time on gaining understanding. When traders have no model at all, it's easy to get them to use the very first model available. Once they have something they rely on, it's much harder to get them to accept an improvement.

So, they simply stuck to using the Black-Scholes single-volatility framework for valuing exotics, even though it produced a flat volatility surface. To compensate, they put all their inventive energy and intuition into picking the "right" single volatility to use in the wrong model. One senior trader insisted that even if the implied tree model were correct and the Black-Scholes model were wrong, he would always be able to think his way through to the correspondingly appropriate single volatility that, when inserted into the wrong model, would nevertheless produce the correct value for an option. I was therefore very pleased one day to discover that there were certain exotic options whose correct value in the implied tree model lay completely outside the range of values we could obtain from the Black-Scholes model, no matter what single volatility we entered into it. For these options there was simply no appropriate single volatility that gave the correct answer from the wrong model. I showed these examples to the traders with great glee and some vindictiveness. It was merely a minor victory, as it failed to alter anyone's behavior.

By 2000, when I worked on approving the use of all models at Goldman, the tide had begun to turn. Increasingly, at Goldman and its competitors, trading desks were obligated to provide some justification that the models they used were appropriate for their market. Nevertheless, in the tug of war between traders and risk managers, traders usually have greater pull.

One day in late 1994 the tension between traders and quants led me to do something particularly stupid. I had spent all day dealing with impatient demands for systems support that I couldn't provide. That evening I took a limo out to Kennedy airport to catch a flight to Vienna, where I was scheduled to give a talk on implied trees at a conference at the OTÖB, the Austrian options exchange. Boarding my plane, I sat down in my business-class aisle seat and finally relaxed. I was frustrated by the constant battles at work, and swore that I would be pushed around no longer.

As I unwound before takeoff, a family of three boarded the plane at the last minute and began taking their seats, none of which were contiguous. The father, a gentleman of about fifty, took the window seat on my right, his son sat across the aisle from me, and his wife sat farther towards the front of the plane. As I flipped through the pages of the OTÖB conference program, the father asked the flight attendant if there were a set of three contiguous seats for his family. Finally, after about ten minutes of unsuccessful agitation, he turned to me and asked if I would switch aisle seats with his son. Still smarting from being pushed around all day, I remembered my "no more Mr. Nice Guy" promise to myself. I was seated in the aisle seat I had requested and I wasn't about to give it up for anyone. Turning to him with misplaced firmness, I said, "I'm sorry, but I'd rather stay where I am."

As we took off for Vienna, I was appalled at my pointless recalcitrance. Both my seat and his son's seat were on the aisle. I was gaining nothing by being stubborn. And worse, I had now condemned myself to sit for ten hours next to someone to whom I had been unnecessarily objectionable. Guilt began to overwhelm me as I debated with myself how to undo what I had done.

While I writhed, I continued looking through the conference schedule. Then, I noticed, the man on my right extracted a similar schedule from his briefcase and began to look at it, too. I glanced at his face again, and suddenly realized I was sitting next to Bob Merton himself, the developer of continuous-time financial modeling, a Harvard professor and also a partner at Long-Term Capital Management. I had seen his picture just that morning on the inside flap of the cover of his famous book *Continuous Time Finance* when I had been reading about jump-diffusion models.

I turned to him shamefacedly and apologized for my rudeness. By now his son had fallen asleep, and there was no point in exchanging seats, so we talked for a couple of hours about the history of options pricing models. Though Bob was very gracious, I felt mortified at having displayed this unpleasant part of my character, and for the duration of the conference I found myself instinctively avoiding him and his family. Next time, I promised myself, I would be tough on the people who deserved it.

Though Mark, Bruno, and Iraj and I were among the first theorists to use local volatility to tackle the smile, various other people had similar ideas. In particular, I came across a closely connected paper by Avi Bick, an Israeli finance professor at Simon Fraser University in Canada. In November 1994, speaking at an NYU conference *Derivatives: The State of the Art*, I was buoyed to hear Gary Gastineau, himself the author of an options text, comment that our model would make markets more liquid by making options pricing more accurate. Although we did live to see local volatility become a household word and a textbook topic, I discovered that it was much more difficult than I had imagined to create a truly successful financial model.

Local volatility was an improvement on Black-Scholes in that it could account for the smile, but it had three genuine failings. First, our new model excluded the possibility that an index or stock could jump, and most market participants nowadays regard that possibility as the main factor determining the shape of the very short-term volatility smile. Our very first attempt to model the smile had indeed involved such jumps. We were never fond of jump models—since jumps are too violent and discontinuous to be hedged, when you include them you lose much of the coherence of the Black-Scholes model. But jumps are real, and omitting them made our model less realistic.

Second, implied trees were difficult to calibrate. Often, as you tried to build progressively finer-meshed trees for better computational accuracy, the local volatility surface grew wild, displaying unrealistic peaks and troughs as it varied from point to point. Over time we developed methods for smoothing these fluctuations, but the need to smooth them made it difficult to automate the production of implied trees for the desk. These waves and troughs were themselves a partial consequence of having excluded jumps; we were trying to model a violent phenomenon with a tranquil diffusion, something that was bound to make calibration unstable.

Finally, our model ignored the random nature of volatility itself. Iraj and I tried to enhance our implied tree model a few years later by adding a random component to the local volatilities, but it made calibration and calculation even more complex and unwieldy.

Over time we discovered that it is possible to obtain a smile with local volatility, jumps, random volatility, or some mixture of all three. So, local volatility and implied trees didn't become "the" single model of the smile. Years later, at a dinner in Manhattan discussing the past, Mark Rubinstein and I both laughed ruefully at the mismatch between what we had expected and the way things turned out.

Nevertheless, I was ultimately satisfied. Iraj and I had been among the first to propose a consistent model of a new and strange phenomenon; we had created a new framework and vocabulary, and we had done it from the front lines, on Wall Street, not from a leisurely research position in academia. The model was somewhat simplistic, as all models are, and it did not tell the whole story, but it was a plausible, self-consistent little world that captured one true and essential feature of equity volatility markets: Volatility tends to increase when markets fall. Local volatility models have become part of the standard arsenal of tools used by academics and practitioners.

During the 1990s, volatility smiles spread to almost all other options markets. Wherever there was fear of large market moves that could hurt investors—downward for equities, upwards for gold, in either direction for many currencies and interest rates—there smiles and skews appeared, and our model became a key tool in explaining at least some of these features. By the new millenium, smile models were ubiquitous, with *Risk* magazine conferences devoting entire sessions, year after year, to these issues. In the Firmwide Risk area at Goldman Sachs, I ran a team of about twelve PhDs in the Derivatives Analysis group that had to approve the prices set and the models used throughout the firm's derivatives businesses, and we soon found that every desk had its own smile model (all of them different), and that most of our work involved the verification of these models. The models differed from desk to desk because their markets differed; each market had its own characteristic smile for its own idiosyncratic reasons. Equity markets feared a crash; gold markets, after years of low prices, feared a sudden upward move; in interest-rate markets, bond investors feared high rates that would devalue their assets, while insurance companies, who often guaranteed their clients a minimum rate of interest, feared low rates that would diminish their incoming cash flow; in currency markets, investors feared a move outside some stable band. Each fear, based on bitter experience, corresponded to a different pattern and required a different model. There was no single model for the smile.

Years ago, when I first became aware of the smile and hoped to find the "right" model, I used to ask colleagues at other firms which model they thought was correct. But now there is such a profusion of models that I ask more practical questions—not "What do you believe?" but rather "When you hedge a standard S&P 500 option, do you use the Black-Scholes hedge ratio, something larger, or something smaller?" Local volatility models produce smaller hedge ratios, while stochastic volatility models tend to produce larger ones. The differences between the models are even more dramatic for exotic options.

In 2003, at a derivatives meeting in Barcelona, I led a small round-table discussion group on the smile. There were fifteen of us, traders and quants from derivatives desks all over the world. I asked everyone my simple question: When you hedge an S&P 500 option, would you use the Black–Scholes hedge ratio, something larger, or something smaller? I was surprised that ten years after the first smile models appeared, with the smile a fact of life in almost every derivatives market, after thousands of published papers, there was still no consensus on how to respond to it.

There still isn't. Though we know much more about the *theories* of the smile, we are still on a darkling plain regarding what's correct. A decade of speaking with traders and theorists has made me wonder what "correct" means. If you are a theorist you must never forget that you are traveling through lawless roads where the local inhabitants don't respect your principles. The more I look at the conflict between markets and theories, the more that limitations of models in the financial and human world become apparent to me.

Chapter 15

The Snows of Yesteryear

■ *Wall Street consolidates* ■ *Clothing goes casual* ■ *Moving*
from equity derivatives to firmwide risk ■ *The bursting*
of the Internet bubble ■ *Taking my leave* ■

L ife in the first half of 1990s was a bit too good to last. The atmosphere in Quantitative Strategies was rousing—we were an eclectic
bunch of ex-physicists, ex-mathematicians, and computer programmers, with our own individual interests but all of us were passionate about
finance. Most of the time we were one happy family—the quants taught
financial theory to programmers who in turn taught programming style
to the quants. Best of all, we worked closely with traders such as Dan
O'Rourke to bridge the gap between academic theory and trading practice. Our body was in the business world but our head was inspired by
academia. It was a rich existence.

To top it off, we had ample resources because we worked for traders
who understood that spending money on research and development is
not a zero-sum game. We believed that our models and systems were the
best on Wall Street. But business is cyclical. After the punishing rise in
interest rates of late 1994, power shifted from our traders to our salespeople, who had difficulty imagining that investment in new models
and trading systems could lead to more business. Instead, they regarded
research as an expense. Lacking the skill to distinguish indulgence from
necessity, they demanded that each investment, no matter how small, be
authorized by someone "on the business side" who could determine its

merit and need. But authorization requires authority, and few salespeople had the time and interest to acquire it. Instead, they held meetings.

In the short run, it was merely time that was wasted; over the longer haul, opportunities were lost. While the business grew our infrastructure stagnated. Now traders began to stay late into the evening to handle ever larger numbers of transactions with antiquated systems. Eventually, our models suffered, too. Then, as our models and software failed to stay state-of-the-art, our self-respect declined. Soon I found myself spending more and more of my time consoling the discontented in our group. Money could no longer keep them happy when daily life ceased to be rewarding. Slowly but steadily I could feel the need for change growing within me, too.

There was one elementary fact that many of our bosses were unable to grasp: We were building these models and systems not just because *somebody* authorized it, but rather because *we* thought they were the right thing to do, because these questions fascinated us. We saw a problem, discerned a need, became absorbed, and tackled it. It was all-engrossing. Struggling to resolve the paradoxes of convertible bond models that had to combine credit and equity risk, or trying to figure out how to model the smile, I would find myself thinking about the problems in mental pictures while I showered or took a run in the park. Sometimes I lay in bed unable to put the picture out of my mind. We worked hard out of passion, pride, and the pleasure of being thanked, recognized, and appreciated; of course, we also worked for money, but money alone wasn't enough.

The investment banking universe had changed, too. In 1985 you could look for a quantitative research job at Goldman, Salomon, First Boston, Prudential, Drexel, Shearson, Lehman, E. F. Hutton, DLJ, Smith Barney, Paine Webber, Bankers Trust, Chase, Chemical, Citibank, and Mocatta Metals, to name just a few among the large and reasonably respectable banks and trading firms. Almost none of these firms exists as an independent entity anymore. By 2000 the bigger fish had swallowed up the smaller ones, and Citigroup, Morgan Stanley, Merrill, and Goldman faced off in a competition for business and capital around the globe.

To compete, the firms had grown unavoidably larger. When I began working at Goldman in 1985, the firm employed fewer than 5,000 souls; when I ate my daily lunch in the cafeteria of the 85 Broad Street building that housed all our New York employees, I could recognize many of them. After the layoffs of 1994 there were about 10,000 employees throughout the firm. By late 1999, as the millennium drew to a close, we had become a publicly listed company with a workforce of over 20,000 people. At every quarterly managing directors meeting I heard company leaders recite the mantras that more than half the people in the firm had been there less than two years, that growth was necessary to stay competitive, and that we had to figure out new ways to maintain our culture.

And there really was a culture. Goldman was a little more gentle, a touch more thoughtful, a jot more tolerant of intellectual diversity. You could talk to anyone if you needed to—there was little standing on ceremony. If you were good at something, you could be different. Even programmers and quants were paid a modicum of respect for their skill and contribution. People seemed to understand that all of these activities, in their different ways, benefited the firm, helped attract employees and customers, and helped make money.

After the IPO, quotidian life changed. The aristocratic old guard with whom I was familiar, Bob Rubin, Jon Corzine, and Roy Zuckerberg among them, had left to make their imprint on politics or enjoy their personal lives. With its newly minted shares of stock to disperse, Goldman began to raid other firms' talent and buy other firms' businesses. As we grew into a large public company, the flow of information inside the firm became more constricted and the hierarchy more stratified. None of this was necessarily bad; it simply went with the territory. I still liked Goldman better than any other place I considered.

Appearances were changing, too. In late 1999 the Nasdaq was heading towards its precipitous peak, and each day there were new cracks in the Berlin wall of Wall Street's formal business attire. Each new day another firm announced that casual clothing was henceforth *de rigueur*. Each new morning saw formerly navy-suited partners come to work in manifestly casual trousers and sports jackets over open-necked shirts. At Goldman, the first to crumble was the historically more plebeian currency and commodities division. Fixed income fell rapidly thereafter. Equities, the last bastion, at first gave in only to casual Fridays. One principled person in my group continued to wear a suit each Friday; when someone asked him why he wasn't going casual, he replied that it was bad enough to wear a uniform every day, but that wearing different uniforms on different days was too much. After a few weeks of casual Fridays, Equities fell, too, and the Velvet Revolution was over. From then on it was all casual, all the time.

The intent, of course, was to continue attracting the best young graduates to staid old investment banking in the face of competition from hipper dot-coms. On recruiting trips for Goldman we discovered that many MBA students were leaving their studies in mid-course to join new get-rich ventures. Even the undergraduates we interviewed weren't as sharp as they had been in previous years. Striking back, Goldman distributed free fruit and soft drinks each day, and, in case that didn't suffice, they further provided concierge services to junior employees working too hard to afford the time to attend to their own needs.

Finally, the hot thing in equities in the late 1990s was going after retail customer flow and electronic distribution. Investment banks, traditionally wholesalers, had to catch up fast. For the next few years, I could see, the valuation side of the business was going to take a back seat to issues of technology. So, by late 1999, a little weary of intermediating between discontented quants and resource-starved traders, I thought about change.

But how to move? On the day when I left Goldman for Salomon Brothers in 1988, Scott Pinkus had offered me the chance to move to another position within the firm. When I asked him why he hadn't broached it earlier, he explained that it would have been poaching. It was bad form to try to recruit someone from another department.

The inverse held, too. If you wanted to move to another area, you weren't supposed to set about it openly—that was putting your needs before those of the business, a bad character trait. Condoning this would have opened the floodgates. To be culturally correct, you were supposed to sit down with your boss and then, after politely explaining your need for different horizons, ask him: Is it okay with you if I explore other opportunities?

But this meant showing your hand—it was difficult to tell someone you didn't want to work for him or her anymore. Instead, in practice, you approached the person you did want to work for and asked discreetly if a position was available for you in his or her area. Then, if there was interest, you met several times to discuss possibilities. Finally, if you both wanted to proceed with the transfer, you went to your current boss and asked: Is it okay with you if I explore other opportunities?

In late 1999 I spoke to several senior people I knew around the firm and asked about possibilities. One of them was Bob Litzenberger, the head of Firmwide Risk Management at Goldman Sachs and a former well-known Wharton professor. His group's job was to monitor and report the risk of the entire firm and all of its subdivisions; Bob was well suited to lead it. He was immensely broad and knowledgeable, the author of well-known papers who had also worked in several derivatives trading firms. He also had the will for it; to control the risk carried by the well-paid heads of powerful trading desks you had to be tough. Concealed behind Bob's deceptively mild facade lay a necessarily stubborn will.

It took only a few meetings to establish that Bob was keen to have me join Firmwide Risk; for my part, I was eager to move. He needed someone who was a derivatives expert because many of the more subtle risks to the firm lay in the complex, exotic, high-margin, over-the-counter options traded by Goldman. We quickly agreed to move forward. Then, other opportunities having been explored, we rolled back the odometer. The next day I went to ask my current boss: Is it OK with you if I explore other opportunities?

In early January 2000 I departed Equity Derivatives for Firmwide Risk.

The Firmwide Risk group that I joined was located in the division of Operations, Finance, and Resources (OF&R). It was a service division and it wasn't glamorous—Resources meant Personnel, Controllers, and Legal, all essential but nevertheless auxiliary to the firm's main business activities. OF&R was a strange locus for quants, a home so foreign to mathematics and modeling that it was difficult to tempt experienced strategists to come and work there.

Despite its dull location, Firmwide Risk tackled important problems. Like insurance companies, trading desks at investment banks make money by taking calculated risks for a fee. Our major task was to measure the magnitude of the current risk of every desk, each division, and the entire firm in a systematic and uniform way, helping to decide which risks were inappropriate. Each desk ran its own risk management system, but we were responsible for coordinating the bigger picture.

Most days, a desk was likely to gain or lose small amounts, but there was always some chance of a potentially large loss. To quantify the notion of risk, we and almost everyone else on the Street used the so-called daily VaR, or Value at Risk, the dollar loss threshold above which greater losses would occur with a probability no larger than 0.4 percent, or 1 chance in 250. This corresponded to about one trading day in a year. VaR is therefore the 99.6 percentile loss. So, for example, a VaR of $50MM for the Equities Division meant that there was only a one-in-two-fifty chance that more money than this would be lost on any given day in the year.

Invented in 1994 by the J. P. Morgan bank, VaR is an unsatisfactory risk metric that has somehow become an industry standard. We esti-mated our daily VaR by running nightly simulations of the changes in the prices of the portfolio held by each trading desk. These simulations were huge computer programs that used the past statistics of each desk's assets to estimate the distribution of possible values the portfolio might take in the future. With those estimates we could predict the distribu-tion of each desk's portfolio value a day later. We produced VaRs for each desk, then for each group of desks in a common trading area, then for each division, and finally for the entire firm, generating a hierarchy of potential one-day losses that gave a view of the firm's riskiness from top to bottom.

Each day, like clockwork, we computed and reported the VaR for the firm and its parts. Several times a week senior members of our group met with each division's risk committee, and once a week, in an unpleasantly early 7:30 A.M. global conference call, we met with the central risk com-mittee who fine-tuned the entire firm's risk by setting limits on VaR. During turbulent times they lowered the cap and during quiet times they raised it. The aim was to take the appropriate amount of risk for the eco-nomic environment, not to eliminate it. No risk, no return.

VaR is not a panacea, and there are many legitimate objections to its use. Most importantly, VaR by its nature uses statistical distributions to project the firm's value into the future, and statistics are inevitably based upon the past. But the past doesn't repeat itself verbatim; people learn enough from their past experiences to make new mistakes as they struggle between greed and the effort to avoid the old ones.

VaR is also too simplistic: it's not possible to capture the profit-and-loss potential of a complex distribution of future portfolio values in a single number, because very different distributions can have the same 99.6 percentile. We are ignorant of the true probabilities—the extreme tails of stock and bond price distributions, not to mention the overall distributions of complex securities like swaptions or weather derivatives, are poorly understood and may not even be stationary.

Even if you insist on representing risk with a single number, VaR isn't the best one. Percentiles don't reflect the psychology of risk perception very well—two different securities can each have their own small percentile losses that combine to produce a greater percentile loss for the portfolio. The VaR of a portfolio can therefore be greater than the VaR of its components, in counterintuitive contradiction with the idea that diversification diminishes risk.

As a result, though we used VaR, we didn't make it our religion. We were pantheists, praying to many parallel risk gods. For example, we had all lived through various market meltdowns—the 1987 stock market crash, the 1998 Russian default crisis—whose reoccurrence would cause great losses even though we had no idea of their probability. Thus, the firm imposed a bound on the positions on each desk so that they could lose no more than a tolerable amount in a repetition of such events. These and other stress-test limits based on similar experienced or imagined catastrophes were imposed over and above the VaR limits.

I think we did a pretty good job by taking a many-sided view of risk, but it was a never ending enterprise. Each year we collected more data to improve our statistics. Each year the simulations were enhanced to better reflect the behavior of familiar markets. And, whenever Goldman entered a new business—energy or weather derivatives, for example—that had no history, we strived to create an imagined history and statistics that would reflect the risk we perceived. So much of financial modeling is an exercise of the imagination.

Though most of Firmwide Risk focused on VaR, I didn't have much to do with it. I found it useful but inelegant work, aimed more at an audience of regulators rather than traders. Instead, I spent most of my time in Firmwide Risk as head of the Derivatives Analysis group, a collection of about twelve PhDs in New York, London, and Tokyo. Our mission was to ensure that every trading desk's derivative deals were "marked to market" accurately.

Marking to market is the act of assigning to each security in your portfolio a price that reflects its current market value. You have a very good idea of the value of a share of Microsoft, which trades millions of times a day at a publicly listed price. Marking it to market is easy. But the derivatives trading desks at Goldman (and most other investment banks) had developed increasingly large positions in long-term or exotic over-the-counter derivative securities, tailored to satisfy the needs of particular customers. It was harder to mark them to market. It's much simpler to price a new pair of Levi's than a secondhand, custom-tailored Christian Lacroix evening dress.

Our firm owned hosts of illiquid derivatives in the interest-rate, equity, currency, commodity, energy, and credit markets. Some structured products spanned many markets—we traded yen-denominated bonds whose coupons would increase if the S&P 500 index rose. To manage this position you had to hedge changes in Japanese and American interest rates, the yen, and the S&P 500.

There *were* no current market prices for such securities. Quants and traders "marked them to model," which meant they figured out their value by means of carefully calibrated models, developed with mathematics and written in computer code that was then embedded in front-office risk management systems. And there was no secondary market for most of these exotics—you had to keep them on your books until they expired, and hedge them by means of the same model along the way.

What is the fair value of an illiquid security that you have to hold for several years? This was an immensely significant and practical question, because the value of these securities determines the company's earnings, its stock price, and the bonuses of the traders that manage them.

The trading desks typically valued their illiquid positions using their own models. But this involved a moral hazard; when a trader's year-end bonus depends upon the value of a security whose price is both obscure and under his control, he may be tempted to embellish his profit when payday approaches.

The Derivatives Analysis group was the firm's model police: Our job was to confirm that the billions of dollars of exotic or illiquid derivatives were being marked fairly. It's an honorable and important task, one that requires both knowledge and wisdom. That first year in Firmwide Risk I saw a plethora of idiosyncratic and illiquid securities on the firm's books in New York, London, and Tokyo. The Equities Division was long out-of-the-money, four-year calls and short out-of-the-money puts on individual technology stocks, sold to them by insiders who were hedging the stock they had received when their firm went public. The value of these options was somewhat uncertain because there was no listed market at those distant expirations and strikes. The fixed-income division had much more complex swaptions on their books, similar to those yen-denominated bonds with coupons indexed to the S&P 500. The commodities desks traded long-term barrier options on gold, structured to help mining companies hedge their future profits against gold price declines. All of these markets manifested volatility smiles that made the accurate valuation of these highly complicated securities difficult and uncertain.

Slowly it began to dawn on me that what we faced was not so much *risk* as *uncertainty*. Risk is what you bear when you own, for example, 100 shares of Microsoft—you know exactly what those shares are worth because you can sell them in a second at something very close to the last traded price. There is no uncertainty about their current value, only the risk that their value will change in the next instant. But when you own an exotic illiquid option, uncertainty precedes its risk—you don't even know exactly what the option is currently worth because you don't know whether the model you are using is right or wrong. Or, more accurately, you know that the model you are using is both naive and wrong—the only question is *how* naive and *how* wrong.

No one truly knows the precise value of a stock option that cannot be traded. Its value depends on what you can squeeze out of it by hedging its underlying stock through all its future random price changes to expiration. And this depends on the nature of the randomness and on the particular strategy employed to hedge against it, both of which cannot be totally determined in advance.

Faced with uncertainty, I took a many-worlds view of derivatives values. I assumed that the future could be one of several foreseeable worlds, and that there was consequently a range of possible values one could legitimately assign to the option. In one future world, for example, stock volatility might decrease as stock prices increased. In another, volatility might simply be random. In each of a host of plausible different worlds, all consistent with today's observations, you can work out the correspondingly appropriate theoretical model and then use it to value the option. You can then compare the desk's mark-to-model value with the spectrum of many-worlds values, and see whether it lies inside their range. If it does, then it's reasonable and can be allowed as a mark. But if it doesn't, you negotiate with the desk to either justify or amend its estimate. Furthermore, since there is a range of plausible values, we recommended that Goldman hold in reserve an amount equal to the average mismatch between the range of plausible values and the desk's actual mark. This reserve represented a portion of their expected profit to be held in escrow against the possibility that their model or hedging strategy was wrong. It would be released only when the trade was finally unwound and the true market value of the option would finally be realized and revealed.

This was the strategy we adopted for appraising the firm's exotic and illiquid derivatives, which we regarded in the same way that an art dealer might think about his inventory of impressionist painting. Suppose an art dealer's agent has acquired a valuable Renoir painting for $10 million when he believes it to be worth $13 million, and now asks to be paid a bonus of ten percent of the expected profit of $3 million, or $300,000. It would be foolish of the dealer to pay the bonus until the Renoir has been sold. Until then, the painting's value is not merely risky, but uncertain. Illiquid option or illiquid painting, you shouldn't count your chickens until they're hatched.

The more I thought about it, the more that appraisal seemed like the right metaphor for options valuation. When you want to estimate the value of an antique that hasn't changed hands in a long time, you compare it to analogous *objets d'art* that have been auctioned more recently. The more I dealt with estimating the value of the panoply of option structures and models we came across, the more I believed that options valuation was really valuation by analogy.

I recalled that as a child in bible school, I had learned the story of Hillel, a famous sage, who was asked to recite the essence of God's laws while standing on one leg. "Do not do unto others as you would not have them do unto you," he is supposed to have said. "All the rest is commentary. Go and learn." I believe that you can summarize the essence of quantitative finance on one leg, too: "If you want to know the value of a security, use the price of another security that's as similar to it as possible. All the rest is modeling. Go and build."

Financial economists grandiosely refer to this law as the *law of one price*, which states that securities with identical future payouts, no matter how the future turns out, should have identical current prices. It's the essential—perhaps the only—principle of the field. To estimate the value of an illiquid security, you find a set of similar liquid securities, with known market prices, whose payouts match those of the illiquid security under all circumstances. The best estimate for the value of the illiquid security is then the value of the set of liquid securities with the same payouts.

Where do models enter? It takes a model to show that the illiquid security and the liquid portfolio have identical future payouts under all circumstances. Your model must specify what you mean by "all circumstances," and you must show that the replicating portfolio, in every future circumstance, has the same payout. Most of the mathematical complexity in finance involves the elaboration of this single principle.

Models are only models, toylike descriptions of idealized worlds. Simple models envisage a simple future; more sophisticated models incorporate a more complex set of future scenarios that can more closely approximate actual markets. But no mathematical model can capture the intricacies of human psychology. Watching traders occasionally put too much faith in the power of formalism and mathematics, I saw that if you listen to the models' siren song for too long, you may end up on the rocks or in the whirlpool.

In September 2000 I was elected Financial Engineer of the Year by the International Association of Financial Engineers (IAFE). I was the first and, thus far, only practitioner to receive this award, lucky to be temporarily in the company of the previous winners: Robert Merton, Fischer Black, Mark Rubinstein, Stephen Ross, Robert Jarrow, John Cox, and John Hull, all renowned contributors to the field who had made their major contributions while in academic life. I considered myself fortunate to have been able to make a small mark after a late start.

As a practitioner I had always been hands-on. What I had enjoyed most was research, the primary work that no one has done before, carried out for a small number of people in trading who were genuinely interested in the result. Now, in Firmwide Risk at a large firm, I had to accustom myself to doing secondary research, merely helping to validate the results of other quants on the desk who had taken the first crack at a problem. I was also part of a large bureaucracy. Each week I went to two fixed-income risk meetings, one equities risk meeting, one firmwide risk committee meeting, at least two Derivatives Analysis group meetings, and a meeting of all the managers in Firmwide Risk. Then there were three different meetings with three different controllers for equities, fixed income, and currencies and commodities respectively, as well as the periodic meeting of all the VPs in Firmwide Risk.

That was when times were good. By mid-2000, after the bursting of the technology bubble and the subsequent decline in all stock markets, I had many more meetings with discouraged young quants in my group who foresaw a very limited upside. By early 2001 I was spending a large fraction of my time trying to cheer up disgruntled but talented people.

There was one real perquisite to being a senior person in Firmwide Risk—you got to participate in the firm's central risk meeting once a week and watch all the biggest big shots in action as we listened to the state of our business prospects and discussed current events and strategies. I was invited to hear Wesley Clark address us on Iraq, more than a year before the invasion. In the end, however, I was an outsider. Running the firm was their world, not mine. I liked smaller worlds and I preferred working on more specific and detailed topics. Soon, I knew, I would move on.

Every Tuesday morning I held a global call at 10 Hanover Square with all the senior people in Derivatives Analysis. At 8:00 A.M. New York time they called in from London and Tokyo. One Tuesday, as we sat around the speakerphone discussing deals we were vetting, I glanced at the window and saw sheets of paper cascading out of the sky. I thought it looked like an archaic ticker-tape parade for returning astronauts or victorious Yankee teams, but it was too early for a parade. Then someone came running in to say an airplane had struck the World Trade Center. We switched on the television perched high in the corner of my office, and saw the flaming tower, listened to the reports of an accidental collision. Then, a few moments later, we heard a thunderous bang through my window as we simultaneously saw the other tower on TV burst into flame. It was instantly clear we were under attack.

Outside the building we regrouped, watching the horrific flames and smoke pour from the towers. I had visions of waves of subsequent airplanes careening in to strike more buildings. Crowds of us set off for the long walk north, careful to walk neither too close to the unprotected FDR Drive nor too close to attractive targets such as the Pan Am building. By the time we reached Chinatown we heard of the towers' collapse and the strike on the Pentagon. By 3 P.M. I reached Sonya's school on the Upper East Side, where they were releasing students only into the care of their parents.

Lower Manhattan was like a war zone for the next few months—burnt air and blockaded streets patrolled by New York City policemen and scared-looking and out-of-shape members of the National Guard. I took a cab daily from the West Side to Gracie Mansion, itself surrounded by sand-filled dump trucks, and a ferry from there down the East River to the South Street Seaport. Working and living in Manhattan was oppressive; you had no respite from the expectation of the next assault. Helicopters patrolled the night sky. People woke at 3 A.M. like clockwork to watch CNN. I noticed the palpable relief when I spent a weekend in the country or the suburbs—one felt briefly safe there. The first day I noticed a lightening of spirits in Manhattan was more than two months after September 11, on the Wednesday before Thanksgiving, when suddenly the city seemed just slightly festive.

Normally it takes me years to make up my mind about a transition. Now it took only two months of vacillation before I decided that I was ready to leave Goldman Sachs. The best times I had had there were when I worked in small groups of traders and quants with a strong joint purpose—with Peter Freund's desk when we developed BDT, and with Iraj and Dan O'Rourke when we built equity risk systems and developed our implied tree model. I decided to take a year off, write a book, and then return to work, either in academia or at a job in a smaller investment firm. On June 7, after my farewell party, more than 17 years after I started at Goldman, I went home for good. The next morning I went for a run in Central Park at 11 A.M., the best time for running. I hadn't done this in several years.

A week later I received an email at home from someone in my old Quantitative Strategies group who hadn't been able to attend my party. He and I had had occasional fierce battles over software standardization.

Like most quants, he was foreign born. "In retrospect," he wrote, "Working in your QS has been [*sic*] my happiest years in Goldman. Very often, I deeply regret not having recognized fully what a privilege it was to work next to (sometimes with) you and your colleagues. As time goes by, I realize how lucky I was to be able to work in the atmosphere of the high intellectual standards that you set, with extraordinary talented people that gathered around you. I missed the times, and the opportunities that I did not take a full advantage of."

The snows of yesteryear inevitably melt, and there's nothing sad about it. I was ready for something new.

■ *Chapter 16* ■

The Great Pretender

■ *Full circle, back to Columbia* ■ *Physics and finance redux* ■ *Different endeavors require different degrees of precision* ■ *Financial models as* gedanken *experiments* ■

A year later, in the fall of 2003, I had come full circle, time present and time past present in time future. I was back at Columbia, a professor and director of the program in financial engineering in the Mudd building on 120th Street and Amsterdam Avenue, a mere 100 yards east of Pupin where I spent so many years getting my PhD. I was also working part-time with a fund of funds, a firm that invests clients' money in a portfolio of hedge funds.

As I teach, I am struck again by the difference between what can be taught in school and what can be learned on the job. When I started on Wall Street, I simply assumed it made good sense to apply the techniques of physics to financial modeling. In particle physics people dreamed of GUTs (Grand Unified Theories) and strings and TOEs (Theories of Everything). The tools they used—differential calculus, partial differential equations, Fourier series, Monte Carlo simulations, even Hilbert spaces—at first seemed as appropriate for describing the movements of stocks and yield curves as they did for particles and fields.

Looking at the motion of yield curves in the mid-1980s, I saw no reason why financial theorists shouldn't shoot for their theory of everything, too. Why shouldn't one set of equations describe the motions of all interest rates, producing one rational set of fair prices for all interest-rate-sensitive securities? If you had asked me where quantitative finance was headed, I would have hoped for the discovery of that theory.

Seventeen years on, I say without regret that things aren't the way I expected. There is no unified theory. Models must necessarily be pragmatic, and traders typically use a variety of similar but slightly inconsistent models—one for Treasury bonds, another for corporates, a third for caps, a fourth for swaptions—even though all these securities depend on the same underlying interest rates. Though we aspire to it, we don't expect comprehensiveness. The best quants know that it is unattainable.

Newcomers to the field find it hard to swallow. One French student in my course recently wrote in his evaluation that, although the course gave him a good feel for the way quantitative finance is practiced, he is "still not convinced that an *ab initio* model in finance (like the sophisticated ones in other fields) to explain almost everything does not exist." Physicists new to finance, as I did, imagine a grand unified theory can be found. Many finance academics who should know better also seem to imagine it can be done, but they don't live in the real world. It isn't really possible. And it's not a question of computational power—even infinitely fast computers won't do the trick. The problem is deeper.

The techniques of physics hardly ever produce more than the most approximate truth in finance, because "true" financial value is itself a suspect notion. In physics, a model is right when it correctly predicts the future trajectories of planets or the existence and properties of new particles, such as Gell-Mann's Omega Minus. In finance, you cannot easily prove a model right by such observations. Data are scarce and, more importantly, markets are arenas of action and reaction, dialectics of thesis, antithesis, and synthesis. People learn from past mistakes and go on to make new ones. What's right in one regime is wrong in the next.

As a result, physicists turned quants don't expect too much from their theories, though many economists naively do. Perhaps this is because physicists, raised on theories capable of superb divination, know the difference between a fundamental theory and a phenomenological toy, useful though the latter may be. Trained economists have never seen a really first-class model. It's not that physics is "better," but rather that finance is harder. In physics you're playing against God, and He doesn't change his laws very often. When you've checkmated Him, He'll concede. In finance, you're playing against God's creatures, agents who value assets based on their ephemeral opinions. They don't know when they've lost, so they keep trying.

In his textbook *Derivatives*, Paul Wilmott, an applied mathematician turned quant, writes that "every financial axiom I've ever seen is demonstrably wrong. . . . The real question is *how* wrong is the theory, and how useful is it regardless of its validity. Everything you read in any theoretical finance book, including this one, you must take with a generous pinch of salt." I couldn't agree more. In fact, the very title Wilmott chose for his later book, *Wilmott on Derivatives*, aptly illustrates his understanding of the point. The "Wilmott" in the title implies that a difficult subject is being explained by an authority, but it also suggests that the subject matter itself lacks the coherence of true science. True science does not need this kind of authority—one cannot imagine a 1918 textbook called *Einstein on Gravitation*! Unlike finance, the theory of gravitation gets its weight from the ineluctability of its arguments and its ability to account for previously inexplicable anomalies. Gravitation needs no Einstein to lend it gravitas. Personality plays a larger part in economic writing because truth's part is smaller.

So, why is it that the methods of physics work less well in finance?

As a physicist, when you propose a model of Nature, you're pretending you can guess the structure created by God. It sounds eminently plausible. Every physicist believes he has a small chance of doing so, or else he wouldn't be in the field. Perhaps it's possible because God Himself doesn't pretend. But as a quant, when you propose a new model of value, you're pretending you can guess the structure created by other people. When you try out a new yield curve model, you're implicitly saying something like "Let's pretend people in markets care only about the level of future short-term interest rates, and that they expect them to be distributed normally." As you say that to yourself, if you're honest, your heart sinks. You're just a poor pretender and you know immediately there is no chance at all that you are truly right. When you take on other people, you're pretending you can comprehend other pretenders, a much more difficult task.

But doesn't God make people, too? Is there really a conflict between individuals and Nature? These are ancient questions. Schrödinger, the unconventional father of the probability wave equation in quantum mechanics, wrote a short summary of his personal views on determinism and free will in the epilogue to *What is Life?*, a compilation of his influential lectures on the physico-chemical basis of living matter. "My body functions as a pure mechanism according to the Laws of Nature," he wrote. "Yet I know, by incontrovertible direct experience, that I am directing its motions, of which I foresee the effects, that may be fateful and all-important, in which case I feel and take full responsibility for them." The only way he could reconcile these two apparently contra-dictory experiences—his deep belief in the susceptibility of Nature to human theorizing and his equally firm sense of the individual autonomy that must lie beneath any attempt to theorize—was to infer that "I—I in the widest meaning of the word, that is to say, every conscious mind that has ever said or felt 'I'—am the person, if any, who controls the 'motion of the atoms' according to the Laws of Nature."

Schrödinger was following in the steps of the long line of earlier German philosophers who thought that all the various worldly voices referring to themselves in conversation as "I" were not really referring to independent I's, but to the same universal I—God or Nature.

Nevertheless, it's the unpredictable I's—people like you and me—who determine financial value. Fischer Black once wrote of financial theo-ries that:

> In the end, a theory is accepted not because it is confirmed by conventional empirical tests, but because researchers persuade one another that the theory is correct and relevant.

I would go even further than this. From the viewpoint of someone who works with traders, I like to think of financial models as analogues of the way quantum and relativity physicists in the early part of the last century used *gedanken* experiments. *Gedanken* experiments—German for thought experiments—were imaginary investigations, a sort of men-tal stress-testing of the physical world, conducted in your head because they were too difficult to do in practice. Their aim was to force your conceptual picture of the world into a contradiction. Einstein imagined what he would see sitting on the edge of a moving light beam in order to get insight into the contradiction between a Newtonian observer and Maxwell's description of light. Would the light wave still seem to undulate from peak to trough when you sat on one of its peaks? Similarly Schrödinger, in order to highlight the radical, counterintuitive nature of quantum mechanics, imagined an unobserved cat sealed in a box containing a radioactive atom that, on decaying, would trigger a Geiger counter to release a poison. Would the cat, like an unobserved electron oscillating continuously between different quantum states, swing from alive to dead and back again?

I think this is the right way to use mathematical models in finance. Models are only models, not the thing in itself. We cannot, therefore, expect them to be truly right. Models are better regarded as a collection of parallel thought universes you can explore. Each universe should be consistent, but the actual financial and human world, unlike the world of matter, is going to be infinitely more complex than any model we make of it. We are always trying to shoehorn the real world into one of the models to see how useful an approximation it is.

You must always ask: Does the model give you a set of plausible variables to describe the world, and a set of relationships between them that permits its analysis and investigation? You're always trying to make a limited approximation of reality, using variables that people can comprehend, so that you can say to yourself or your boss, for example, "I was short emerging-market volatility, so we lost money when the crisis came." Good theories, like Black-Scholes, provide a laboratory of ideas in which you can work out the likely consequences of possible causes. They give you a common language with which to quantify and communicate your feelings about value.

The right way to engage with a model is, like a fiction reader or a really great pretender, to temporarily suspend disbelief, and then push it as far as possible. The success of the theory of options valuation, the best model economics can offer, is the story of a Platonically simple theory, taken more seriously than it deserves and then used extravagantly, with hubris, as a crutch to human thinking. "If a fool would persist in his folly, he would become wise," wrote Blake in *The Marriage of Heaven and Hell*. This is what quants have done with options theory.

A little hubris is good. But then, when you're done modeling, you must remind yourself that you're theorizing about I's, and that, though God's world can be divined by principles, humanity prefers to remain mysterious. Catastrophes strike when people allow theories to take on a life of their own and hubris evolves into idolatry. Somewhere between these two extremes, a little north of common sense but still south of idolatry, lies the wise use of conceptual models. It takes judgment to draw the line.

Meanwhile, fundamental physics and its visions of ten-dimensional strings seem to get steadily more arcane, and quantitative finance becomes progressively more refined and detailed. Being a scientist can sometimes be depressing. Surrounded by younger versions of yourself, you are constantly confronted by the mismatch between the dreams of youth and the facts of maturity.

I once read J.P.S. Uberoi's biography of Goethe,[1] one of the last people to make contributions to both art and science. Goethe's *Theory of Colours* is a unified examination of the interior and exterior characteristics of light and color, conducted with an awareness of the observer himself. According to Uberoi, scientists tend to regard Goethe as a poet who strayed beyond his proper place. His critics said he mistakenly thought of Nature as a work of art, being qualitative and personal where he should have been quantitative and impersonal. But Goethe was not so naive as to think that Nature is a work of art, wrote Uberoi. Rather, he believed that the *description* of our knowledge of Nature should be a work of art.

I like to think in Goethean terms of what we do in quantitative finance: We try to make as beautiful and truthful a description as we can of what we observe. We're involved in intuiting, inventing, or concocting approximate laws and patterns. We combine both art and science in creating understanding. We use our intuition, our scientific knowledge and our pedagogical skills to paint a picture of how to think qualitatively, and then, within limits, quantitatively, about the world of human affairs, and in so doing, we influence and are influenced by other people's thoughts. There's not much more one could ask for in this life without being wishful.

---

[1] J.P.S. Uberoi, *The Other Mind of Europe: Goethe as a Scientist*, Oxford University Press, Delhi (1984).

Acknowledgments

I am most indebted to Pamela van Giessen, my editor at John Wiley & Sons, Inc., who, several years ago, let me persuade her that writing a book about what it's like to be a quant was a good idea. From then on she provided inspiration, enthusiasm, guidance, and advice, on the big picture as well as on details. I'm thankful for her interest and patience; it is very unlikely I would have seen this endeavor through to its end without her.

Jennifer MacDonald at Wiley also provided useful help, as did the people at PV&M Publishing Solutions, in particular Joanna Pomeranz, Matt Kushinka, and Gabriella Kadar.

The kind encouragement I received from family, friends, and, sometimes, from relative strangers who later became friends, played a truly large part in my completing this book. Writing is a lonely pleasure, and a small amount of other people's enthusiasm can have a disproportionately large and beneficial impact. I am pleased to thank Beverly Bell, Steve Blaha, Richard Cohen, Nancy Cohen, Joshua Derman, Shulamit Derman, Sonya Derman, Michael Goodkin, Marc Groz, Ruth Jowell, Mike Kamal, Robert Kiernan, Mark Koenigsberg, Bob Long, Helga Nagy, Nassim Taleb, and Don Weingarten. Their positive words had more effect on me than they may realize, and I'm grateful to them. I am especially thankful to Ray Bacon, who encouraged me and offered helpful comments on the manuscript.

Finally, above all, I am pleased to thank my wife Eva, who patiently and carefully read and commented on large parts of the manuscript, and give me thoughtful suggestions, good advice, and moral support throughout its writing.

About the Author

Emanuel Derman is a principal and Head of Risk at Prisma Capital Partners and a professor and Director of the Program in Financial Engineering at Columbia University. He was formerly a managing director at Goldman, Sachs & Co., which he joined in 1985 after an initial career in academic life and at AT&T Bell Laboratories. He is the co-creator of the widely used Black-Derman-Toy interest rate model and the Derman-Kani local volatility model. Among his many awards and honors, he was named the SunGard/IAFE Financial Engineer of the Year in 2000 and was appointed to the Risk Hall of Fame in 2002. He has a PhD in theoretical physics from Columbia University and is the author of numerous articles in elementary particle physics, computer science, and finance.

Index